The Macroeconomics of Monetary Union

The CFA Franc Zone currently comprises a group of fifteen francophone African countries that developed after various colonies, having achieved political independence from France in the late 1950s and early 1960s, chose to retain close economic links with their former colonial power. The CFA Franc is linked to the French Franc and Euro, and is a prime example of cross-national monetary union.

David Fielding uses macroeconomic theory and econometric modelling techniques to address the policy issues relating to the CFA Franc Zone. Within this methodological framework, the book analyses the ways in which the monetary institutions of the CFA, which are unique among developing economies, influence macroeconomic development and policy formation. The three main themes are:

- The impact of the fixed exchange rate regime on monetary and fiscal policy within the CFA and the way in which external shocks impact on members of the Zone.
- The impact of monetary institutions peculiar to the CFA on monetary and fiscal policy.
- The consequences of these impacts for economic performance and growth.

The Macroeconomics of Monetary Union will be of particular interest to researchers in development macroeconomics and illustrates to advanced students how modern economic and econometric techniques can be applied to address policy issues in developing countries.

David Fielding is Reader in Economics at the University of Leicester. He is also an External Fellow of the Centre for Research in Economic Development and International Trade at the University of Nottingham and a Research Associate of the Centre for the Study of African Economies at the University of Oxford.

Routledge studies in development economics

The Macroeconomics of Monetary Union
An Analysis of the CFA Franc Zone

David Fielding

Routledge
Taylor & Francis Group

LONDON AND NEW YORK

For Jo, Anna and Matthew

First published 2002 by Routledge
2 Park Square, Milton Park, Abingdon, Oxfordshire OX14 4RN

Simultaneously published in the USA and Canada
by Routledge
711 Third Avenue, New York, NY 10017

First issued in paperback 2015

Routledge is an imprint of the Taylor and Francis Group, an informa business

© 2002 David Fielding

Typeset in 11/13 Times New Roman by Newgen Imaging System (P) Ltd., India

British Library Cataloguing in Publication Data
A catalogue record for this book is available from the British Library

Library of Congress Cataloging in Publication Data
A catalogue record for this book has been requested

ISBN 13: 978-0-415-75850-5 (pbk)
ISBN 13: 978-0-415-25098-6 (hbk)

Contents

Figures

Tables

Acknowledgements

Permission has been granted for reproduction of material from the following previously published papers:
"Determinants of investment in Kenya and Côte d'Ivoire", *Journal of African Economies*, vol. 2, pp. 299–328, 1993, (OUP)
"Investment in Cameroon 1978–88", *Journal of African Economies*, vol. 4, pp. 29–51, 1995, (OUP)
"Asymmetries in the behaviour of members of a monetary union: a game-theoretic model with an application to West Africa", *Journal of African Economies*, vol. 5 pp. 343–65, 1996, (OUP)
"Interest, credit and liquid assets in Côte d'Ivoire", *Journal of African Economies*, vol. 8, pp. 448–78, 1999, (OUP)
"How does a central bank react to changes in government borrowing? Evidence from Africa", *Journal of Development Economics*, vol. 59, pp. 531–52, 1999, (North-Holland)
"Monetary discipline and inflation in developing countries: the role of the exchange rate regime", *Oxford Economic Papers*, vol. 52, pp. 521–38, 2000, (OUP)

1 An introduction to the institutions and members of the CFA Franc Zone

The analysis of the costs and benefits of monetary union – the sharing of a single currency and a single central bank by different countries – is currently at the forefront of both academic economics and policy debate. The main focus of attention has been the newly formed European Monetary Union (EMU), the economic impact of which – given its short life – is largely a matter for speculation. However, monetary unions are by no means a new phenomenon. At the end of the Second World War, with the European empires largely intact, many economies around the world participated in monetary unions based on the Pound Sterling, Escudo, Guilder and Franc.

As the various colonies achieved political independence in the late 1950s and early 1960s, most of these monetary unions were dissolved, the new nation states preferring complete economic independence, with their own currencies and independent central banks. Economically, they distanced themselves from each other as well as from their former colonial rulers. However, an exception to this general rule arose in western and central Africa, where most of the states newly independent from France chose to retain close economic links with the colonial power. They retained the shared currency of French colonial Africa, and continued to adhere to the existing central banks. In the light of contemporary economic arguments for and against international monetary union, it is interesting and informative to compare the economic development of this 'CFA' with that of other developing countries. In this book, we will consider evidence on the various ways in which CFA membership influences economic performance.

In this chapter we will review and highlight those elements of CFA institutions that are likely to have an economic impact. Here, we need to be careful to distinguish between what the Zone appears to guarantee on paper, and what actually happens. In practice, some principles are not strictly adhered to, so the distinction between the institutions of members and non-members becomes blurred. The distinctions that remain, even in practice, will inform econometric analysis in later chapters that is designed to quantify the positive and negative aspects of CFA membership.

1.1. The institutions of the CFA

The African CFA – the Communauté (or Cooperation) Financière Africaine (CFA) – currently consists of fifteen countries, all but one of which are situated in West and Central Africa. The CFA is the major component of the worldwide CFA, which also includes Monaco and some French overseas territories. The cornerstone of the CFA is the use of currencies that the French Treasury guarantees to exchange for French Francs (now Euros) at a fixed rate.[1] In continental Africa, member states are grouped into two regions, each of which has one central bank issuing a single currency (both currencies are called the CFA Franc, CFAF) that is convertible with the French Franc (FF) at a rate of 100 CFAF : 1 FF.

The CFA evolved from the monetary institutions of the last phase of French colonial Africa. In 1955, five years before independence, the Metropolitan French authorities devolved the right to issue currency onto two newly created institutions: the Central Bank of Equatorial African States and Cameroon, later renamed the Bank of Central African States (BEAC), and the Central Bank of West African States (BCEAO). These banks issued their own notes for use in French Equatorial Africa (including Cameroon) and French West Africa (including Togo). Their headquarters were originally in Paris, but later moved to Yaoundé in Cameroon and Dakar in Sénégal.

On independence, the banks retained their function and their currencies, and the French Treasury continued to guarantee convertibility at 50 CFAF : 1 FF.[2] All of the newly independent Central African states: Cameroon, Centrafrique, Congo Republic, Gabon and Chad, adhered to this monetary union under the auspices of the BEAC. These were joined in 1985 by the former Spanish colony of Equatorial Guinea. In West Africa, Togo and Guinea-Conakry seceded from the monetary union on gaining their independence, although Togo rejoined the union in 1963. The other states: Côte d'Ivoire, Dahomey (later Bénin), Upper Volta (later Burkina Faso), Mali, Mauritania, Niger and Sénégal, formed the Economic and Monetary Union of West African states (UEMOA) under the auspices of the BCEAO. Mali, however, was independent of UEMOA from 1962 to 1984, issuing its own CFA Franc, convertible at a rate of 100 CFAFM : 1 FF. Also, Mauritania completely seceded from the CFA in 1973. The former Portugese colony of Guinea-Bissau joined the union in 1997. In a parallel organisation in Southern Africa, the states of Madagascar and Comoros shared a central bank issuing CFA Francs, although Madagascar seceded from the CFA in 1973. The current CFA in Africa is therefore organised into three regions: the UEMOA monetary union, the BEAC region monetary union, and Comoros. In the rest of this book we will focus on the two monetary unions, the institutional and regulatory characteristics of which are described below.

1.1.1. Economic characteristics guaranteed in the CFA constitutions

The two monetary unions constitute a complex array of contractual obligations on the part of the African states and France. Appendix 1.1 summarises the beaurocratic structure of the two monetary unions. Here we review those features of the CFA constitutions that are likely to affect economic policy and economic performance. What are the commitments made, and are they binding in practice?

The obligations fall into two categories. First, there are the constitutional 'principles' designed to achieve the goal of complete financial integration between member states. Under this heading fall the guarantees of convertibility between CFA and French Francs, and the fixed exchange rate. Maintenance of the principles implies a heavy obligation on the part of France, with some obligations on the part of the CFA. Second, there are the administrative structures to which member states bind themselves, and which prevent (or at least, which are designed to prevent) African states free riding on French guarantees, and on each other. These entail considerable loss of economic sovereignty on the part of the African states.

The constitutions of the central banks of the CFA describe the principles and institutional structures of the union. More details are to be found in Bathia (1986) and Vizy (1989). We will concentrate below on the details of the revised CFA constitutions of 1972–3, which devolved policy-making authority from the French Treasury to the central banks.[3] The members of the CFA and France agree to act to ensure the following economic conditions.

(i) *Guaranteed convertibility.* Article 2 of the BEAC constitution states that the union is based on France's guarantee of unlimited convertibility of CFA Francs. Article 1 of the UEMOA accord stipulates that France will help member states to ensure the free convertibility of their currency. In practice, this means that the French Treasury will exchange CFA Francs for French Francs on demand. It also agrees to provide the CFA central banks with as many French Francs as are needed to ensure the smooth running of the zone's financial system. The scrabble for foreign exchange that typifies many African economies is absent from CFA members.

If this guarantee of convertibility were absolute, then there would be no parallel market for forex. The official and 'parallel' exchange rates would be the same. However, the rates do diverge somewhat. This divergence was particularly marked in 1988, when the official CFAF/ US Dollar rate was 285.25 : 1, and Ivorian Francs were selling at a rate of 360 : 1 on parallel markets.[4] The main reason for this divergence is probably that although the French Treasury guarantees convertibility now at a certain exchange rate, there is a finite risk that the CFA Francs will be devalued, or that one or more countries will secede from the union. When rumours are rife, the implied risk of holding CFA Francs means that there is not full convertibility in practice. Nevertheless, the official and parallel market rates for CFA Francs are always of the same order of magnitude, which is in itself a major achievement, compared with other African currencies.

(ii) *A fixed exchange rate.* From 1948 to 1994, Article 9 of the BEAC constitution and Article 2 of the UEMOA convention stipulated a fixed rate of 50 : 1. The rate has been changed only once – to 100 : 1 – in January 1994. The devaluation of the French Franc in August 1969 prompted the members of the CFA to negotiate a system of compensation for French devaluations. Each year, the French Treasury would compensate for any loss of exchange by the CFA due to falls in the value of the French Franc–SDR rate, crediting the 'Operations Accounts' of the central banks accordingly. (See below for a description of these accounts.) This agreement has been carried over into the floating exchange rate system, the Operations Accounts being credited when the French Franc depreciates. If the French Franc appreciates, the accounts are not debited, but the calculated gain by the CFA is deducted from any future credits.

Again, there is a fixed exchange rate *de jure*, the sustainability of which will be credible as long as the pressure for devaluation does not become too large. This will depend on the external balances of the member states of the two unions, an issue to which we shall return.

(iii) *Free transferability.* Article 10 of the BEAC constitution states that 'transfers of funds between member states and France will be unrestricted'. Similarly, Article 6 of the UEMOA accord describes the 'freedom of financial relations between France and members of the Union'. This obligation on the part of the African states is not without qualification, and the practice of member states is not always in harmony with the principle, a point to which we will return in later chapters.

(iv) *Harmonisation of rules governing currency exchange.* Article 14 of the BEAC constitution stipulates that 'with the exception of modifications necessitated by local conditions... states will try to implement the exchange policy of the CFA'. Article 6 of the UEMOA accord notes that the 'uniform regulation of the external financial relations of member states... will be maintained in harmony with that of the French Republic'. These regulations cover such things as the remittance of salaries abroad (i.e. outside the CFA), foreign investment and borrowing from abroad. Again, with the relaxation of currency restrictions in France in order to conform to EU regulations, there has been some divergence from the idea of complete harmonisation of Franco-African exchange regulations.

1.1.2. Regulation of the CFA monetary system

The administrative structures of the CFA are built around the BEAC and the BCEAO, which are the only institutions in the region granted with the power to issue CFA currency. They also implement monetary policy, and finance and regulate government and private banking activity. The regulations the central banks are empowered to enact concern particular monetary aggregates. Overall control of monetary creation is sought through the close monitoring and regulation of the different components of the money stock. The CFA constitutions make the central banks' roles and powers very clear; what is not so clear is how effective the central banks actually are in controlling the financial system.

We might stylise the monetary system of either zone in the following way:

$$MON - CTE - NGD - E \cdot NFA - OAS \equiv 0 \qquad (1.1)$$

$$M_Q + CTE - E \cdot NFA_{\mathrm{PB}} - PCR - NGD_{\mathrm{PB}} \equiv 0 \qquad (1.2)$$

Equation (1.1) is the central bank's balance sheet and equation (1.2) the private sector banks' balance sheet. MON (the money base) and M_Q (quasi-money, net of cash reserves) are the components of the money supply, and form part of banks' liabilities. NFA and NFA_{PB} are the net foreign assets of the central bank and the private banking system respectively (E is the exchange rate); NGD and NGD_{PB} are net indebtedness of the governments of the zone to the central bank and the private banking system respectively. The main foreign creditor of CFA governments is the IMF. IMF funds are directed through the central bank, so IMF credit is counted as NGD and corresponds to negative NFA. CTE is net central bank credit to private banks. PCR is credit allocated by the banking system to the private sectors of each economy. It can be disaggregated into credit rediscounted by the central bank and that credit which is not rediscounted. OAS is a balancing item discussed in more detail in Chapter 3. The identity (1.1) applies to individual countries as well as to the zone as a whole, the central bank accounts being disaggregated by country.

The administration of the CFA is based on accounts held by the central banks in Paris ('Operations Accounts'). The central banks are required to hold 65 per cent of their foreign assets (NFA) with the French Treasury. Similar restrictions guide the regulation of private banks' foreign assets (NFA_{PB}). These assets represent the pooled foreign reserves of the zone. The BEAC and the BCEAO each have accounts. Moreover, each central bank imputes shares in the Operations Account to each country, based on national economic and financial data.[5] This facilitates the calculation of balance of payments statistics for each country. The rises and falls in the net foreign assets of each country correspond to surpluses and deficits on the balance of payments. A key feature of the Operations Accounts is that they can be in debit, the CFA as a whole receiving credit from France. The interest payments on this credit are very low: 1 per cent for a deficit less than FF 5 million, 2 per cent for the FF 5–10 million range and for over FF

10 million the mean Banque de France intervention rate for the quarter, which is usually around 6–8 per cent. However, the burden on France of financing the system is not great, since the total money supply of the CFA amounts to only about 3 per cent of the money supply of France.

The administrative structures of the CFA are designed to 'harmonize' the monetary policy of member states, so that the French guarantees are feasible, i.e. institutional restrictions prevent countries free riding on the system. Without any controls, free riding would be easy. For example, without any institutional constraints, governments could create large current account deficits each year by increasing borrowing from private banks to finance government consumption of imports. This would take the form of a reduction in the net foreign assets of private banks (NFA_{PB}), to acquire the forex to pay for the imports, and a corresponding increase in NGD_{PB} as the private banks hand over the money. The government has generated a substitution of domestic assets for foreign ones in the domestic banking system, leaving the money supply unchanged. The consumption of the imports is financed by an increase in the country's debit on the Operations Account, a debt on which interest payments are negligible.

The central banks have a number of measures at their disposal aimed at preventing the deterioration of the Operations Accounts, and thus the extent to which CFA members are indebted to the French treasury.

1 The central banks provide rediscount facilities to financial institutions of member states. These facilities can be restricted in an attempt to reduce the total credit created by these institutions ($NGD_{PB} + PCR$). Rediscount levels are set for each country, placing an upper bound on the total amount of rediscount credit allocated by the central bank to that country in a particular year. The assumption has been that these levels will control total credit creation, since banks will consider it too risky to lend more than a certain multiple of their rediscount facility. However, an important limitation of these rules has been the exclusion of short-run agricultural credit from the rediscount limits.

2 The central banks can also operate a procedure called *ratissage* – 'raking in'. This involves the compulsory deposit of foreign assets of public and private bodies in the central bank in exchange for CFA Francs. The presumable motivation for this is to prevent governments running up foreign assets abroad while becoming

increasingly indebted with respect to the Operations Account, a practice that the 65 per cent rule is meant to prevent. However, *ratissage* is seldom used.

3   The central banks also control a wide range of interest rates in the domestic economy, which could in theory be raised to discourage borrowing by private agents and encourage saving. However, CFA documents emphasise that interest rate policy is intended to promote long term saving. Interest rates are not perceived as a short run adjustment tool.[6]

4   The other key tool for controlling African deficits is the '20 per cent rule'. Credits to government from the central banks (*NGD*) are limited to 20 per cent of the government's fiscal receipts for the previous year. If the government wants to increase its expenditure, it must increase its revenue. Thus, if the 20 per cent limit is a binding constraint, there is a link between credit creation and the budget deficit and, with government borrowing from abroad making up such a large fraction of total borrowing, between credit creation and the current account deficit.

The most important tools for preventing free riding are the private credit limits (1) and the 20 per cent rule (4). However, both of these tools are limited in scope, the first because of the exclusion of short-run agricultural credit and the second because 20 per cent has turned out to be a very generous limit that seldom represents a binding constraint. The consequences of these limitations are explored in more detail in Chapters 3 and 4.

1.2.   The economic impact of CFA institutions

1.2.1.   Existing evidence

The institutions and regulations described above could have an impact on economic performance in several ways. In the rest of this book we will discuss evidence of the impact on economic performance of the different elements of the constitutions of the two monetary unions. Before listing these elements, it is important to point out that there already exists some empirical evidence on the impact of CFA membership on economic performance.

A number of studies have sought to determine whether membership of the CFA promotes or retards economic growth. Since economic data are usually available only annually in African countries, and the significance of economic determinants of short-run performance is difficult to evaluate in the presence of highly variable geographical factors (for example, rainfall, humidity and temperature), these studies tend to concentrate on long run growth trends. The major studies comparing income growth rates are Devarajan and de Melo (1987), Plane (1988) and Elbadawi and Majd (1992). The main obstacle to obtaining significant statistical results is the great diversity in the economies inside and outside the CFA. Devarajan and de Melo's solution is to estimate a GLS model of the log of gross national product of seventy-four LDCs for the period, 1960–82. The model is of the form,

$$y_{it} = b_0 + b_1 D + g_0 T + g_1 DT \tag{1.3}$$

where y_{it} is log GNP of the ith country in year t, D is a dummy variable for membership of the CFA and T is a time trend. The model is estimated for eleven categories, grouping together oil importers and exporters, and countries with *ex ante* low and high per capita GNP, for Sub-Saharan Africa as well as for the whole sample. In general, aggregate growth of CFA members is significantly lower than the aggregate for the rest of the sample, but this does not take account of the possibility of more adverse climatic and geographical conditions in Africa than elsewhere. When CFA members are compared with just the rest of Sub-Saharan Africa, statistically significantly better performance by CFA members appears for the high income countries and for the high and low income countries pooled, while there is no statistically significant difference for low income countries alone. Comparing two sub-samples, 1960–73 and 1973–82 (before and after the move to floating exchange rates in the international economic system and the reform of the BEAC/BCEAO) reveals more information. In the first period, the one significant result for Sub-Saharan Africa is that low-income CFA members grew more slowly, while in the second period the one (highly) significant result is the faster growth of high-income CFA members.

This approach is open to the criticism that its treatment of the factors determining economic growth is rather crude, allowing for no quantification of the effects of natural resources and geography on growth. It would not be difficult to compile a long list of possibly significant omitted variables.

Plane (1988) tries to avoid this criticism by beginning with a general model of economic growth for sixty-one LDCs for the period, 1962–81, and for two sub-periods. (The partition is between 1970 and 1971.) The dependant variable in the cross-country regression is the average rate of growth of GNP over the period. Significant explanatory variables include *ex ante* population and population growth rate, a dummy for aridity of climate, variation in terms of trade, *ex ante* per capita GNP, the proportion of mineral extraction output in GDP, infant mortality rate and the proportion of the population with primary education. Plane then tests whether the cross-country residual is dependant on CFA membership. Although the weighted average of residuals for the CFA is positive, and the residual for Africa outside the CFA negative, the difference is not significant.

This methodology is not itself without drawbacks, however. In particular, Plane makes a number of questionable assumptions about the independence of variables, for example, the independence of CFA membership from such factors as previous macroeconomic performance (there has been some movement in and out of the CFA, and this may be determined partly by economic factors). Also, although the average residuals for each of the country groups are calculated using weights reflecting the size of each country, the original 'baseline' equation used to calculate the 'norm' for income growth gives each LDC equal weighting: the figure for Bhutan counts as one observation as does the figure for India.

Elbadawi and Majd (1992) address the problem of the non-independence of CFA membership from other determinants of growth. They use instrumental variables to estimate the likelihood of CFA membership in a Probit equation, and then go on to estimate economic growth by country as a function of the instrumental variable estimate plus other explanatory variables. The most striking, and seemingly contradictory conclusion of this study is that while CFA membership had a positive influence on growth in the 1970s, the contribution of CFA membership to growth has been negative in the late 1980s.

However, the studies described above do not shed any light on the mechanisms by which the institutions of the CFA might affect the performance of its members' economies. Indeed, Plane's paper excludes a number of possible connections a priori, by assuming the independence of explanatory variables from CFA membership. If we are to explain the seemingly contradictory results of the existing papers that use a CFA dummy, we need to embed the impact of CFA institutions in a structural framework that shows how these institutions affect economic performance. The next section outlines the ways in which the rest of this book will address this problem.

1.2.2. The structure of this book

The following chapters in the book concentrate in turn on the following three key areas. The aim of each chapter is to draw out the mechanisms at work in the links between CFA membership and economic performance.

(i) *The impact of the fixed exchange rate on inflation.* Maintaining an exchange rate peg against the French Franc entails a major potential benefit and a major potential disadvantage. The potential benefit is that the peg constitutes a credible commitment to a long-run inflation rate equal to that of France (i.e. much lower than the African average). The potential advantage of the CFA peg compared with a unilateral peg is that financial authorities can quite easily renege on a unilateral peg, which undermines its use as a commitment indicator. In a country locked into the institutions of the CFA, reneging would be much more difficult since it would entail quitting the zone entirely, or negotiating a change in the rate with all of the country's partners. This is not to say that the CFA peg represents a completely credible commitment: as discussed above, the possibility of future devaluation has affected the CFA in the past. Evidence on the potential benefit of CFA membership in terms of a credible commitment to low inflation informs the content of Chapter 2.

(ii) *The impact of the regulatory system on monetary policy and the monetary transmission mechanism.* Chapter 2 is concerned with long-run monetary growth and inflation, and focuses on the impact of the exchange rate peg as a disciplining device. Chapters 3–5 provide more evidence on the macroeconomic consequences of the institutional and regulatory environment in which CFA monetary policy is conducted, and have more of a short-run focus. Chapter 3 will focus on the determination of the different components of the central bank's balance sheet in equation (1.1) above. We will estimate a policy reaction function for the BCEAO that explains the evolution of those components of the balance sheet the central bank can control, and compare the behaviour implicit in the function with that of two non-CFA central banks (in Kenya and Tanzania). Comparison of the policy reaction functions in different institutional and regulatory environments will shed light on the particular impact of the CFA.

Chapter 4 is concerned with the interaction of monetary and fiscal policy of CFA members, and involves an exploration of the free riding problem mentioned above. The CFA constitutions are designed to prevent any CFA government free riding on France or on other CFA members. As we have already suggested, these constitutional arrangements might not be completely watertight. Chapter 4 will examine the extent to which the free riding problem exists, and who the main culprits and victims of the problem are.

While Chapters 3 and 4 are concerned with monetary policy, Chapter 5 focuses on the monetary transmission mechanism. The institutional characteristics of the CFA are likely to impact on the private sector's demand for financial assets. This in turn will influence the effectiveness of the CFA central banks' own monetary policy. In order to illustrate the role of institutions in conditioning asset demand, we will focus on the case of Côte d'Ivoire, a country for which economic and financial data are relatively abundant.

(iii) *The impact of currency convertibility, transferability and exchange harmonisation on investment and growth.* To the extent that the CFA is successful in guaranteeing that these characteristics are actualised, we ought to observe a substantial degree of financial openness and access to international capital markets among CFA members. The hypothesis that CFA membership promotes openness – and so better investment and growth performance – will be tested in several ways. Chapter 6 will investigate the degree of financial integration between the CFA and France by measuring the magnitude of (and causes of) differences in the real opportunity cost of borrowing between the two regions. Chapter 7 will use time-series data from two relatively data-abundant countries (Côte d'Ivoire in the UEMOA and Kenya outside the CFA) in order to pursue the consequences for investment of differing degrees of financial openness in representative CFA and non-CFA countries. Chapter 8 complements Chapter 7 by employing cross-section data on African investment performance over a wide range of countries. Data limitations mean that the approach taken is more reduced-form than in Chapter 7, but we will be able to quantify the marginal impact of CFA membership in explaining long-term variations in investment across a wide range of countries.

Appendix 1.1: CFA administrative structures

The BEAC zone

At the apex of the BEAC structure is the *Comité monétaire* (Monetary Committee). This is composed of the finance ministers of member states, and meets annually. Its role is restricted to oversight of the application of the rules and policies of the zone. There is also a *Comité monétaire mixte* (Mixed Monetary Committee), which is composed of Monetary Committee members plus French representatives, also meeting annually. The main policy-making body is the *Conseil d'administration* (Administrative Council). This is composed of four Cameroonian representatives, two from Gabon, one from each other member state and three from France. Decisions are made by a simple majority vote, except for major decisions, which require a three-fourths majority. This meets regularly to decide on general BEAC policy and to check the bank's statement of accounts. Under the Administrative Council are the *Comités monétaires nationaux* (National Monetary Committees). Each committee is made up of BEAC officials and national representatives sponsored by the government. This assesses the general financial needs of the economy, as a basis for setting upper bounds on credit allocated to private banks and enterprises. Decisions are taken at the level of the individual firm, with the setting of limits on the quantity of credit to the firm from private banks that the BEAC will rediscount. Individual officials of the BEAC: the Governor, Censors and National Directors, have a purely administrative role.

The UEMOA zone

The highest authority in the BCEAO is the *Conference des chefs d'état* (Conference of Heads of State). This meets at least once a year to decide on issues not resolved by the *Conseil des ministres* (Council of Ministers). Decisions require a unanimous vote. The Council of Ministers (two from each country) decides general BCEAO policy. In recent years, much of its time has been taken up by credit arrangements with international organisations such as the IMF and World Bank. Again, a unanimous vote is required. It plays a much more active role than its BEAC counterpart. The Council of Ministers nominates the Governor of the BCEAO, who serves for a period of six years. Endowed with more authority than the Governor of the BEAC, he implements not just the decisions of the councils, but also his own decisions in areas the councils do not have time to cover. The UEMOA Administrative Council and *Comités nationaux du crédit* (National Credit Committees) are similar to the BEAC Administrative Council and National Monetary Committees, although with less authority, since the higher organs of the administration play a more active role.

Notes

1 Because convertibility has always been the responsibility of the French treasury, and not the Banque de France, France's membership of the EMU had very minimal institutional consequences for the CFA.
2 The rate changed to 100 : 1 in January 1994.
3 See de la Fournière (1973) for an account of the CFA before the 1973 reforms.
4 Figures are taken from African Analysis (May 1988).
5 The net position of the central bank is not identical to the sum of the net positions of member states, since some assets of the bank are not disaggregated by country.
6 See for example Secrétariat du Comité de la Zone Franc (1990).

References

Bathia, R. (1986) 'The west African monetary union: An analytical survey', *IMF Occasional Paper 35*.

de la Fournière, X. (1973) *La Zone Franc*, Paris: Presses Universités de France.

Devarajan, S. and de Melo, J. (1987) 'Evaluating participation in African monetary unions', *World Development*, 15.

Elbadawi, I. and Majd, N. (1992) 'Fixed parity of the exchange rate and economic performance in the CFA zone', *World Bank Policy Research Working Paper 830*.

Plane, P. (1988) 'Performances comparées en matiere de croissance économique', in Guillaumont, P. and Guillaumont, S., *Strategies de Développement Comparées*, Paris: Economica.

Secrétariat du Comité Monétaire de la Zone Franc (1990) *La Zone Franc Rapport*, Paris.

Vizy, M. (1989) *La Zone Franc*, Paris: CHEAM.

2 CFA membership, exchange rate pegs and inflation*

The CFA's adherence to a fixed exchange rate removes one degree of freedom in monetary policy. Given that its members are small open economies and price-takers on world markets, the CFAF prices of tradable goods (and hence the corresponding inflation rates) are given. This is not necessarily a disadvantage: there is a body of macro-economic theory that predicts that pre-commitment to a fixed exchange rate will help in reducing inflation. Monetary policymakers in countries in which such a pre-commitment is absent will not be able to achieve inflation rates as low as those adhering to a fixed exchange rate. In this chapter we will first review the theoretical foundation for this idea, and then outline an empirical model that will allow us to investigate whether there is any evidence whether exchange rate pegs in general – and the CFA in particular – help in reducing inflation.

2.1. Why does pre-commitment matter?

The theoretical basis for the advantages of pre-commitment derives from the model of Kydland and Prescott (1977). In this model the level of aggregate output depends positively on the gap between actual and expected inflation, so the government always has some incentive to increase the rate of monetary expansion and generate extra inflation. (In the traditional version of the model, the government values monetary

---

*This chapter is based on the article 'Monetary discipline and inflation in developing countries: The role of the exchange rate regime', *Oxford Economic Papers*, **52**: 521–38, written jointly with M.F. Bleaney. By permission of Oxford University Press.

expansion and inflation because it leads to higher output; but the same kind of results appear in a model where the government's incentive is that it can finance a larger budget deficit by printing money at a faster rate.) If the private sector is aware of this incentive then they will (correctly) anticipate a high inflation rate; and if the government is unable in some way to pre-commit itself to a low inflation policy then it will never be possible to reach an equilibrium with low inflationary expectations and low actual inflation.

The simplest form of the model consists of two equations. The first is a 'surprise supply curve', which embodies the relationship between aggregate output and unanticipated inflation:

$$y = y^* + \beta \cdot [\pi - \pi^e] \tag{2.1}$$

where y is actual output, y^* the natural rate of output, π actual inflation and π^e the inflation rate anticipated by the private sector.[1] The second is a government objective function. In the government's ideal world, output would be equal to some target rate $\alpha \cdot y^*$, where $\alpha > 1$, and inflation would be equal to zero. Any deviation of inflation or output from these targets generates a welfare loss (L). The government can control inflation through the rate of monetary expansion that it sets, and sets inflation to minimise L. The most tractable loss function is a quadratic one:

$$L = \tfrac{1}{2} \cdot [y - \alpha \cdot y^*]^2 + \tfrac{1}{2} \cdot k \cdot \pi^2 \tag{2.2}$$

The parameter k reflects the relative importance to the government of achieving low inflation. Substituting (2.1) into (2.2) we have:

$$L = \tfrac{1}{2} \cdot [\beta \cdot [\pi - \pi^e] - [\alpha - 1] \cdot y^*]^2 + \tfrac{1}{2} \cdot k \cdot \pi^2 \tag{2.3}$$

Taking inflationary expectations (π^e) as given, and minimising L with respect to π, the government's optimal policy rule is:

$$\pi = \beta \cdot [[\alpha - 1] \cdot y^* + \pi^e \cdot \beta]/[k + \beta^2] \tag{2.4}$$

The key assumption here is that the government acts when inflationary expectations have been set. In other words, the government can adjust the rate of monetary expansion more quickly than the private sector can adjust its expectations. Now, if the private sector knows the problem that the government is facing, i.e. it knows the policy rule represented by equation (2.4), then it can form its expectations so that the actual inflation rate is correctly predicted. In other words, $\pi = \pi^e$. Substituting the equality $\pi = \pi^e$ into equation (2.4) yields:

$$\pi = [\alpha - 1] \cdot y^* \cdot \beta/k \qquad (2.5)$$

This implies a welfare loss equal to:

$$L^* = \tfrac{1}{2} \cdot [[\alpha - 1] \cdot y^*]^2 + \tfrac{1}{2} \cdot k \cdot [[\alpha - 1] \cdot y^* \cdot \beta/k]^2 \qquad (2.6)$$

Since actual inflation equals expected inflation, the government gains no benefit from the positive inflation rate. It would have been better to set $\pi = 0$, in which cases the welfare loss would have been:

$$L = \tfrac{1}{2} \cdot [[\alpha - 1] \cdot y^*]^2 < L^* \qquad (2.7)$$

However, a zero inflation rate is not an equilibrium in this model. It would never be rational for people to anticipate a zero inflation rate – if they did, the government would always have an incentive to set a positive inflation rate, as indicated by equation (2.4). The only inflation rate that is rational to expect is the one given by equation (2.5): any other expectation will turn out to be incorrect.

One way out of the problem is for the government to find some way to pre-commit itself to a low inflation rate: in other words, to set a low inflation rate and remove the possibility that it can adjust the inflation rate once expectations have been set. In the industrialised world this has led governments to institute central banks that are operationally independent from the elected government, and that are set the objective of achieving low inflation.

In the developing world, however, this is unlikely to be politically feasible. Few countries have the political institutions that would make such independence credible. The CFA represents an alternative form of pre-commitment. Although the CFA central banks are not operationally independent from the governments of member states, they do have to set monetary policy within the framework of a fixed exchange rate. If the exchange rate cannot depreciate when the money supply expands, such expansion is likely to lead to painful Balance of Payments deficits.[2] The fixed exchange rate therefore represents a deterrent to monetary expansion. Such a deterrent could in principle be created by any fixed exchange rate regime, but the problem with unilateral pegs – as opposed to membership of the CFA – is that they can always be revoked. A unilateral peg is unlikely to be as successful on average in keeping inflation low. Recent empirical work by Ghosh *et al.* (1995) and Anyadike-Danes (1995) suggests that inflation is significantly lower under pegged exchange rate regimes, but they do not distinguish between CFA members and other pegged regime countries.

In this chapter we will present an empirical model that allows us to test the extent to which CFA membership leads to lower rates of monetary expansion, as compared with unilateral peg regimes and flexible exchange rate regimes. We will also investigate whether the inflation rate is correspondingly lower. The distinction between the impact of exchange rate regimes on monetary expansion and their impact on inflation is necessary because the exchange rate regime can alter the structure of the monetary transmission mechanism. As theoretical models[3] of small open economies predict, the choice of exchange rate regime affects the rate of inflation for a given rate of monetary expansion, because some excess money emerges as a Balance of Payments deficit, rather than as higher prices. Although this deficit is likely to require correction in the long term, the two effects ought to be distinguished in an empirical investigation into the deflationary power of adherence to a pegged exchange rate. As we show below, the choice of exchange rate regime influences both the intercept and the slopes of the money market equilibrium equation, adding an extra layer of complexity to the exercise.

We will address these issues by estimating a two-equation model on cross-country data for eighty LDCs. The first equation, examining the monetary discipline hypothesis, is a model of the rate of monetary growth. Because this model uses monetary expansion rather than inflation as a dependent variable, it is free from the interpretational ambiguities of other exchange rate discipline models. The second equation explores the marginal effect on inflation of adherence to a pegged exchange rate regime (for a given rate of monetary expansion) in the context of an empirical model that is consistent with the theoretical literature. Because the theoretical basis of the second model is rather more complex than that of the first, the next section reprises the theory of exchange rates and inflation determination in small open economies.

2.2. Monetary expansion and inflation in a stylised small open economy

In order to examine the links between inflation, monetary growth and the exchange rate regime we take a simple stylised monetary model, similar to that discussed by Frenkel and Mussa (1985). The main point of exploring such a model is to see what impact the exchange rate regime has on inflation for a given rate of monetary expansion. Although this kind of model is by no means new to the literature, its detailed predictions regarding the structure of the relationship between money and prices have not been made explicit. The innovation we make is to specify log-linear functional forms for relationships that have generally been left imprecise in the literature; this permits the derivation of predictions about the impact of the exchange rate regime on the different parameters of the money market equilibrium equation.

The model consists of a money demand equation, equations determining the allocation of consumption between imports, exportables and nontradables, a supply equation defining output of exportables and nontradables, and an equilibrium condition for the nontraded sector. Under the managed exchange rate regime, the nominal exchange rate is treated as exogenous, whereas under a flexible exchange rate regime it adjusts to equate the value of imports and exports.

Consumption in the model is allocated between three goods: an imported commodity, an exportable and a nontraded commodity. For clarity of exposition, the ratio of each in total expenditure is held fixed, though this makes no substantial difference to the results. If nominal money demand is proportional to total consumption, then monetary equilibrium can be expressed as:

$$m = \varphi + \gamma \cdot [p_N + c_N] + [1 - \gamma]$$
$$\cdot \{e + \kappa \cdot [p_M + c_M] + [1 - \kappa] \cdot [p_X + c_X]\} \qquad (2.8)$$

where m represents the (exogenous) money stock, p_N the domestic price of nontraded goods, c_N consumption of nontraded goods, p_M the (exogenous) dollar price of imports, c_M consumption of imports, p_X the (exogenous) dollar price of exportables, c_X consumption of exportables, e the nominal exchange rate, γ the ratio of nontraded good consumption to total expenditure and κ the ratio of import consumption to total tradables consumption; all variables are expressed as logarithms. Traded and nontraded consumption levels are related by the equation:

$$c_N = \kappa \cdot c_M + [1 - \kappa] \cdot c_X + \gamma' \qquad (2.9)$$

where $\gamma' = \log(\gamma) - \log(1 - \gamma)$. Similarly,

$$c_M = c_X + \kappa' \qquad (2.9a)$$

where $\kappa' = \log(\kappa) - \log(1 - \kappa)$. Two commodities are produced: non-traded goods (output $= y_N$) and exportables (output $= y_X$). In Appendix 2.1 we derive production functions for any period t of the form:

$$y_N = \theta_N \cdot [p_N - e - p_X] + \alpha_{Nt} \qquad (2.10)$$

$$y_X = \theta_X \cdot [e + p_X - p_N] + \alpha_{Xt} \qquad (2.11)$$

where θ_N and θ_X are exogenous parameters and α_N and α_X are exogenous output growth rates. In addition, we have a nontraded goods market clearing condition:

$$c_N = y_N \qquad (2.12)$$

The determination of equilibrium prices will depend on the exchange rate regime. In the managed exchange rate case the trade balance is not necessarily equal to zero, and we can solve equations (2.8)–(2.10) and (2.12) for p_N. (The other endogenous variables in the system are $\{\kappa \cdot c_M + [1 - \kappa] \cdot c_X\}$, c_N and y_N.) Assuming for simplicity that $\alpha_N = \alpha_X = \alpha$, we have:

$$p_N = \{m - \varphi - \alpha \cdot t + [1 - \gamma] \cdot [\gamma' - \kappa \cdot p_M] + [\gamma + \theta_N - 1] \cdot e$$
$$+ [\theta_N - [1 - \kappa] \cdot [1 - \gamma]] \cdot p_X\}/[\gamma + \theta_N] \qquad (2.13)$$

This implies equilibrium values of y_X (via equation (2.11)) and $\{\kappa \cdot c_M + [1 - \kappa] \cdot c_X\}$; equation (2.9a) then implies values of c_X and c_M and hence a value for the trade deficit.

The consumer price index (cpi) can be represented as:

$$p = \gamma \cdot p_N + [1 - \gamma] \cdot \{e + \kappa \cdot p_M + [1 - \kappa] \cdot p_X\} \qquad (2.14)$$

This implies that:

$$p = \{\gamma/[\gamma + \theta_N]\} \cdot \{m - \varphi - \alpha \cdot t + [1 - \gamma] \cdot \gamma'\}$$
$$+ \{\theta_N/[\gamma + \theta_N]\} \cdot \{e + [1 - [1 - \gamma] \cdot \kappa] \cdot p_X + [1 - \gamma] \cdot \kappa \cdot p_M\}$$

(2.15)

which can also be expressed as:

$$p = \{\gamma/[\gamma + \theta_N]\} \cdot \{m - \varphi - \alpha \cdot t + [1 - \gamma] \cdot \gamma'\}$$
$$+ \{\theta_N/[\gamma + \theta_N]\} \cdot \{e + p_M\}$$
$$+ \{[1 - [1 - \gamma] \cdot \kappa] \cdot \theta_N/[\gamma + \theta_N]\} \cdot x$$

(2.16)

where $x = p_X - p_M$ represents the terms of trade. The rate of inflation can be derived by differentiating equation (2.16) with respect to t. Assuming that φ is constant, we have:

$$\pi = dp/dt = \{\gamma/[\gamma + \theta_N]\} \cdot \{dm/dt - \alpha\}$$
$$+ \{\theta_N/[\gamma + \theta_N]\} \cdot d[e + p_M]/dt$$
$$+ \{[1 - [1 - \gamma] \cdot \kappa] \cdot \theta_N/[\gamma + \theta_N]\} \cdot dx/dt$$

(2.17)

This equation decomposes inflation into three sources: monetary growth over and above real output growth, import price inflation and changes in the terms of trade.

In the flexible exchange rate case e is endogenous, and there is a trade balance equation:

$$\kappa \cdot [p_M + c_M] + [1 - \kappa] \cdot [p_X + c_X] = p_X + y_X$$

(2.18)

Solving equations (2.8)–(2.10), (2.12) and (2.18) and substituting into the definition of the cpi. in equation (2.14) we have:

$$p = m - \varphi - \alpha \cdot t - \{\kappa \cdot \theta_N/[\theta_N + \theta_X]\} \cdot x - \gamma'$$
$$\cdot [\gamma - \theta_X/[\theta_N + \theta_X]]$$

(2.19)

and inflation is:

$$\pi = dp/dt = dm/dt - \alpha - \{\kappa \cdot \theta_N/[\theta_N + \theta_X]\} \cdot dx/dt$$

(2.20)

Table 2.1 Sources of inflation under alternative exchange rate regimes

	Managed rate	Floating rate
The coefficients on sources of inflation		
Monetary growth – Real output growth	Positive < 1	Unity
Import prices	Positive < 1	None
Terms of trade	Positive < 1	Negative > −1
The effect of γ on the value of the coefficients		
Monetary growth – Real output growth	Positive	None
Import prices	Negative	None
Terms of trade	Ambiguous	None

Comparison of equations (2.17) and (2.20) illustrates some of the stylised differences which one might expect to find between managed and flexible exchange rate regimes, and which are summarised in Table 2.1. In the flexible exchange rate regime, a 1 per cent increase in the money stock leads to a 1 per cent increase in prices; in the managed exchange rate regime, the resulting increase in prices is only $\gamma/[\gamma + \theta_N]$ per cent, because some of the monetary expansion is translated into a deterioration of the trade balance. If most expenditure is on imports (γ is small) and the nontraded goods supply curve is shallow (θ_N is large), then monetary expansion has relatively little effect on prices.[4] However, the same remarks are true of the disinflationary effect of real economic growth, represented by α: higher growth has a less than proportional impact on inflation in a managed exchange rate regime.

There are also differences in the impact of changes in terms of trade on domestic inflation. For a given import price level, the terms of trade improvement in a managed exchange rate regime leads to higher domestic prices, because the export price rise draws factors out of nontraded goods production, leading to higher nontraded goods prices. In a flexible exchange rate regime terms of trade improvements lead to exchange rate appreciation (without such appreciation there would be a trade surplus), reducing the domestic price of traded goods and so aggregate domestic prices. As a result the overall impact of a change in the export price is negative.

Moreover, for a given terms of trade the impact of import prices varies between managed and flexible exchange rate regimes. In the former, the elasticity is $\theta_N/[\gamma + \theta_N]$ and in the latter it is zero. In the fixed exchange rate case a rise in γ (a fall in the share of imports in total expenditure) reduces the elasticity; this effect is non-linear and depends on the slope of the nontraded goods supply curve.

For a given rate of monetary growth, the effect on inflation of adherence to a managed exchange rate regime is a priori indeterminate. There is a gain through the reduced impact of monetary expansion on inflation, but a loss due to the increased impact of import price inflation, and a reduction in the deflationary effect of any real economic growth.

2.3. Empirical results

This section consists of two parts. The first is a cross-country model of the rate of monetary growth in LDCs. This model is designed to test whether pegged exchange rate countries (and particularly the CFA countries) do really benefit from a nominal anchor and mitigate the time inconsistency problem outlined in Section 2.1. The second, employing the results summarised by equations (2.17) and (2.20) in Section 2.2, is a model of inflation conditional on this rate of growth. Data are taken from the World Bank World Development Indicators CD-ROM (1996), and cover the period 1980–89. There are eighty LDCs (listed in Appendix 2.2) with adequate data for this period, once potential outliers (countries with annual inflation rates in excess of 50 per cent) have been excluded; longer sample periods would entail a substantial reduction in the number of countries included. The regression equations use average values of each variable for each country over the sample period, rather than a panel of annual observations. This allows us to avoid modelling the short-run dynamics of inflation, and concentrate on the equilibrium effects discussed in the previous section.

In each empirical model, the sample is divided into two groups. The first (fifty-two countries) consists of those countries characterised by Ghosh *et al.* (1995) as having pegged exchange rates over the whole sample period; this group includes both CFA members (nine countries) and others (forty-three countries). The second (twenty-eight countries) consists of those characterised as having a flexible or 'intermediate' exchange rate regime for at least part of the sample period. A caveat to the results reported below is that this second group is somewhat heterogeneous. Many of the governments in the group have engaged in some form of exchange rate intervention, so they cannot be regarded as exemplifying the 'pure' floating exchange rate case. Nevertheless, it is reasonable to suppose that the second group is much closer than the first to the paradigm represented by theoretical floating exchange rate models, and that there are stylised differences between the two groups corresponding to those discussed in the theory above.

2.3.1. The determinants of monetary growth

If adherence to a managed exchange rate regime instils monetary discipline, then we should observe a lower mean rate of monetary growth among the managed exchange rate sample, after allowing for other factors that might influence monetary policy. If CFA membership leads to an especially high degree of discipline, then the mean should be even lower for the CFA countries in the sample. We control for the other factors by estimating monetary growth equations that include measures of country size, openness to international trade and central bank independence for both of our samples. The pegged exchange rate sample also includes a dummy for membership of the CFA. The variables in our monetary growth regression are:

- The mean rate of growth of GDP, in real domestic currency, $\mu(dy/dt)_i$
- The log of mean GDP, in real US$, $\mu(y)_i$
- The log of the mean ratio of the value of exports plus imports to nominal GDP, $\mu(z)_i$
- A dummy variable for membership of the CFA Franc Zone, CFA_i
- The Central Bank Independence index of Cukierman *et al.* (1992), CBI_i.

The dependent variable is the mean rate of growth of M1 (narrow money). Because the variance of regression residuals varies systematically with the exchange rate regime, we estimate two separate regressions for the two samples. The last of the explanatory variables is available only for a subset of thirty-seven countries (twenty managed and seventeen floating exchange rate regimes), so there are four regression equations in total: for the smaller managed exchange rate sample including the Central Bank Independence (CBI) variable, for the larger managed exchange rate sample excluding this variable, and similarly for the floating exchange rate samples. Each explanatory variable is scaled so that it has a mean of zero and a variance of unity over the whole sample of eighty countries (thirty-seven countries for

Table 2.2 Summary statistics for variables of interest

	Means	SDs
Flexible exchange rate group		
$\mu(dp)$ inflation	0.214	0.129
$\mu(dm)$ monetary growth	0.227	0.114
$\mu(z)$ openness	−0.552	0.622
$\mu(dy)$ output growth	0.028	0.024
$\mu(y)$ total output	22.53	2.160
Managed exchange rate group		
$\mu(dp)$	0.091	0.054
$\mu(dm)$	0.103	0.058
$\mu(z)$	−0.405	0.598
$\mu(dy)$	0.026	0.026
$\mu(y)$	22.91	1.660

the regressions including Central Bank Independence index (CBI_i). The difference between the intercepts of the managed and floating exchange rate samples is therefore a measure of the impact of the exchange rate regime at the mean values of other conditioning variables, and the size of each coefficient is an indicator of the relative importance of the corresponding variable. Sample means and standard deviations are reported in Table 2.2.

A higher *per capita* income growth will allow a faster rate of monetary expansion for a given level of inflation, so one ought to expect a positive coefficient on $\mu(dy/dt)_i$. The coefficients on $\mu(y)_i$ and $\mu(z)_i$ could be interpreted in various ways. One argument is that it is easier to raise tax revenue from more open economies (because the administrative costs of import and export duties are lower than those of other taxes), and from larger economies (because of administrative economies of scale), so their governments are less likely to need to raise revenue from inflation seigniorage. In this case the coefficients should be negative, and this is indeed what we find. Membership of the CFA ought to be associated with a lower rate of monetary growth: quitting the monetary union in order to devalue is a politically and economically costly step, and any re-pegging of the CFAF exchange rate is difficult because it requires the agreement of all the union's members; so there is no way of avoiding a larger external deficit if monetary expansion increases. (The CFA Franc has been re-pegged only once, in 1994, which is outside our sample period.) A greater degree of CBI ought to be associated with lower monetary growth, for the reasons discussed in Cuckierman *et al.* (op. cit.).[5]

Table 2.3 presents the results of the monetary growth equations. Note that these treat the exchange rate regime as an exogenous variable. Appendix 2.3 discusses tests of this assumption, employing a Probit model for the exchange rate regime. The null hypothesis of exogeneity cannot be rejected.

Table 2.3 Monetary growth equations[a]

Variable	Coeff.	Std. err.	t-value	HCSE
Managed exchange rate group (52 countries)				
Intercept	0.10829	0.00736	14.717	0.007631
$\mu(dy/dt)^{b}$	0.01511	0.00746	2.026	0.007256
$\mu(y)^{b}$	0.00658	0.00896	0.735	0.006540
$\mu(z)^{b}$	−0.01936	0.00868	−2.231	0.009697
CFA[b]	−0.01407	0.00589	−2.388	0.003651
$R^2 = 0.2783$ $\sigma = 0.05156$ *RESET test: F(1,46) = 1.7544 [0.1919]*				
Flexible exchange rate group (28 countries)				
Intercept	0.22722	0.01739	13.064	0.016577
$\mu(dy/dt)^{b}$	−0.01538	0.02119	−0.726	0.020992
$\mu(y)^{b}$	−0.05103	0.01717	−2.973	0.021614
$\mu(z)^{b}$	−0.05847	0.01963	−2.978	0.015091
$R^2 = 0.4543$ $\sigma = 0.0893$ *RESET test: F(1,23) = 2.0208 [0.1686]*				
Managed exchange rate group (20 countries)				
Intercept	0.09611	0.00750	12.821	0.00914
$\mu(dy/dt)^{b}$	0.01811	0.00712	2.546	0.00801
$\mu(y)^{b}$	−0.00681	0.00960	−0.709	0.00761
$\mu(z)^{b}$	−0.02803	0.00823	−3.407	0.00912
CFA[b]	−0.01383	0.00949	−1.457	0.01058
CBI[b]	0.00481	0.01032	0.467	0.01334
$R^2 = 0.6874$ $\sigma = 0.0291$				
Flexible exchange rate group (17 countries)				
Intercept	0.23049	0.02464	9.354	0.025490
$\mu(dy/dt)^{b}$	−0.02860	0.02601	−1.100	0.022637
$\mu(y)^{b}$	−0.04028	0.02140	−1.882	0.027688
$\mu(z)^{b}$	−0.03564	0.02366	−1.507	0.018168
CBI[b]	0.03401	0.03161	1.076	0.022520
$R^2 = 0.4923$ $\sigma = 0.0929$				

[a] $\mu(dy/dt)$ is the average GDP growth rate for each country, $\mu(y)$ the average GDP level (in logs), $\mu(z)$ the mean ratio of imports plus exports to GDP (in logs), *CFA* a dummy for CFA Franc Zone membership and *CBI* the central bank independence index. The RESET test is calculated by adding squared fitted values of the LHS variable to the regression equation.
[b] Indicates normalisation of the variable on its sample cross-country mean.
    HCSE: Heteroscedasticity-corrected standard error.

The small-sample equations including CBI_i do not generate significant coefficients on this variable, and other coefficients are insignificantly different from those in the larger samples. These results cast some doubt on the importance of CBI in LDCs. In what follows, we base our interpretation on the top half of Table 2.3, which excludes the *CBI* variable.

In the managed exchange rate sample, all other variables except $\mu(y)_i$ are significantly different from zero. A rate of growth one standard deviation higher than the sample average can be expected to lead to a monetary growth rate 1.5 percentage points higher. Similarly, a ratio of imports plus exports to GDP one standard deviation higher than the sample average can be expected to lead to a monetary growth rate 1.9 percentage points lower. The CFA term is of the same order of magnitude (-1.4 per cent), so all three factors are of roughly equal importance; if an untransformed dummy is used then the coefficient is -4.9 per cent, indicating the average impact of CFA membership on money growth. In other words, CFA membership does seem to be associated with lower monetary growth than in other managed exchange rate regime countries, once one has controlled for other exogenous national characteristics.

In the flexible exchange rate sample, $\mu(y)_i$ is significant but $\mu(dy/dt)_i$ is insignificant. An aggregate income level one standard deviation above the sample mean can be expected to lead to a monetary growth rate 5.1 percentage points lower, and a ratio of imports plus exports to GDP one standard deviation above the sample mean to a monetary growth rate 5.8 percentage points lower. So monetary growth in the flexible exchange rate sample is much more sensitive to the size and structure of the economy. This goes some way to explaining the higher standard deviation of monetary growth in the flexible exchange rate group reported in Table 2.2 (11.4 per cent v. 5.8 per cent). The difference in mean monetary growth rates between the two groups (22.7 per cent v. 10.3 per cent) is very similar to the difference between the intercepts of the equations in Table 2.3 (22.7 per cent v. 10.8 per cent). In other words, differences in monetary growth rates between the two groups are not explained by differences in $\mu(dy/dt)$, $\mu(y)$ or $\mu(z)$. An 'average' country displaying the mean values of these variables can be expected to have a rate of monetary growth 11.9 percentage points higher if it has a flexible exchange rate regime, as compared with a non-CFA managed regime country. (The gap *vis-à-vis* the CFA is an extra 4.9 percentage points.)

How this translates into differences in inflation rates will be seen below.

2.3.2. The determinants of inflation

The theoretical model in Section 2.2 indicates that the structure of the relationship between inflation and monetary growth will vary across exchange rate regimes, so it is appropriate to estimate two inflation equations, one for each regime group. Moreover, equation (2.17) indicates that the effect of mean monetary expansion ($\mu(dm/dt)_i$), real growth ($\mu(dy/dt)_i$), import price inflation ($\mu(d[e+p_M]/dt)_i$) and terms of trade growth ($\mu(dx/dt)_i$) may depend on the share of nontraded goods in consumption in managed exchange rate regimes. Equation (2.20) suggests that in a 'pure' float this share is unimportant, and that for a given terms of trade import price growth does not affect domestic inflation. However, to the extent that the flexible exchange rate sample countries have not all operated 'pure' floats, as assumed in the theoretical model, the import price and the nontradeables share effect will also be a factor in the flexible rate case.[6]

Therefore, the set of explanatory variables should include not only the terms listed above, but also these terms interacted with a measure of the share of nontraded goods (or alternatively, of tradeables) in total consumption. It is difficult in practice to identify just those goods consumed that are traded, so the empirical measure of γ must be a proxy. One way of capturing this kind of effect is to use trade data to construct a general measure of openness: a relatively high level of import consumption ought to be associated with a low level of nontradeables' consumption, and a high level of export production with a low level of nontradeables' production. So the ratio of exports plus imports to GDP is likely to be (negatively) correlated with γ. It is this variable, $\mu(z)_i$, which is used in the results reported below. Note that in the regression reported in Table 2.4 a constant has been added to the $\mu(z)_i$ variable, which is a logarithm, so that its minimum observed value is zero; otherwise increasing openness could not have a monotonic impact on the different inflation elasticities.[7]

One caveat to the results is that there is no variable in the empirical model capturing the slope of the aggregate nontraded goods supply curve (θ_N), which can in theory affect the impact of the RHS variables on inflation. Estimates of aggregate nontradeables' production functions are few and far between in LDCs, and given the data limitations,

Table 2.4 Inflation equations[a]

Variable	Coeff.	Std. err.	t-value	HCSE
Managed exchange rate group (52 countries)				
Unrestricted				
Intercept	0.01968	0.02917	0.674	0.03145
$\mu(z)$	0.00164	0.01603	0.103	0.01513
$\mu(dm/dt)$	1.00100	0.29634	3.378	0.27602
$\mu(z) \cdot \mu(dm/dt)$	−0.35734	0.18757	−1.905	0.15117
$\mu(dy/dt)$	−1.59310	0.52073	−3.059	0.54873
$\mu(z) \cdot \mu(dy/dt)$	0.76245	0.30103	2.533	0.28540
$\mu(d[e+p_M]/dt)$	0.09935	0.29558	0.336	0.28148
$\mu(z) \cdot \mu(d[e+p_M]/dt)$	0.18567	0.20504	0.906	0.16299
$\mu(dx/dt)$	−0.07266	0.35712	−0.203	0.30345
$\mu(z) \cdot \mu(dx/dt)$	−0.02837	0.23566	−0.120	0.18440

$R^2 = 0.8270$ $\sigma = 0.0248$ *RESET test:* $F(1,41) = 0.0745$ *[0.7863]* $SC = -6.85$
$HQ = -7.08$

Variable	Coeff.	Std. err.	t-value	HCSE
Restricted				
Intercept	0.02431	0.00724	3.359	0.00667
$\mu(dm/dt)$	1.04450	0.10173	10.267	0.06185
$\mu(z) \cdot \mu(dm/dt)$	−0.38225	0.07780	−4.913	0.06013
$\mu(dy/dt)$	−1.55100	0.41998	−3.693	0.37293
$\mu(z) \cdot \mu(dy/dt)$	0.73867	0.24377	3.030	0.19119
$\mu(z) \cdot \mu(d[e+p_M]/dt)$	0.25102	0.06145	4.085	0.06017

$R^2 = 0.8238$ $\sigma = 0.0239$ *RESET test:* $F(1,45) = 0.1296$ *[0.7206]* $SC = -7.13$
$HQ = -7.27$ $\mu(dm/dt)$ exogeneity test: $t = -0.302$

Variable	Coeff.	Std. err.	t-value	HCSE
Flexible exchange rate group (28 countries)				
Unrestricted				
Intercept	0.10167	0.07501	1.355	0.06543
$\mu(z)$	−0.07133	0.05272	−1.353	0.04497
$\mu(dm/dt)$	1.07220	0.25570	4.193	0.26929
$\mu(z) \cdot \mu(dm/dt)$	−0.08030	0.20750	−0.387	0.20194
$\mu(dy/dt)$	−2.55430	1.05770	−2.415	0.96215
$\mu(z) \cdot \mu(dy/dt)$	1.23460	0.61578	2.005	0.53941
$\mu(dp_M/dt)$	−1.09130	1.06030	−1.029	1.10990
$\mu(z) \cdot \mu(dp_M/dt)$	1.15890	0.84626	1.369	0.68879
$\mu(dx/dt)$	−1.32980	1.18390	−1.123	0.95398
$\mu(z) \cdot \mu(dx/dt)$	0.81468	0.84680	0.962	0.59956

$R^2 = 0.9450$ $\sigma = 0.0353$ *RESET test:* $F(1,17) = 2.2611$ *[0.1510]* $SC = -5.94$
$HQ = -6.27$

Table 2.4 (Continued)

Variable	Coeff.	Std. err.	t-value	HCSE
Restricted				
Intercept	0.10317	0.04436	2.326	0.04231
$\mu(z)$	−0.07635	0.02290	−3.334	0.02004
$\mu(dm/dt)$	0.99720	0.06718	14.843	0.07093
$\mu(dy/dt)$	−2.70660	0.81722	−3.312	0.78790
$\mu(z) \cdot \mu(dy/dt)$	1.35220	0.41483	3.260	0.39589
$\mu(z) \cdot \mu(dp_M/dt)$	0.39411	0.20352	1.936	0.19464

$R^2 = 0.9439$ $\sigma = 0.0338$ RESET test: $F(1,21) = 1.0913$ [0.3081] SC = − 6.30
HQ = − 6.50 $\mu(dm/dt)$ exogeneity test: $t = 1.123$

Elasticities at mean $\mu(z)$	m	y	p_M
Managed exchange rate group	0.46	−0.41	0.38
(Standard errors)	(0.13)	(0.41)	(0.09)
Flexible exchange rate group	1.00	−0.82	0.55
(Standard errors)	(0.07)	(0.77)	(0.31)

a SC: Schwartz Criterion, HQ: Hannon–Quinn Criterion. Variables are as in Table 2.3; in addition, $\mu(dm/dt)$ is the mean rate of growth of M1, $\mu(d[e + p_M]/dt)$ the mean growth rate of import prices in domestic currency, $\mu(dp_M/dt)$ the mean growth rate of import prices in US$ and $\mu(dx/dt)$ the mean rate growth rate of terms of trade.
$\mu(dm/dt)$ exogeneity test: $t = 1.123$.

reliable estimates could not be expected for more than a handful of countries. The empirical model assumes that the countries in each sample share a common θ_N.[8]

The estimated equation for the managed exchange rate sample, corresponding to equation (2.17), is:

$$\mu(dp/dt)_i = [1 + \mu(z)_i] \cdot [a_0 + a_1 \cdot \mu(dm/dt)_i + a_2 \cdot \mu(dy/dt)_i$$
$$+ a_3 \cdot \mu(d[e + p_M]/dt)_i + a_4 \cdot \mu(dx/dt)] + \varepsilon_i \quad (2.21)$$

The equation for the flexible exchange rate sample, which allows for some deviation from the pure float and is consistent with both the managed and flexible rate paradigms, is:

$$\mu(dp/dt)_i = [1 + \mu(z)_i] \cdot [a_0 + a_1 \cdot \mu(dm/dt)_i + a_2 \cdot \mu(dy/dt)_i$$
$$+ a_3 \cdot \mu(dp_M/dt)_i + a_4 \cdot \mu(dx/dt)] + \varepsilon_i \quad (2.22)$$

where ε_i is the equation residual. Note that in these regressions, the variables are not scaled to mean zero, and that the nominal exchange rate is not included on the right hand side of the flexible exchange rate sample equation. To ensure that all sample observations of $\mu(z)_i$ are non-negative, a constant is added to this variable so that its minimum observation is zero. If the flexible exchange rate sample conforms to the 'pure' floating rate paradigm then in equation (2.15) we will observe that $a_1 = a_2 = 1 - a_3 = 1$.

Table 2.4 presents the regression results for each regime group. Many of the parameters in the unrestricted estimates of equations (2.21) and (2.22) reported in the table have high standard errors, since the variables interacted with $\mu(z)_i$ exhibit some collinearity. It is therefore likely that the second set of results reported in the table, in which the set of explanatory variables is restricted so as to minimise the Schwartz and Hannon–Quinn Criteria, provide better estimates of standard errors. It is these results that we discuss below. Table 2.5 summarises the results in a format that corresponds to the predictions in Table 2.1 above.

As the theoretical model of the previous section predicts, the impact of monetary growth on inflation in the managed exchange rate sample depends negatively on $\mu(z)_i$ (i.e. positively on γ). The estimated value of $dp/dm = 1.04 - 0.38 \cdot \mu(z)_i$. At the mean value of $\mu(z)_i$, $dp/dm = 0.46$, which is significantly different from both zero and unity. Similarly, the negative impact on inflation of real income growth is smaller when $\mu(z)_i$ is larger: $dp/dy = 0.74 \cdot \mu(z)_i - 1.55$. This finding is also consistent with the theoretical model. At the mean value of $\mu(z)_i$ $dp/dy = -0.41$.

Table 2.5 Sources of inflation under alternative exchange rate regimes results

	Managed rate	Floating rate
(i) The coefficients on sources of inflation		
Monetary growth – Real output growth	Positive < 1	Approx. unity
Import prices	Positive < 1	Positive < 1
Terms of trade	Insignificant	Insignificant
(ii) The effect of the tradeables share of consumption on coefficient values		
Monetary growth – Real output growth	Negative	Negative
Import prices	Positive	Positive
Terms of trade	Insignificant	Insignificant

Compare with Table 2.1. Results that conflict with the predictions for a pure floating exchange rate regime, and indicate some similarity with the predictions for a managed exchange rate regime, are shown underlined.

Also as predicted, the magnitude of the impact of import prices depends positively on $\mu(z)_i$: $dp/d[e + p_M] = 0.25 \cdot \mu(z)_i$, and at the mean value of $\mu(z)_i$: $dp/d[e + p_M] = 0.38$. These results are consistent with the stylised facts discussed in Section 2.2 and summarised in Table 2.1, except that the absolute values of the coefficients on dm/dt and dy/dt differ slightly; a possible explanation for this is that dy/dt is an imprecise measure of factor supply growth. Otherwise, the restricted regression is strongly supportive of the model in Section 2.2 and explains a large fraction of the sample variance of inflation rates.

The results for the flexible exchange rate sample are also broadly consistent with the predictions of Table 2.1, though the sample does exhibit some of the features of the managed exchange rate paradigm. As predicted, the coefficient on monetary growth is 1.00. $\mu(z)_i$ has no significant impact on this value but (a departure from the flexible exchange rate paradigm) the coefficient on the import price index is significant and positive in openness, and so negative in γ: $dp/dp_M = 0.39 \cdot \mu(z)_i$; at the mean value of $\mu(z)_i$ this is equal to 0.55.

Similarly, the real output growth coefficient does depend on openness: $dp/dy = 1.35 \cdot \mu(z)_i - 2.71$; at the mean value of $\mu(z)_i$ this is equal to -0.82. As noted above, this group of countries is not restricted to those engaging in pure floating exchange rate regimes, so it is not surprising that elements of the managed exchange rate paradigm appear in this regression. Nevertheless, the key prediction of the theory, that the gearing of inflation to monetary growth is substantially higher in a flexible exchange rate regime, is borne out by the data: the gearing coefficient is significantly higher in the flexible exchange rate case.

One final point is made in Table 2.4. The addition of the residuals from the regressions reported in Table 2.3 to the regressions reported in Table 2.4 constitutes a test for the exogeneity of dm/dt to dp/dt (see Engle and Hendry, 1993). As the exogeneity test statistic shows, the coefficients on these residuals are insignificant, i.e. the null that dm/dt is exogenous cannot be rejected.

The estimated marginal impact of adherence to a managed exchange rate regime is summarised in Table 2.6. The table estimates the expected

Table 2.6 Marginal effects of the exchange rate regime on inflation

Variable	Constant	dm/dt	dy/dt	dp_M/dt	Sum
Effect	0.079	0.079	-0.011	0.004	0.151

difference between the rate of inflation in a flexible regime and the rate in a managed exchange rate regime, at mean values of dm/dt, dy/dt, dp_M/dt and $\mu(z)_i$ and assuming that the managed exchange rate is constant, by summing the difference between the effects of dm/dt, dy/dt and dp_M/dt reported in Table 2.4. The sum of the effects is 15.1 per cent, which implies that *for a given rate of monetary growth*, there is an extra benefit of adherence to a managed exchange rate regime.

This extra potential benefit is substantial, but one should remember that it depends on the nominal exchange rate remaining fixed in a pegged exchange rate regime. In practice, pegged exchange rates are frequently adjusted, and the average annual rate of devaluation in our sample is 5.1 per cent. (For the CFA countries there was no devaluation within the sample, but there was a 100 per cent devaluation in 1994.) As Table 2.2 indicates, real rates of monetary growth have in fact been very similar on average across exchange rate regimes. Nominal monetary growth has been on average 12.4 per cent faster under flexible exchange rates, which is virtually identical to the average difference in inflation rates (12.3 per cent): there is no evidence, on average, of the extra benefit described above. This is consistent with the conjecture that over the span of a decade (the length of the dataset used in this study), the disequilibrium effects of excess monetary growth in a fixed exchange rate regime (and in particular, balance of payments deficits) need to be corrected, either by devaluation or the tightening of monetary policy.

Nevertheless, for both the CFA and for other managed exchanged rate regimes, there is a potential short-run benefit in the difference in the structure of the monetary transmission mechanism: the impact on inflation of increases in the rate of monetary expansion can be delayed for some time, at the expense of a Balance of Payments deficit. For example, a temporary increase in CFA members' fiscal deficits could be monetised without generating much of an increase in the rate of inflation, if the increase in the rate of growth of the money supply were reversed in the medium term.

2.4. Summary and conclusion

The choice of exchange rate regime can be expected to make a substantial difference to the process determining the rate of inflation in developing countries. Not only is adherence to a managed exchange rate regime likely to be associated with a lower rate of monetary expansion but it also results in less inflation for a given rate of monetary expansion, at least in the short term. We find both of these effects to be statistically significant. According to our estimates, those countries that are able to maintain a fixed exchange regime without resorting to devaluation can be expected to have an inflation rate 19.1 percentage points lower than the average rate for flexible exchange rate countries. Of this, we estimate 11.9 percentage points as the 'monetary discipline' effect (lower monetary growth) and 7.2 percentage points as the price-controlling effect of a fixed exchange rate regime, for a given rate of monetary expansion. Since the latter is a disequilibrium phenomenon, it is offset over the long run by exchange rate devaluations.

We also find that the monetary discipline effect is significantly greater in the CFA than in other managed exchange rate regime countries. The extra benefit for the CFA is 4.9 percentage points. This could be interpreted as the result of a greater degree of credibility of low-inflation policy in the CFA than in other managed exchange rate regimes. Because CFA members are tied into an institutional framework that it would be very costly to break out of, the probability of abandonment of the peg in favour of a float is particularly low. Hence average expected inflation (and with Rational Expectations so also average actual inflation) is particularly low. Further, our study only covers a ten-year period. This limitation of the time frame (which is data-driven) is likely to underestimate the benefit of CFA membership, relative to a unilateral peg. Very few LDCs have been able to maintain a peg for as long as the CFA, and so very few have benefited from the monetary discipline effect for such a long time.

In the last few years there has been a move away from managed exchange rates to more flexible systems, partly as a result of persistent external deficits (Agénor and Montiel, 1996). The results here suggest that such a move is not without costs. Flexible exchange rate regimes have in the past, and may still be, a cause of high monetary growth rates and high inflation.

Appendix 2.1: Derivation of the production functions in Section 2.2

In order to derive the production functions (2.10) and (2.11), we assume that output in each sector is a log-linear function of employment of a single factor of production, l:

$$y_N = \beta_N \cdot [l_N - 1] \qquad (A2.1)$$

$$y_X = \beta_X \cdot [l_X - 1] \qquad (A2.2)$$

where y_N and l_N represent output and employment in the nontraded goods sector and y_X and l_X represent output and employment in the export sector. Both β_N and β_X are assumed to be less than unity. Equivalence of marginal products in the two sectors implies:

$$e + p_X - [1 - \beta_X] \cdot l_X = p_N - [1 - \beta_N] \cdot l_N \qquad (A2.3)$$

Approximating the factor market clearing condition as:

$$l = \delta \cdot l_X + [1 - \delta] \cdot l_N \qquad (A2.4)$$

where δ represents the share of the total factor supply employed in the export sector, we can use equations (A2.1) – (A2.4) to derive production functions of the form:

$$y_N = \theta_N \cdot [p_N - e - p_X + \eta_N \cdot l] \qquad (A2.5)$$

where

$$\theta_N = \beta_N \cdot \{1 - \beta_N + [1 - \beta_X] \cdot [1 - \delta]/\delta\}^{-1}, \quad \eta_N = [1 - \beta_X]/\delta$$

$$y_X = \theta_X \cdot [e + p_X - p_N + \eta_X \cdot l] \qquad (A2.6)$$

where

$$\theta_X = \beta_X \cdot \{1 - \beta_X + [1 - \beta_N] \cdot \delta/[1 - \delta]\}^{-1},$$
$$\eta_X = [1 - \beta_N]/[1 - \delta]$$

If the supply of the factor of production grows at a constant rate of ζ, then in any period t:

$$y_N = \theta_N \cdot [p_N - e - p_X] + \alpha_N \cdot t \qquad (A2.7)$$

$$y_X = \theta_X \cdot [e + p_X - p_N] + \alpha_X \cdot t \qquad (A2.8)$$

where

$$\alpha_N = \zeta \cdot \theta_N \cdot \eta_N, \quad \alpha_X = \zeta \cdot \theta_X \cdot \eta_X.$$

Appendix 2.2: The countries included in the sample

Algeria	Chile[a]	Ethiopia	India[a]	Malaysia	Paraguay
Surinam	W. Samoa[a]	Bahamas	Colombia[a]	Fiji	Indonesia[a]
Mauritius	Philippines[a]	Syria	Congo D.R.[a]	Bahrain	Congo Rep.[b]
Gabon[b]	Iran	Morocco[a]	Sénégal[b]	Tanzania[a]	Zambia[a]
Bangladesh	Costa Rica[a]	Gambia[a]	Jamaica[a]	Burma	Seychelles
Thailand	Zimbabwe	Barbados	Ghana[a]	Kenya	Côte d'Ivoire[b]
Nepal	S. Leone[a]	Togo[b]	Lesotho	Belize	Dominica
Guatemala	S. Korea[a]	Niger[b]	Singapore[a]	Tonga	Rwanda
Burkina[b]	Dom. Rep.[a]	Guyana[a]	Kuwait	Nigeria[a]	Solomon Is.[a]
Trinidad	St.Vincent	Burundi	Ecuador	Haiti	Liberia
Pakistan	Somalia[a]	Turkey[a]	Sudan	Cameroon[b]	Egypt
Honduras	Madagascar[a]	Panama	S. Africa[a]	Uruguay[a]	Swaziland
Centrafrique[b]	El Salvador	Hong Kong[a]	Malawi	P.N.G.	Sri Lanka[a]
Venezuela	Vanuatu				

a Indicates inclusion in the flexible exchange rate sample.
b Indicates a CFA member.

Appendix 2.3: The regime exogeneity test

In order to test the assumption that adherence to a managed exchange rate regime (R_i) is exogenous to the rate of monetary growth, we construct a Probit model of the form:

$$R_i = \Phi(\mu(y)_i, \mu(s)_i, \mu(dp_M/dt)_i, \mu(dx/dt)_i,$$
$$\sigma(dp_M/dt)_i, \sigma(dx/dt)_i) + u_i \qquad (A2.9)$$

where all variables are defined as in the text, $\mu(s)_i$ is the mean ratio non-exported services to GDP and $\sigma(\cdot)$ represents a standard deviation. The results are reported in Table 2.A1. Addition of the residual, u_i, from this equation to a switching regression corresponding to the Table 2.3 regressions:

$$\mu(dm/dt)_i = [1 + R_i]$$
$$\cdot [a_0 + a_1 \cdot \mu(y)_i + a_2 \cdot \mu(dy/dt)_i + a_3$$
$$\cdot \mu(z)_i] + a_4 \cdot CFA_i + \nu_i \qquad (A2.10)$$

generates a residual t-ratio of 1.33. So the null of exogeneity of the regime cannot be rejected.

Table 2.A1   The Probit model of regime adherence

Variable	Coeff.	Std. err.	t-value	Prob.
Intercept	6.9989	2.5313	2.765	0.0072
$\mu(y)$	−0.2451	0.0981	−2.498	0.0147
$\mu(s)$	0.9267	0.5916	1.567	0.1215
$\sigma(dx/dt)$	3.9346	2.4184	1.627	0.1081
$\mu(dx/dt)$	−10.0010	6.9283	−1.443	0.1532
$\sigma(dp_M/dt)$	−7.1446	2.6760	−2.670	0.0093
$\mu(dp_M/dt)$	−4.1352	7.6194	−0.543	0.5890

Notes

1 See Lucas (1972) for a motivation for such a relationship.
2 This argument is based on the Monetary Approach to the Balance of Payments. See Mundell (1968).
3 The genre of model which we have in mind includes those of Mundell (1971), Berglas (1974), Dornbusch (1974) and Frenkel and Mussa (1985).
4 If the assumption that nontraded goods demand is independent of p_N were relaxed then the slope of the demand curve would also be relevant.
5 Region-specific dummies are insignificant when added to the regression equations.
6 There is a difference between the unrestricted equation for the managed exchange rate sample and that for the flexible rate sample. Because in the latter we cannot assume the exogeneity of the nominal exchange rate, the import price inflation term used is $\mu(dp_M/dt)$, not $\mu(d[e + p_M]/dt)$.
7 So the means for $\mu(z)$ in Table 2.2 are no longer relevant.
8 If θ_N did vary across countries, and was at all correlated with any of the RHS variables in the model, the correlation would most likely be a negative one with the openness index $\mu(z)_i$, i.e. a positive correlation with γ (because a higher θ_N is likely to lead to a relatively high level of nontradeables' production). So any bias in the coefficients would most likely be on the $\mu(z)_i$ terms. Since θ_N and γ have opposite effects in the theoretical model, the estimates of the γ effects via $\mu(z)_i$ would be biased downwards. So our estimates might understate the importance of openness in the determination of inflation.

References

Agénor, P-R. and Montiel, P. (1996) *Development Macroeconomics*, Princeton, NJ: Princeton University Press.

Anyadike-Danes, M. (1995) 'Comment on "Measuring the independence of central banks and its effect on policy outcomes" ', *World Bank Economic Review*, **9**: 335–40.

Berglas, E. (1974) 'Devaluation, monetary policy and border tax adjustment', *Canadian Journal of Economics*, **7**: 1–11.

Cukierman, A., Webb, S. and Neyapti, B. (1992) 'Measuring the independence of central banks and its effect on policy outcomes', *World Bank Economic Review*, **6**: 353–98.

38   *CFA membership, exchange rates and inflation*

Dornbusch, R. (1974) 'Real and monetary aspects of the effect of exchange rate changes', in Aliber, R. (ed.) *National Monetary Policies and the International Financial System*, Chicago, IL: University of Chicago Press.

Engle, R. and Hendry, D. (1993) 'Testing superexogeneity and invariance in regression models', *Journal of Econometrics*, **56**: 119–39.

Frenkel, J. and Mussa, M. (1985) 'Asset markets, exchange rates and the Balance of Payments', in Jones, R. and Kenen, P. (eds) *The Handbook of International Economics*, Amsterdam: North-Holland.

Ghosh, A., Gulde, A-M., Ostry, J. and Wolf, H. (1995) 'Does the nominal exchange rate regime matter?', *IMF Working Paper WP/95/121*.

Kydland, F. and Prescott, E. (1977) 'Rules rather than discretion: The inconsistency of optimal plans', *Journal of Political Economy*, **85**: 473–92.

Lucas, R. (1972) 'Expectations and the neutrality of money', *Journal of Economic Theory*, **4**: 103–24.

Mundell R. (1971) *Monetary Theory*, Pacific Palisades, CA: Goodyear.

3 Short-run monetary policy formation

Comparing the CFA with anglophone Africa*

In Chapter 2 we examined the impact of CFA membership on long-run monetary growth and inflation. We said nothing about the influence the CFA has on monetary policy in the short run. In this chapter we will focus on the short run, and look at the differences between monetary adjustment in the CFA and monetary adjustment in non-CFA countries. This will be a more data-demanding exercise than the previous one, so we will be using data from just three countries to illustrate our arguments. The countries featured here are Côte d'Ivoire in the CFA, Kenya and Tanzania. Analysis of data for a wider range of countries is beyond the scope of this chapter. Nevertheless, comparison of the Ivorian economy (one of the largest in the CFA) with two non-CFA African economies that have a similar structure is likely to provide some indication of the impact of CFA membership on Côte d'Ivoire's smaller neighbours.

3.1. Monetary policy and fiscal shocks

The theoretical analysis in this chapter begins with two different parts of the development economics literature, both concerned with the determinants of growth. The first analyses the causes and consequences of variability in government revenue (e.g. are Lim, 1983; Greenaway and Milner, 1991; Chambas, 1994; Bleaney et al., 1995). Revenue in LDCs is typically more variable than elsewhere, and revenue in

*Reprinted from Fielding, D. (1999) 'How does a central bank react to changes in government borrowing? Evidence from Africa', *Journal of Development Economics*, **59**: 531–52, with permission from Elsevier Science.

Sub-Saharan Africa the most variable. This is partly explained by a higher degree of dependence on tariffs combined with highly volatile terms of trade. If the government does not have adequate access to short term borrowing facilities, then high revenue instability will lead to high variability in expenditure and the provision of public goods, with potentially disastrous consequences for economic development. This is one of the arguments for the replacement of tariffs by internal indirect taxes, a policy that has been vigorously pursued by the World Bank.

The second investigates the impact of price instability on economic growth. Unexpected changes in the rate of inflation can impede development in several ways. To the extent that they create uncertainty about real interest rates, they are likely to deter investment and thus growth (see e.g. Hartman, 1972; Ferderer, 1993). On the other hand, interest rate variability might also discourage domestic saving (Thirwall, 1974) which will *ceteris paribus* weaken the Balance of Payments and exacerbate debt-financing problems.

These two areas are linked in a way that has been largely ignored. All governments have recourse to borrowing from their central bank; they have at least this way of maintaining a smooth consumption pattern in the face of variable income; and there is some evidence to suggest that variations in revenue in African countries are only partially passed on to expenditure.[1] What might deter the use of this facility is the possibility that the central bank will monetise variations in government debt, which might be inflationary. The government is then faced with a trade-off between variability in expenditure and variability in inflation, both of which are harmful. If variations in borrowing are not translated into variations in the money supply, then the trade-off does not exist; short-term borrowing from the central bank to smooth public consumption is costless, and revenue instability is not a cause for concern. In assessing the costs of revenue instability, it is therefore essential to determine how the central bank responds to changes in government borrowing.

We will investigate these issues using data from Côte d'Ivoire, Kenya and Tanzania. All are low-middle income petroleum importers, whose governments are highly dependent on import and export taxes for revenue, which is consequently highly variable. The two anglophone countries have complete monetary independence, all monetary policy being conducted by a national central bank. In all three countries a large part of the increase in the government debt held by the central bank has been monetised in the long run. In Côte d'Ivoire net government debt increased by CFAF 239 billion and currency in circulation by CFAF

231 billion over the period 1970–90. The corresponding figures for Kenya are Sh 17.5 billion and Sh 10.1 billion; for Tanzania the figures are Sh 34.4 billion and Sh 30.4 billion. Cross-country differences in these long-run figures are analysed in Chapter 2. Here, we are concerned with the variations around the long run. The character of these variations will depend on the nature of the relationship between government borrowing and money creation. Consider the following three possibilities:

A   The money stock is highly geared to government debt. Not only does long-run monetary growth depend on long-run growth in government debt: short run fluctuations in debt are translated into short-run monetary fluctuations.

B   The money stock is not highly geared to government debt, and over the medium run follows a different deterministic process, the central bank being able to accommodate differences between the trend in debt and the trend in the money stock by adjustment of other assets in its portfolio. However permanent adjustment of these other assets is infeasible and over the long run the trend in monetary growth must be adjusted to bring it into line with the trend in the growth of debt. There is some variability in the monetary growth path due to these structural breaks.

C   The money stock is not highly geared to government debt, and because the long run trend it follows is not substantially different from the trend in debt, the adjustments necessary in (2) are not required. Hence the variability of the money stock is relatively low.

Figures 3.1–3.3 plot the annual rates of growth of currency issue and consumer prices for each country, along with real changes in the central bank's net claims on the government. The figures show that in no country is there a simple one-for-one Cagan relationship between government borrowing and monetary expansion in the short run: periods in which borrowing was strikingly high (e.g. Côte d'Ivoire in 1979–81; Kenya in 1980, 1988, 1992 and 1995; Tanzania in 1978–80 and 1985–86) did not always experience correspondingly high monetary growth and inflation.[2] Nevertheless, it is possible that the three central banks differed in the degree of success they had in insulating the domestic economy from borrowing shocks. Summary statistics suggest that Kenya had more success than the other two: the ratio of the standard deviation of the real level of the currency stock (detrended and deseasonalised) to that of net government debt over the sample period

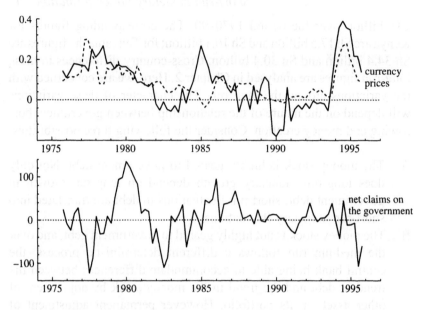

Figure 3.1 The annual rate of growth of currency issue and consumer price for Côte d'Ivoire.

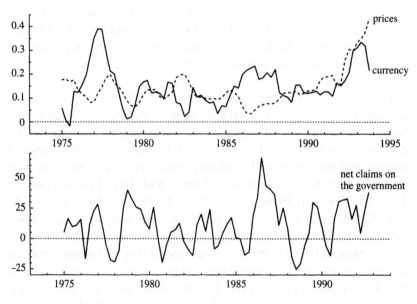

Figure 3.2 The annual rate of growth of currency issue and consumer price for Kenya.

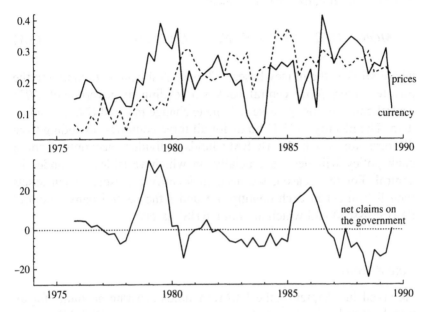

Figure 3.3 The annual rate of growth of currency issue and consumer price for
Tanzania.

was 0.27, compared with 0.44 in Tanzania and 0.58 in Côte d'Ivoire.
However, we need to examine more rigorous evidence for such a
difference than can be derived from summary statistics or eyeballing
the time-plots. It remains to be seen whether the differences can be
attributed to differences in systematic policies implemented by each
central bank, and to differences between the CFA on the one hand and
the two national central banks on the other. In order to test the hypothesis that the differences in monetary variability do result from different
policies, we will outline and estimate a model of central bank behaviour. Before doing this, it is necessary to look in more detail at the
components of the central bank balance sheet, in order to determine
which variables form the bank's choice set.

3.2. Modelling central banks' policy choices

3.2.1. *Disaggregation of central bank assets and liabilities*

In order to model a central bank's behaviour, we need to disaggregate
its assets and liabilities. Recalling equation (1.1) in Chapter 1, we know

that the central bank's balance sheet is:

$$MON - CTE - NGD - E \cdot NFA - OAS \equiv 0 \qquad (3.1)$$

where MON is the money base, CTE is central bank net lending to the private sector, NGD central bank net lending to government, NFA central bank net foreign assets, E the exchange rate and OAS a residual item. The identity in (3.1) holds for all three countries, including Côte d'Ivoire, for which the BCEAO holds individual accounts. Central bank policy will depend crucially on which variables are under its control. For this reason, we need to identify precisely which assets (and liabilities) in each country are under the central bank's control ('LHS' assets) and which are not ('RHS' assets).

Côte d'Ivoire

As noted in Chapter 1, the UEMOA holds separate accounts for all members and is in charge of money creation in each. BCEAO control over both public and private borrowing is very limited. The constitution of the BCEAO stipulates that the annual change in gross lending to a government cannot exceed 20 per cent of the previous year's fiscal receipts. Aside from this rule, the central bank authorities in Dakar have no control over the level of gross borrowing set in Abidjan. Moreover, this rule has never been a binding constraint for the Ivorian government, which has been able to run up a large level of debt without the increase in any one year ever exceeding 15 per cent of past fiscal receipts. There is no control at all over government deposits. In this respect, the BCEAO is not different from most African central banks. However, it is unusual in the extent to which its control over private borrowing is limited. Until 1990 the BCEAO had a constitutional obligation to refinance all short run agricultural credit given to farmers by commercial banks. There was no upper bound on this type of credit. Since then, upper bounds on refinancing have been introduced, but actual lending to commercial banks fell below this notional upper bound only in the second half of 1991. During the period we will consider, lending to private banks was beyond central bank control (Secrétariat du Comité Monétaire de la Zone Franc, 1991). In principle there is some control over reserve deposits, since liquidity ratio rules require private banks to hold a certain fraction of their assets in the form of reserve deposits. However, evidence suggests that Ivorian banks are seldom at the frontier of this constraint.

By contrast, the central monetary authorities of the UEMOA are accorded absolute control over decisions regarding currency issue in each member state and changes in the net foreign asset position of each state. Any change in *NFA* is accommodated by the Operations Account. Ivorian *NFA* can and has been negative for long periods of time over the 1970s and 1980s. Note also that the rules of the system require central bank net foreign assets to be held in French Francs, and that the exchange rate, E, is fixed.

The residual assets term in the BCEAO balance sheet is very small, and is composed mainly of interbank transactions that do not fit easily into any other category. Given the heterogeneous nature of this term, we should consider the possibility that it is used as a policy instrument by the central bank. This leaves us with three policy instruments for the BCEAO: *MON, NFA* and *OAS. NGD* and *CTE* are beyond its control; E is a constant.[3]

Since Côte d'Ivoire is part of a monetary union, we ought not to assume a priori that movements in Ivorian assets and liabilities are independent of those in other member states. Since the BCEAO must ensure that equation (3.1) holds for each country, an increase in other governments' borrowing from the central bank cannot affect the Ivorian money stock and net foreign assets in the same way that an increase in Ivorian government borrowing does. When the Ivorian government borrows more the BCEAO, the net response of other Ivorian assets and liabilities (d*MON*/d*NGD*, etc.) must sum to unity; when other governments borrow more, the net Ivorian response must sum to zero. Nevertheless, there might be reasons for adjusting the Ivorian balance sheet in reaction to changes elsewhere in the UEMOA region. As noted in Appendix 1.1 of Chapter 1, the organisational structure of UEMOA and the BCEAO gives each of the seven member states an equal voice at each level of the hierarchy, both at the general policy-making level (the *Conference des chefs d'état* and *Conseil des ministres*) and at the administrative level (the *Conseil d'administration*). This means that BCEAO policy with respect to Côte d'Ivoire might be influenced by the interests of the other countries. When, for example, there is an expansion of borrowing from the BCEAO elsewhere in the union, necessitating monetary expansion elsewhere, the *Comité national du crédit du Côte d'Ivoire*, which is responsible for accommodating changes in Ivorian borrowing from the BCEAO, but is under the direct control of the *Conseil d'administration*, might order some monetary expansion in Côte d'Ivoire, in order to prevent, or at least mitigate, asymmetric price shocks across the union.[4] The formal modelling of this process is discussed in the next section.

Kenya and Tanzania

In the case of Kenya and Tanzania the issues are not quite so clear-cut. Levels of lending to the government are decided 'in consultation with' central bank officials. However, Cuckierman *et al.* (1992) characterise the central banks of Kenya and Tanzania as having little control over government borrowing decisions. As in Côte d'Ivoire, there is no control over government deposits. In the analysis that follows, *NGD* will be treated as being outside central bank control. By contrast, currency issue is within the constitutional scope of the central bank, and can be treated as a financial policy instrument.

Control over lending to the private sector is much more extensive. There are no constitutional rules stipulating how much credit the central bank provides to private banks. This decision is left to central bank officials. In this respect, the case of Kenya and Tanzania differs from that of Côte d'Ivoire, and *CTE* will be treated as a potential financial policy instrument. Since most of the residual asset, *OAS*, appears to consist of central bank lending directly to private enterprises this will also be treated as a potential policy instrument.

There is an additional financial policy instrument in Kenya and Tanzania, since during the period in which we will be interested the exchange rate was managed as a crawling peg. To the extent that increases in net borrowing from the central bank are offset by devaluations (if only because the resulting increase in aggregate demand worsens the balance of payments) E should be treated as a policy instrument, and $E \cdot NFA$ should be decomposed into that part which has resulted from past changes in NFA ($NFA(0) + \int_t E(t) \cdot dNFA(t)$, henceforth $NF1$) and that which has resulted from changes in E ($\int dE(t) \cdot NFA(t)$, henceforth $NF2$). In Kenya and Tanzania MON, $NF1$, $NF2$, CTE and OAS are treated as policy instruments. NGD is assumed to be entirely beyond central bank control.

3.2.2. The policy model

In this section we sketch out a simple model to illustrate how central bank preferences about the value of the assets and liabilities it does control will determine the values actually observed. This model is based on the assumption that the central bank has a target value for each asset, and that deviations from the target reduce central bankers' utility. These targets may not be given: they may trend over time, or they may depend on the macroeconomic environment. The countries included in this study have a fixed exchange rate regime and a private sector with limited access to capital markets, so the macroeconomic variables of key interest are likely to be the current account (or its integral, the economy's stock of net foreign assets) and the supply of credit to the private sector. For a given vector of asset levels set by the central bank these variables (and hence central bank targets) are likely to depend primarily on aggregate income, in the following ways:

1   If wider real domestic monetary aggregates (M) are proportional to real MON ($M = k \cdot MON$), and if there is a Monetary Approach to the Balance of Payments equation relating M to real private sector foreign assets (F) and real income (Y):

$$F + M = F + k \cdot MON = \gamma \cdot Y \qquad (3.2)$$

then a target ratio of F to Y ($(F/Y)^* = \lambda$) implies a target level of MON which is proportional to income:

$$MON^* = (\gamma - \lambda) \cdot Y/k \qquad (3.3)$$

A target level of F independent of Y ($F = F^*$) would imply a target level of MON equal to:

$$MON^* = (\gamma \cdot Y - F^*)/k \qquad (3.3a)$$

Similarly, there may be a target level for the stock of net foreign assets held by the central bank (NFA, the other component of the economy's total stock of net foreign assets), either in absolute terms or as a function of income.

2   If commercial banks' lending to the private sector is proportional to CTE ($L = h \cdot CTE$) and if there is a target level of L (L^*) which is proportional to income, because firms are perceived to require a level of credit proportional to their output ($L^* = \delta \cdot Y$), then (in countries where the central bank can control it) there will be a target

level of *CTE* equal to:

$$CTE^* = (\delta/h) \cdot Y \tag{3.4}$$

A similar rule may determine lending by the central bank to non-bank private sector institutions incorporated in *OAS*.

Actual values of central bank assets might be derived as follows. The central bank has a target value for each asset (A_j) that it controls, denoted by A_j^*. For liabilities such as *MON* A_j will be negative; A_j^* might be fixed, or follow a trend (with or without structural breaks), or depend on aggregate income in the ways outlined in equations (3.2)–(3.4). Any gap between A_j and A_j^* reduces the central bank's utility, and marginal disutility is increasing in the gap. A simple loss function with these properties is:

$$L = \frac{1}{2} \cdot \left[\sum_i \left(\frac{1}{\alpha_i} \right) \cdot (A_i - A_i^*)^2 \right] \tag{3.5}$$

where the α_i are weights representing the relative importance of achieving a particular target. L is minimised subject to the central bank balance sheet constraint:

$$\sum_i A_i + A = 0 \tag{3.6}$$

where A represents the assets beyond the control of the central bank. If we impose the normalisation $\Sigma_i \alpha_i = 1$ then minimisation of L subject to equation (3.6) implies that for each asset:

$$A_j = A_j^* + \alpha_j \cdot \left[A - \sum_i A_i^* \right] \tag{3.7}$$

This relationship might be estimated on time series data by an equation of the form:

$$A_j(t) = \beta_j(Y(t), D, t) + \alpha_j \cdot A(t) + u_j(t) \tag{3.8}$$

$$\sum_i \beta_i = 1 + \sum_i \alpha_i = 0$$

where D represents possible structural breaks in the β_j, $u_j(t)$ a residual and

$$\beta_j = A_j^* - \alpha_j \cdot \sum_i A_i^* \tag{3.9}$$

Note that the sign of β_j need not be the same as that of A_j^*. Nor need the sign of $\partial\beta_j/\partial Y$ be the same as that of $\partial A_j^*/\partial Y$: for example, even if desired *CTE* rises with income, actual *CTE* may fall if increases in net foreign assets are even more desirable. The model parameters α_j can be recovered directly as the gearing coefficients on $A(t)$ in equation (3.8); the parameters A_j^* can be recovered indirectly.[5]

If a relatively large weight is put on achieving the target value of *MON*, for example, the corresponding α_j coefficient and the gearing of *MON* to A will be very small; we will observe policy which approximates to case (B) or (C) in Section 3.1. If the vector of A_i^* targets (and hence the vector of β_i terms) is constant then *MON* will be constant; if they follow a deterministic trend then *MON* will follow a deterministic trend; if they vary with incomes, then so will *MON*. Case (B) will occur when the targets set for the medium term are not feasible in the long term (for example, very low *NFA* may be politically acceptable in the medium term but not in the long term): in this case structural breaks will appear in the A_i^* and β_i (or possibly in the α_i) as the central bank adjusts its policy. Of course structural breaks could also occur as a result of genuine changes in central bank preferences. If such breaks do not occur, then we will observe case (C).

While in Kenya and Tanzania there is a single RHS asset, *NGD*, in Côte d'Ivoire there are two RHS assets, *NGD* and *CTE*. The model estimated below will allow the central bank to react differently to changes in each asset. The reason for allowing this is that changes in *CTE* might affect the A_i^* and β_i: if theBCEAO perceives short run agricultural credit to farmers to be an alternative to currency as a way of financing the agricultural cycle[6] then when such credit (and hence *CTE*) rise, the BCEAO might value reductions in *MON*. This could offset any increase in *MON* as a response to a rise in central bank assets *qua CTE*.

A further modification in the case of Côte d'Ivoire is to include net borrowing from other UEMOA members (*NLO*) as an argument of the $\beta_j(\cdot)$ functions. When borrowing rises elsewhere in the union, possibly leading to monetary expansion elsewhere, the central bank might wish to increase the Ivorian money stock, for the reasons discussed above. In order to accommodate this Ivorian net foreign assets (or perhaps other assets) will have to increase.

In the next section we will present an empirical model based on equations of the form of (3.8) using data from the three countries in our sample. Before doing so, it is worthwhile to deal with two possible caveats in the interpretation of the results. First, the selection of LHS and RHS variables is made on a priori grounds; it is possible that this selection will be incorrect. For example, the government and central bank might conceivably make decisions about debt and money creation jointly, so all assets should be treated as LHS assets and $A = 0$. However, when exogeneity tests are conducted, the null that the RHS assets are exogenous cannot be rejected.

Second, the loss function $L(\cdot)$ might conceivably have a non-quadratic form, so the asset determination equations might not be linear. However, when non-linear terms are added to the equations reported below they are not jointly significant, i.e. the loss function is not significantly non-quadratic.

A final point to note is that NGD is not equal to total government debt: the government in each country borrows not only from the central bank, but also from the domestic private sector and from abroad. Total government borrowing might be another argument of the $\beta_j(\cdot)$ functions. For example, the central bank might think it worthwhile to offset any increase in foreign debt incurred by central government by increasing its own net foreign asset stock, which would require compensating adjustment to other assets and liabilities (increasing the money stock, for instance). However, data limitations prevent the inclusion of total debt in the estimated $\beta_j(\cdot)$ functions. The solution to this problem is discussed at the end of the next section.

3.3. Model estimation

3.3.1. Estimating the long-run central bank reaction functions

The aim of this section is to estimate the model described above and encapsulated in equation (3.8). The main coefficients of interest will be the α_i and the determinants of the β_i, which indicate the structure of central bank policy. The assets and liabilities used as variables in the model are: MON, NFA (disaggregated into $NF1$ and $NF2$ in Kenya and Tanzania), CTE, NGD and OAS. These are measured in real domestic currency units at 1990 consumer prices. MON, NFA and OAS are taken to be endogenous in each country; NGD and Y are taken to be exogenous. CTE is exogenous just in Côte d'Ivoire. Note that $NF1$ is calculated on quarterly data as $NFA(0) + \sum_t E(t) \cdot \Delta NFA(t)$ and $NF2$ as $\sum_t \Delta E(t) \cdot NFA(t)$; this approximation may mean that the restrictions in equation (3.8) do not necessarily hold.

The quarterly data for assets, income and prices are taken from various editions of the IMF *International Financial Statistics.*[7] The sample period is 1975(1)–1993(4) for Côte d'Ivoire, 1975(1)–1995(4) for Kenya and 1975(1)–1989(2) for Tanzania. In Kenya and Tanzania, the limits on the series result from data availability. Ivorian data do run to 1995, but the CFA devaluation in January 1994 represents a structural break too close to the end of the series for us to be confident that we have modelled it correctly.

Before proceeding to estimate equations of the form of (3.8) it is necessary to establish the order of integration of each variable. Augmented Dickey–Fuller test statistics for the variables in levels indicate that the null that each series is I(1) can be rejected in favour of stationarity only for Ivorian income and Kenyan OAS. The null that the first differences of the other variables are I(1) can be rejected in every case. This means that relationships between the assets must be estimated by cointegration techniques. Moreover, in Côte d'Ivoire it is inappropriate to search for an equilibrium relationship between any of the I(1) assets and income.[8]

We have yet to take account of a final factor which might explain changes in asset stocks: there may be structural breaks in the A_i^* or α_i. With a large enough sample the existence of structural breaks might be determined by testing for parameter instability in a VAR consisting of assets and income. However in a sample of seventy observations such tests have low power. Nevertheless we can look at parameter stability in each univariate process. The calculation of one-period forecast Chow tests (confirmed by visual inspection of the series) indicates the existence of breaks in some series in 1980, 1984 and 1987 in Côte d'Ivoire, 1984 and 1992 in Kenya and 1985 in Tanzania, the last two coinciding roughly with the beginning of an exchange rate liberalisation period. These might, a priori, be breaks in the α_i or in the β_i for each series.[9]

On the basis of these preliminary results two ways of estimating equation (3.8) for the n LHS assets are feasible:

1   Estimation of n VARs including a single LHS asset, the RHS assets, Y (except in Côte d'Ivoire), an intercept and trend and dummy variables for the structural break periods (D) interacted with the intercept and trend. Each VAR forms the basis for the estimation of a cointegrating vector in the LHS and RHS assets and Y using the method outlined in Johansen (1988). This vector is interpreted as an

equilibrium central bank policy response equation. Normalising on the LHS asset, the coefficients on the RHS assets are interpreted as the gearing coefficients α_j, and the coefficients on income, trend and the structural breaks as the coefficients $\partial\beta_j/\partial Y$, $\partial\beta_j/\partial t$, $\partial\beta_j/\partial D$ and $\partial\beta_j/\partial(t \cdot D)$. With a larger sample, $n - 1$ LHS assets could be included in the VAR; such an approach here would generate test statistics of very low power. The approach allows equilibrium β_j to be a linear function of t, D, $t \cdot D$ and $Y(t)$. The small-sample properties of this method when slope dummies are included in the VAR are not known, so it would be imprudent to interact D with the RHS assets to allow for structural breaks in α_j. Nor can the restrictions in (3.8) be imposed.

2   Simultaneous estimation of n Engle–Granger regressions (Engle and Granger, 1987) of each LHS asset on the RHS assets, Y and an intercept and trend, allowing for intercept, trend and slope dummies. Such an approach allows for structural breaks in α_j and the imposition of cross-equation restrictions; however, it does not allow for the possibility that there is more than one cointegrating vector (perhaps the level of government debt depends on income) and that the estimated coefficients represent this second relationship.

The approach taken below is to use method (1) unless the estimation results appear not to be robust to changes in sample size or no significant cointegration relationship is found. In such a case, (2) is used instead. Tables 3.1–3.3 below report the estimation results. For Côte d'Ivoire and Kenya these are results from method (1); for Tanzania (where no cointegrating vector is found using method (1)) the results of method (2) are reported.

Table 3.1 reports the results for Côte d'Ivoire, where there are three LHS assets (*MON*, *NFA* and *OAS*), each with their own equation and Johansen rank test statistics, and two RHS assets (*NGD* and *CTE*) plus one argument of the $\beta_j(\cdot)$ function (*NLO*). The reported rank test statistics indicate the existence of a single cointegrating vector between *OAS* and {*NGD*, *CTE*, *NLO*}. In the case of the *MON* and *NFA* VARs, the rank test statistics corresponding to the null, that there is at most one cointegrating vector, is above the 5 per cent critical value; so there appears to be two cointegrating vectors, only the first of which is shown. The second is most readily interpreted as a relationship between *NGD* and *CTE*.

Table 3.1 Estimation results for Côte d'Ivoire. Degrees of freedom corrected Johansen rank test statistics (JRTS)

	Rank	JRTS	5% c.v.
MON	$r = 0$	89.7	54.6
	$r \leq 1$	48.8	34.6
	$r \leq 2$	12.9	18.2
	$r \leq 3$	3.3	3.7
NFA	$r = 0$	72.5	54.6
	$r \leq 1$	36.6	34.6
	$r \leq 2$	12.7	18.2
	$r \leq 3$	2.0	3.7
OAS	$r = 0$	64.0	54.6
	$r \leq 1$	32.5	34.6
	$r \leq 2$	8.5	18.2
	$r \leq 3$	1.2	3.7

*Long-run relationships**

Asset type (j)	NGD gearing coeff. (α_j)	CTE gearing coeff. (α_j)	NLO coeff. ($\partial \beta_j / \partial \mathrm{NLO}$)
MON	0.199[a]	0.084[a]	0.081[a]
−NFA	0.925[b]	0.787[a]	−0.093[a]
−OAS	0.068[a]	0.004	−0.006
Sum	1.192[b]	0.875[b]	−0.018

Note that all LHS variables are listed as liabilities.
a   indicates significantly different from zero and unity at 5 per cent level.
b   indicates significantly different from zero but not unity at 5 per cent level.

The table also shows the gearing coefficients for each LHS asset (since there are three RHS variables, there are three gearing coefficients for each LHS asset). The reported equilibrium relationships indicate that *MON* is not highly geared to *NGD* and *CTE*. The estimated gearing coefficient on *NGD* is 0.20; on *CTE* it is 0.08. Most of the variation in the RHS assets is accommodated by *NFA*, which has gearing coefficients of 0.93 and 0.79 respectively (the first being insignificantly different from unity). *OAS* takes up a much smaller part of the gearing, with point estimates of 0.07 and 0.00. Also in the *MON* equation is a coefficient on net borrowing from the rest of UEMOA equal to 0.08: higher borrowing elsewhere does lead to monetary expansion in Côte d'Ivoire (though the effect is not so great as for Ivorian borrowing), perhaps for the reasons discussed above. The *NLO* coefficient in the *NFA* equation indicates that this monetisation is

Table 3.2 Estimation results for Kenya. Degrees of freedom corrected Johansen rank test statistics (JRTS)

	Rank	JRTS	5% c.v.
MON	$r=0$	39.3	34.6
	$r\leq1$	11.7	18.2
	$r\leq2$	0.2	3.7
NF1	$r=0$	52.3	34.6
	$r\leq1$	10.7	18.2
	$r\leq2$	2.7	3.7
NF2	$r=0$	44.9	34.6
	$r\leq1$	16.7	18.2
	$r\leq2$	1.0	3.7
CTE	$r=0$	47.1	34.6
	$r\leq1$	17.1	18.2
	$r\leq2$	0.2	3.7

Long-run relationships

Asset type (j)	NGD gearing coeff. (α_j)	Y coeff. ($\partial\beta_j/\partial Y$)
MON	0.110[a]	0.100[a]
$-NF1$	0.473[a]	-0.313[a]
$-NF2$	0.026[a]	0.132[a]
$-CTE$	0.377[a]	0.006
(Sum)	(0.986)[b]	(-0.075)

Note that all LHS variables are listed as liabilities.
a indicates significantly different from zero and unity at 5 per cent level.
b indicates significantly different from zero but not unity at 5 per cent level.

Table 3.3 Estimation results for Tanzania. Engle–Granger regression coefficients

Variable	NGD coeff. ($\partial\alpha_j$)	NGD·D coeff. ($\partial\alpha_j/\partial D$)	Y coeff. ($\partial\beta_j/\partial Y$)	t_{ADF}
MON	0.316[a]	-0.239[a]	0.386[a]	-7.33
$-NF1$	0.318[a]	-0.164[a]	0.221[a]	-4.19
$-NF2$	0.043[a]	-0.012[a]	-0.031[a]	-4.97
$-CTE$	0.252[a]	0.056[a]	-0.507[a]	-3.93
$-OAS$	0.079[a]	0.361[a]	-0.079[a]	-4.95
Sum	(1.008)[b]	(0.008)	(-0.010)	

Note that all LHS variables are listed as liabilities.
a indicates significantly different from zero and unity at 5 per cent level.
b indicates significantly different from zero but not unity at 5 per cent level.

accommodated by an increase in net foreign assets. The sum of the *NGD* and *CTE* gearing coefficients is insignificantly different from one, and that of the *NLO* coefficients insignificantly different from zero, supporting the interpretation of the cointegrating vectors as central bank policy equations.

If the equilibrium gearing coefficient on *MON* is quite low, what causes the relatively high monetary variability in Côte d'Ivoire? There are two possible explanations: (1) variability of the actual money stock is much higher than variability of the equilibrium money stock, and (2) the variability is due to the structural breaks. Table 3.4 provides some evidence on this question, showing first the ratio of the sample standard deviation of estimated equilibrium *MON* to that of actual *MON*. This is close to unity, i.e. the variability of actual and equilibrium *MON* are very similar. The table also shows the ratio of the sample standard deviation of a hypothetical equilibrium *MON* without the structural breaks to that of estimated equilibrium *MON*. This ratio equals 0.44, which means that the variability of the hypothetical *MON* is much lower. This suggests that actual *MON* would also be much lower, were it not for the breaks.[10] Côte d'Ivoire approximates to case (B) in Section 3.1: relatively high monetary variability because of structural breaks in the money creation equation. Visual inspection of the time-series for the Ivorian money stock (illustrated in Figure 3.4) confirms this result. The figure shows the nominal money stock in Côte d'Ivoire (in levels).[11] There have been (figure shows) long periods in which the money stock is stable, or even falling slightly, in between periods of rapid expansion, during which the pressure accumulated over the previous years is released. It is the venting of this pressure that causes the high variability in the monetary growth rate.

Table 3.4 Ratios of standard deviations of equilibrium money and actual money stocks[a]

	A	B
Côte d'Ivoire	1.02	0.44
Kenya	0.98	1.07
Tanzania	0.90	1.18

a Standard deviations are calculated around a linear trend in the annual moving average of MON. A = the ratio of the s.d. of the estimated equilibrium *MON* to that of actual *MON*; B = the ratio of the s.d. of the hypothetical no-breaks equilibrium *MON* to that of the estimated equilibrium *MON*.

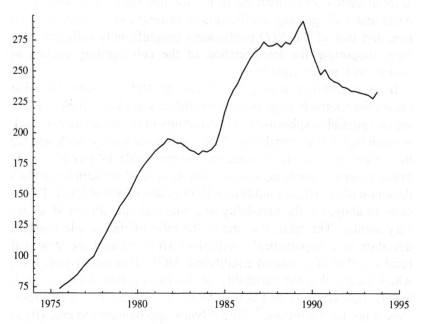

Figure 3.4 Time-series for the Ivorian money stock.

Table 3.2 reports the estimation results for the Kenyan sample. Here there are four LHS variables (*MON*, *NF1*, *NF2* and *CTE*) and one RHS asset (*NGD*); income also appears in the model. *OAS* is stationary and so excluded. The rank test statistics based on each of the four VARs indicate the existence of a single cointegrating vector. These are reported in the table.

Again the equilibrium gearing coefficient on *MON* is quite low (0.11). Most of the gearing to *NGD* is shared between *NF1* (0.47) and *CTE* (0.38); the estimated gearing coefficient for *NF2* of 0.03: all the estimated gearing coefficients together sum to 0.99, which is not significantly different from unity. Changes in income also affect the equilibrium asset levels: a 100 Shilling rise in *Y* leads to an estimated ten Shilling rise in *MON* (as income rises the central bank issues more currency to the private sector) and a 31 Shilling rise in *NF1* (as income rises the central bank acquires more dollar assets). The large rise in *NF1* is accommodated by reductions in *NF2* (currency is revalued, so *E* falls). The sum of the income coefficients is slightly too low: −0.08, when it should be zero; the *NF1* coefficient may be an overestimate, caused by the approximation used in its calculation.

Since the Kenyan VARs include dummy variables too (for 1984 and 1992), it is possible that the structural breaks lead to higher variability in *MON* than would otherwise be the case. However, Table 3.4 shows that this is not so. The hypothetical standard deviation of equilibrium *MON* without the breaks is in fact slightly higher than that of both actual and equilibrium *MON* (the breaks appear to offset sharp changes in *Y*). With low gearing and no monetary instability induced by policy changes, Kenya approximates to case (C) in Section 3.1.

Table 3.3 reports the estimation results for the Tanzanian sample. Here, Engle–Granger regression coefficients are reported for each of the LHS assets. The explanatory variables are *NGD*, *Y* and a deterministic trend, allowing for slope and intercept dummies for 1985. The significant coefficients in the regressions are those on *NGD*, *NGD · D* and *Y*. Dickey–Fuller test statistics for the residuals from these equilibrium equations are significant, indicating that the null of non-cointegration can be rejected.

The estimated equilibrium coefficients suggest that *MON* was highly geared to *NGD* up to the structural break in 1985; then the gearing coefficient fell from 0.32 to 0.08. Similar reductions appear in the gearing coefficients of *NF1* (from 0.32 to 0.16) and *NF2* (0.04 to 0.03). At the same time the gearing coefficients of *CTE* and *OAS* rise (from 0.25 to 0.31 and from 0.08 to 0.44). In the pre-liberalisation period variations in government debt are accommodated mainly by adjustment of the money stock and net foreign assets. In the post-liberalisation period variations in government debt are accommodated mainly by adjustment of net lending to private banks and of *OAS*, the major component of which is lending to non-bank private institutions. One interpretation of this structural break is as a change in underlying preferences: the central bank begins to value monetary stability more highly relative to avoiding crowding out.

Higher income induces the central bank to create more currency (coefficient = 0.39) and to lend more money to banks (coefficient = 0.51) and to other private sector institutions (*OAS* coefficient = 0.08). The second two effects are greater than the first, so net foreign assets must fall when income rises to keep the central bank's books balanced. This case varies from the Kenyan one, in which priority seems to be given to increasing *NFA* when income rises.

Table 3.4 shows that there is very little difference between the variability of the actual money stock and that of the equilibrium money stock and hypothetical equilibrium money stock without the structural break. The relatively high monetary variability indicated in the introduction appears to be due to the high gearing coefficient on *MON* for most of the sample period. So Tanzania is an example of case (A) in Section 3.1.

3.3.2. The role of total government debt

As noted in the previous section, central banks might be affected not only by government borrowing from themselves, but also by total government borrowing. Total borrowing figures, taken from fiscal sources, are available only annually, preventing their inclusion in the quarterly VARs on which the cointegration analysis is based. However, if it can be shown that there is a stable long run relationship between total government borrowing and borrowing from the central bank (at its simplest, this would be manifested in a policy whereby in the long run a constant fraction of government borrowing was from the monetary authorities), then the reaction functions presented in Tables 3.1–3.3 can be seen as reduced form representations of a model in which both *NGD* and total public debt matter.

In order to determine whether such a relationship exists, we use the Engle–Granger method on annual data, regressing *NGD/Y* in each country on a measure of the ratio of total public debt to GDP. For Kenya and Tanzania, the latter is calculated as the cumulative budget deficit (CDF), using fiscal data reported in *International Financial Statistics*. In the case of Côte d'Ivoire, such data are unavailable, so we use public external debt (*PED*), reported in the World Bank *World Debt Tables*, as a proxy. Table 3.5 reports the three Engle–Granger regressions, along with Dickey–Fuller stationarity test statistics for each of the annual series used and for the regression residuals (which is a test for cointegration).

The null of non-cointegration can be rejected at the 5 per cent level in Kenya and Tanzania, and at the 10 per cent level in Côte d'Ivoire; the poorer result in the last case might reflect the use of *PED* as a proxy. The estimated gearing ratios of central bank debt to total debt vary between 13 per cent (Côte d'Ivoire) and 34 per cent (Kenya). In Tanzania and Côte d'Ivoire the time trend is significant in the Engle–Granger regression: over time, borrowing from the central bank in Tanzania appears to be increasing for a given level of total debt; in Côte d'Ivoire it appears to be decreasing. If total public debt does matter to central banks, then Tables 3.1–3.3 do capture the net effect of this in reduced form.

Table 3.5 Public debt to the central bank as a function of total public debt. Stationarity test statistics for debt variables and Engle–Granger residuals[a]

Country	Variable	t_{ADF}	Lag	Trend
Kenya (1972–94)	NGD/Y	0.96	0	X
	CDF/Y	−1.77	0	X
	regression residual	−4.94[b]	1	—
Tanzania (1968–95)	NGD/Y	−2.53	0	X
	CDF/Y	−1.77	0	X
	regression residual	−4.58[b]	1	—
Côte d'Ivoire (1970–93)	NGD/Y	−1.46	0	X
	PED/Y	−2.02	0	X
	regression residual	−3.07[c]	1	—

Regression equations

Kenya	$NGD/Y = -0.030 + 0.338 \cdot CDF/Y$
Tanzania	$NGD/Y = -0.026 + 0.278 \cdot CDF/Y + 0.0037 \cdot t$
Côte d'Ivoire	$NGD/Y = -0.048 + 0.128 \cdot PED/Y - 0.0037 \cdot t$

a t_{ADF} represents the augmented Dickey–Fuller test t-ratio, with the lag column indicating the lag order in the Dickey–Fuller regression and the trend column indicating whether a trend was included.
b represents significance at the 5 per cent level.
c significance at the 10 per cent level.

3.4. Summary and conclusion

We have used data from three African countries to illustrate the different ways in which a central bank might respond to fluctuations in public borrowing. The following stylised facts emerge:

1 Long run growth in public debt must be matched by long run growth of the money supply. Permanent insulation of the money stock from high borrowing is not a sustainable policy, even in the CFA. The case of Côte d'Ivoire illustrates that attempts to pursue such a policy can lead to substantial variability in the money stock over the medium term.

2 However, the money stock can be cushioned from short run fluctuations in debt, by temporary adjustment of other central bank assets. In the country that has insulated its money stock most successfully (Kenya), a large part of short run variations in debt are

translated into variations in central bank foreign asset holdings. Even in the least successful country (Tanzania), some of the variations in debt are absorbed in this way. Côte d'Ivoire is an intermediate case, suggesting that CFA membership is not decisive in determining how successful a country is in this regard.

3   Which other assets the central bank can adjust depends on the institutional constraints it faces. In the anglophone countries, part of the variation in public debt is passed on to net lending to the private sector; this alternative is not available in the CFA. The advantage of CFA membership here is that the supply of credit to the private sector is better insulated from the vagaries of public borrowing. The disadvantage is that, in the absence of efficient use of public net foreign asset adjustment, the money base is likely to be more variable.

The Kenyan case shows that it is possible for an African central bank to prevent variations in public debt from inducing a large amount of monetary instability. In such a case the monetary costs of variations in government borrowing may not be all that high, and when the government's revenue is highly variable its use of central bank accounts for consumption smoothing may not be as costly as a simple model of money creation might predict. Moreover, in Kenya the insulation of the money supply is achieved largely (though not entirely) without recourse to adjustment of claims on the domestic private sector, which, given the credit constraints faced in countries such as Kenya, are potentially just as damaging as monetary fluctuations. Kenya is close to the ideal system in which long run growth in public debt is monetised but all short run fluctuations are accommodated by adjustment of foreign assets. All this is possible outside the CFA: the financial institutional links to a developed country are not necessary.

Other countries have not been so successful, and a substantial part of the variation in government debt has been passed on to the money supply, and to net lending to the domestic private sector. The reasons for the differential degrees of success are not entirely clear. In Tanzania, it may be the case that the long run stock of central bank foreign assets is not large enough to facilitate its extensive use as an absorption mechanism; but there may well be scope for improvements in the management of the central bank balance sheet.[12]

Finally, there is strong evidence that money creation on the balance sheet of one UEMOA member is influenced by the public borrowing of its partners. Although the BCEAO balance sheets for each country are nominally separate, shocks to one are accommodated partly by adjustments in the others. Since money flows freely within the borders of the UEMOA, it is unlikely to make much difference which national balance sheet an extra franc's worth of base money appears on, except perhaps in the very short run. However, the interdependence of the balance sheets emphasises the free-riding problem raised in Chapter 1: public borrowing in one country leads to money creation affecting all. This is the potential problem that we will pursue in the next chapter.

Notes

1 See for example Fielding (1997): in this paper, we estimate that in equilibrium, only 74 per cent of variations in the rate of growth of revenue of countries with low or moderate foreign debt are manifested as variations in the rate of growth of spending. For highly indebted countries, the figure is 91 per cent.

2 The variables and sample periods used in the figures and summary statistics are the same as for the empirical model discussed below. The differenced series shown in the figures are all stationary; the levels, which are the focus of the econometric analysis below, are I(1).

3 In the analysis that follows, central bank accounts related to IMF transactions are excluded. Technically, IMF loans are (foreign) liabilities of the central bank, which creates corresponding assets on central government. This component of *NFA* is beyond direct central bank control, and is therefore excluded from *NFA* and *NGD*.

4 Ivorian-issue CFA Francs are perfect substitutes for the issue of other UEMOA members (which are distinguished only by serial number), so in the long run we would not expect prices in different parts of the UEMOA region to depend on the geographical source of the currency issued. However, such independence might not hold in the very short run.

5 Having estimated the $\beta_i(\cdot)$, A_j^* can be recovered as:

$$A_j^* = [\beta_j/\alpha_j + \sum_{i \neq j} \beta_i/(1 - \alpha_i)]/[(1 - \alpha_j)/\alpha_j + \sum_{i \neq j} \alpha_i/(1 - \alpha_i)]$$

Static asset stock equations of this general form could also be derived as the long run solution to dynamic equations resulting from an intertemporal optimisation problem. Since we will only be presenting the results of a long run econometric model, we do not discuss this alternative in more detail.

6 Farmers need to vary their net financial wealth over the cycle: a short run reduction in net wealth could be achieved by running up agricultural credit (a liability for farmers) or by running down currency holdings (an asset for farmers). If farmers' access to other assets and liabilities is limited, then lower volumes of both agricultural credit and currency in the economy could have deleterious consequences for agricultural production.

7 All the time series employed below are reported as quarterly observations with the exception of income. Income is constructed as terms of trade adjusted GDP, and GDP is reported only annually. The quarterly income series used are the result of an interpolation exercise which is available on request, as are the IFS line numbers

corresponding to the variables named in the text. Note that public debt held by the IMF, which is double-entered in central bank accounts as a foreign liability and a claim on the government, has been subtracted from the measures of *NFA* and *NGD*.

8 The correct identification of the order of integration of each variable is a crucial stage in the analysis. It is somewhat surprising that income and real asset stocks inCôte d'Ivoire appear not to be integrated to the same order, and the exclusion of income from the reported cointegrating vectors for Côte d'Ivoire should be borne in mind as a caveat. However when Ivorian income is included in the VARs on which the cointegration analysis is based the null that the Johansen matrices are not of full rank (i.e. that none of the variables is stationary) can be rejected at the 1 per cent level.

9 Perron stationarity tests including these breaks did not generate results different from the ADF tests. Note that this and subsequent analysis assumes the (weak) exogeneity of the structural breaks, which with a larger sample of countries, and therefore a larger number of observed breaks, might be formally tested. Nevertheless, if (as argued below) the breaks reflect the central bank's response to the accumulated pressure of unsustainable policies in previous periods then weak exogeneity is a valid assumption.

10 The first figure is in fact slightly greater than unity, so the fact that equilibrium is not always reached (*MON* does not even reach the target implied by the 0.2 gearing coefficient when *NGD* changes) provides a little extra insulation from variation in government debt. More detailed dynamic simulations confirming the stylised facts presented here are available on request.

11 The series are shown as annual moving averages, so as to exclude the seasonality.

12 It is not our intention to suggest that management of the central bank's own balance sheet is the only important aspect of monetary policy: control of the money multiplier via management of clearing banks' balance sheets (e.g. with liquidity ratios) is of equal potential importance. However, in the period in which we have considered the liquidity ratios in the CFA were not binding (see for example Secrétariat du Comité Monétaire de la Zone Franc, 1991), and in Kenya the ratio changed only twice, suggesting that it was not used as an active short run policy tool.

References

Chambas, G. (1994) *Fiscalité et Développement en Afrique Subsaharienne*, Paris: Ministère du Développement/Economica.

Bleaney, M., Gemmell, N. and Greenaway, D. (1995) 'Tax revenue instability in subsaharan Africa: Causes and consequences', *Journal of Development Studies*, **31**: 883–902.

Cuckierman, A., Webb, S. and Neyapti, B. (1992) 'Measuring the independence of central banks and its effect on policy outcomes', *World Bank Economic Review*, **6**: 353–98.

Engle, R. and Granger, C. (1987) 'Co-integration, error correction: Representation, estimation and testing', *Econometrica*, **55**: 251–76.

Ferderer (1993) 'The impact of uncertainty on aggregate investment spending', *Journal of Money, Credit and Banking*, **25**: 30–48.

Fielding, D. (1997) 'Modelling the determinants of government expenditure in sub-saharan Africa', *Journal of African Economies*, **6**: 337–90.

Greenaway, D. and Milner, C. (1991) 'Fiscal dependence on trade taxes and trade policy reform', *Journal of Development Studies*, **27**: 95–134.

Hartman, R. (1972) 'The effects of price and cost uncertainty on investment', *Journal of Economic Theory*, **5**: 358–66.

Johansen, S. (1988) 'Statistical analysis of cointegrating vectors', *Journal of Economic Dynamics and Control*, **12**: 231–54.

Lim, D. (1983) 'Instability of government revenue and expenditure in less developed countries', *World Development*, **11**: 447–50.

Secrétariat du Comité Monétaire de la Zone Franc (1991) *Rapport*, Paris.

Thirwall, A. (1974) *Inflation, Savings and Growth in Developing Economies*.

4 Public debt and the strategic interaction of monetary and fiscal policies*

In the last chapter we looked at the response of the BCEAO to changes in government borrowing. We saw that borrowing by one government affects money creation on the account of another. Moreover, regardless of the account to which the money creation is allocated, the free movement of money within the UEMOA means that money creation on any account will affect inflation in all members. So there is a free-riding problem: in the absence of strictly binding limits on public borrowing there is the potential for excessive borrowing on the part of each individual government. Although (as we saw in Chapter 2) CFA membership engenders greater monetary prudence on average than one can expect from countries with their own currency and central bank, the free-riding problem represents a potential inefficiency. Moreover, if some governments create more public debt than others then there is an implicit resource transfer between members of the UEMOA. In this chapter we will investigate the problem further, with particular reference to public borrowing within the BCEAO area.[1] The following section draws out some stylised facts about the nature of the problem. A key feature is that different countries have behaved in very different ways. We then present a simple model to explain why the observed behaviour is the likely outcome of the union's institutions, and discuss the lessons that can be drawn for the future.

*This chapter is based on 'Asymmetries in the behaviour of members of a monetary union: A game-theoretic model with an application to West Africa', *Journal of African Economies*, 5:343–65. By permission of Oxford University Press.

4.1. Evolution of national monetary aggregates in the UEMOA: some stylised facts

If the institutions of the UEMOA engender excessive borrowing on the part of every member state, then this should be manifested in persistent deficits in the Operations Account. In other words, the excessive borrowing will be financed by the French Treasury. The Operations Account represents the pooled net foreign assets of the BCEAO, in other words, that part of total *NFA* over which no individual country has property rights. (Each country's contribution to the Operations Account can nevertheless be imputed as a residual item on the BCEAO national balance sheets.) Recalling the central bank balance sheet identity in Chapters 1 and 3:[2]

$$MON - CTE - NGD - E \cdot NFA - OAS \equiv 0 \qquad (4.1)$$

which holds at both the national and at the union-wide level, and noting that $E \cdot NFA$ can be split into the Operations Account (Z) and national net foreign assets (F), we can see the factors that drive the Operations Account:

$$\Delta Z \equiv \sum_i [\Delta M_i - \Delta CTE_i - \Delta NGD_i - \Delta F_i - OAS_i] \qquad (4.2)$$

where, in general, X_i represents the change in X in country i. There are no institutional restrictions on the value of Z, which could in theory be permanently negative, the French treasury providing the UEMOA with a permanent overdraft facility. (Appendix 4.1 provides details of the overdraft charges.). However, as noted in Chapter 1, there are restrictions on central bank credit to the government that are intended to prevent a continuous decline in Z. In particular, governments are not allowed to borrow more than 20 per cent of the past year's fiscal receipts.

Aggregate UEMOA figures for the 1980s give the impression that these restrictions have prevented excessive borrowing leading to deterioration in the BCEAO's net foreign asset position. Figure 4.1 illustrates the paths of three components of net foreign assets in the UEMOA region: (1) Z, the Operations Account, (2) F, other, country-specific components of net foreign assets of the central bank, the largest and most variable component of which is debt to the IMF, and (3) net foreign assets of private banking institutions (not part of the identity in equation (4.1)).

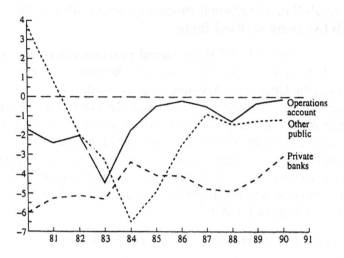

Figure 4.1 Components of UEMOA net foreign assets, 1985 FF billion.

The last of these exhibits very little variability. The first two are consistent with the efficient use, not only of the Operations Account, but also of IMF and other credit. There was a decline in net foreign assets in the early 1980s, following the second oil price shock, and the monetary union experienced Balance of Payments deficits. These deficits were financed partly by Operations Account deterioration. There followed a period of gradual recovery of net foreign assets; by 1990, the Operations Account deficit was a fraction of a per cent of UEMOA GDP.

However, this pattern does not correspond to the pattern for all of the individual countries. Figures 4.2 and 4.3 show the real net foreign asset positions of member states, plotting $E \cdot NFA$ for each country. These exhibit considerable heterogeneity. Of the six countries for which data are available, three (Burkina Faso, Niger and Togo) experienced a temporary decline in net foreign assets after the 1979–80 oil price shock, after which there was a marked recovery. Three (Bénin, Côte d'Ivoire and Sénégal) experienced a permanent decline in net foreign assets after this shock. In order to account for this discrepancy, we must look more closely at the financial aggregates of member states.

Table 4.1a shows a breakdown of the major components of UEMOA net foreign assets (net financial position in the Operations Account and net financial position in the IMF) by member state for 2 years: 1984,

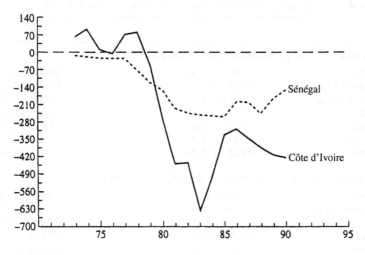

Figure 4.2 Net foreign assets, 1985, FCFA billion (Sénégal and Côte d'Ivoire).

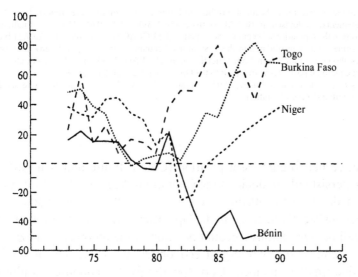

Figure 4.3 Net foreign assets, 1985, FCFA billion (Togo, Burkina Faso, Niger and Bénin).

which was the trough of the region's overall net foreign asset position, and 1990, which was the last observation of the sample, by which time substantial recovery of the region's net foreign asset position had occurred. It shows that two of the three countries with a persistently

Table 4.1a Components of UEMOA official net foreign assets 1984–90[a]

	1990	1984
Operations account in billions of CFA francs (% of GDP)		
Bénin	15.88 (3.0)	−20.00 (−5.1)
Burkina Faso	72.37 (13.1)	45.00 (10.8)
Côte d'Ivoire	−327.68 (−14.3)	−179.00 (−8.4)
Mali	45.57 (8.3)	8.00 (1.8)
Niger	53.85 (8.6)	37.00 (6.0)
Sénégal	−41.69 (−2.9)	−53.00 (−5.2)
Togo	90.45 (25.2)	96.00 (36.0)
Net financial position with respect to the IMF (% of GDP)		
Bénin	−5.18 (−1.0)	0.90 (0.0)
Burkina Faso	−3.33 (−0.6)	3.50 (0.9)
Côte d'Ivoire	−125.13 (−5.4)	−157.40 (−7.4)
Mali	−20.39 (−3.7)	−25.70 (−5.9)
Niger	−22.18 (−3.5)	−16.20 (−2.6)
Sénégal	−88.76 (−6.0)	−95.80 (−9.4)
Togo	−26.32 (−7.4)	−22.60 (−8.5)

a Imputed Operations Account credits and debits by country are reported as 'avoirs (engagements) en devises' in BCEAO statistics (BCEAO, 1980–1990). The sum of national net positions in the Operations Account is not equal to the BCEAO net position (−CFAF 7.31 billion), since some assets consolidated in the Operations Account are not imputed to any country. The figures shown here are taken from official sources (BCEAO, 1990–1). Independent attempts to estimate national positions with regard to the Operations Account have produced a wide variety of figures (see M'Bet and Niamkey, 1993; Krumm, 1987), so the figures in this table should be treated with a degree of caution.

negative net foreign asset position (Côte d'Ivoire and Sénégal) have been persistently in debit on the Operations Account. The third (Bénin) was in debit until 1990, but is now in credit. All the other countries have been consistently in credit in the Operations Account. In 1990, with the overall net Operations Account position of the union close to zero, the large debit of the two largest economies was offset by the credit of the five smaller members. Correspondingly, the countries exhibiting a large decline in net foreign assets in the long run are Côte d'Ivoire and Sénégal. Between 1962 and 1990, net foreign assets in Côte d'Ivoire fell from 3.7 per cent of GDP to −18.8 per cent. In Sénégal, the decline was from 9.0 per cent to −10.2 per cent.

It is instructive to compare the evolution of the Operations Account position of the largest debtor, Côte d'Ivoire, with that of the rest of the union. This is shown in Table 4.1b. In real terms, the Ivorian deficit

Table 4.1b Ivorian and UEMOA operations accounts deficits

GDP year	Ivorian deficit	UEMOA deficit	Difference	Ivorian Deflator
1980	117.8	52.7	65.1	1.00
1982	149.8	77.7	72.1	1.06
1984	179.0	121.7	57.3	1.25
1988	240.1	73.0	167.1	1.26
1990	327.7	7.3	321.1	1.24

Source: BCEAO (1990–91); World Bank (1991).

has been steadily increasing, while the overall UEMOA deficit rose in real terms up to 1984, then fell back to zero. The position of UEMOA less Côte d'Ivoire (the difference between the two deficits) also exhibits a rise and fall, but with an upward trend; moreover, the position is always one of credit. Correspondingly, the net foreign asset position of UEMOA less Côte d'Ivoire and Sénégal rose over the long term, from 4.5 per cent of GDP in 1962 to 11.7 per cent in 1990.

In order to discover the source of the persistently negative contribution of Côte d'Ivoire and Sénégal to the Operations Account, we must look at the components of the money stock in these countries over the 1970s and 1980s. Figures 4.4 and 4.5 show net government debt (*NGD*) and the money stock less credit to the private sector ($M - CTE$): the net financial positions of, respectively, the public and private sectors with respect to the BCEAO. The figures are in billions of CFA francs at 1985 prices. In the wake of the oil price shock, the net financial positions of both public and private sectors deteriorate in the two countries. In the case of the private sector, this is a temporary phenomenon, but in the case of the public sector, there is a permanent decline. That is, the persistently negative net foreign asset position of the two countries is the result of an increase in net government indebtedness, while the long run net financial position of the private sector is approximately constant.

How were the governments of Côte d'Ivoire and Sénégal able to acquire such large liabilities? The main tool for controlling net government debt is the 20 per cent rule: the increase in gross government debt held by the central bank (*DCB*) can be no larger than 20 per cent of past fiscal receipts (*FR*). This means that as long as *FR* are positive *DCB* (and hence net government debt) can rise steadily. Table 4.2 shows the average ratio of *DCB* to *FR* for those countries for which data are available. In all countries, the average value of *DCB/FR* is far less

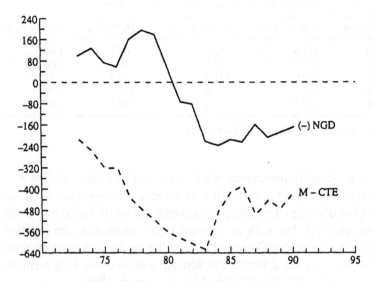

Figure 4.4 Ivorian monetary aggregates, 1985, FCFA billion.

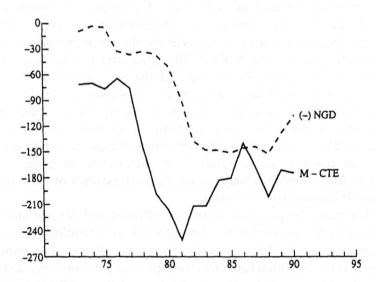

Figure 4.5 Senegalese monetary aggregates, 1985, FCFA billion.

Table 4.2 Fiscal receipts and government debt

	− DCB/FR (%)		
	Maximum	Mean	Time period
Bénin	16	4	1978–89
Burkina Faso	10	3	1978–90
Côte d'Ivoire	23	5	1974–90
Niger	19	5	1978–90
Sénégal	50	10	1976–90
Togo	21	6	1975–90

DCB gross government debt to the central bank.
FR fiscal receipts in the previous financial year. The time periods
are for the longest available continuous series.

Source: IMF (1991); UN Economic Commission for Africa
(1987).

than 20 per cent, and in only one country (Sénégal) has there been
a serious incursion of the rule. This happened in just one year. *DCB/FR*
is typically around 5 per cent. The 20 per cent rule is seldom binding,
and government debt can rise steadily without infringement of the rule.
In particular, it has seldom bound those countries (Côte d'Ivoire
and Sénégal) whose net foreign asset position has been persistently
negative.

The five smaller countries in UEMOA have substantial credit in the
Operations Account (up to 25 per cent of GDP), credit that has over the
long run been financing the debt of the larger countries. France does
not provide any overdraft facility until the Operations Account is
negative, so while the pool is positive the smaller countries bear the
whole brunt of lax policies in their larger partners. In the wake of
external shocks, the magnitude of this inequality has increased.
Meanwhile, the creditors have substantial debts with the IMF (up to 7.5
per cent of GDP). In the next section we will attempt to explain why
this situation has arisen. Given the costs entailed by the IMF debt, not
only in interest payments but also in enforced structural adjustment,
the smaller countries are worse off than with zero IMF debt and less
credit in the Operations Account. The inequalities that arise from this
situation are likely to endanger the political stability of UEMOA.
Moreover, one might wonder whether UEMOA as a whole could be
made better off by a different debt-sharing arrangement. This issue will
also be addressed below.

4.2. Modelling government policy choices in a monetary union: A game-theoretic framework

The experience of the UEMOA over the 1980s suggests several stylised facts:

1   Large members of the monetary union tend to contribute less to pooled foreign exchange reserves than smaller ones.
2   This discrepancy has become larger during a period of BOP adjustment.
3   The asymmetry appears to be due to differences in government behaviour (the institutions designed to prevent this have failed to work).
4   The smaller countries rely more heavily on loans from multilateral donors.

In this section, we present a game-theoretic model of government policy that explains these stylised facts. This model will form the basis for a welfare analysis of government behaviour.

We will begin with a static model to explain 1, 3 and 4. First, we define the contribution of the ith country to pooled foreign exchange reserves:

$$Z_i \equiv M_i - CTE_i - G_i - F_i \tag{4.3}$$

where M_i is domestic money demand, CTE_i the debt of the private sector, G_i net government debt, and F_i non-pooled net foreign assets. The same identity holds for the monetary union as a whole:

$$Z \equiv M - CTE - G - F \tag{4.4}$$

We will assume, to begin with, that M_i, CTE_i and F_i are not influenced by government policy. Real money demand and private borrowing are independent of government policy instruments, and net foreign assets, the major component of which is likely to be debt to the IMF, are beyond the control of the government. This is something of a simplification, since the government may be able to influence domestic inflation or other variables entering into the money demand function, and, at least in the long run, renegotiate its debt to the IMF.

Consider a monetary union in which a government chooses for itself what level of long-run debt to set. A welfare-maximising government will set G_i to maximise the benefits of G_i less the costs. The level of G_i set will thus depend on the form of the cost and benefit functions. In order to make the analysis tractable, we will assume a stylised benefit function for all countries, which is of the form:

$$B_i = a[G_i/s_i]^b, \quad 1 > b > 0 \tag{4.5}$$

where s_i is a scaling parameter reflecting the fact that the different members of the monetary union are of different sizes. Two francs' worth of borrowing to a country of two million people is worth the same as one franc's worth to a country of one million. That $b < 1$ indicates that the benefits of an increase in debt are lower, the higher the level of debt. This is because there are likely to be decreasing returns in the activities for which the borrowed money is used (for example, capital investment projects).

The costs of an increase in government debt, given that M_i, CTE_i and F_i are fixed, are the costs of a reduction in pooled net foreign assets to the individual country. Costs will be some function of $-Z$. Equilibrium G_i will depend crucially on the form which this cost function takes. In particular, it will depend on the way in which the costs of lower pooled net foreign assets (which in the first instance are borne by the central bank) are shared between the members of the monetary union.

Again, a stylised function will be used to represent costs. The fraction of the total costs which an individual country has to bear is denoted by w_i. The monetary value of the costs borne by an individual country is $-Zw_i$. A country's cost function is assumed to be of the form:

$$C_i = c[-Zw_i/s_i]^d = c[(G - h)w_i/s_i]^d \tag{4.6}$$

where $h = M - CTE + F$. Again, a scaling parameter is used: it is as difficult for a country of one million to bear one franc's worth of cost as it is for a country of two million to bear two francs' worth. It is tempting now to impose the restrictions, $a = c$ and $b = d$. However, before imposing restrictions on the cost function, it is necessary to give some consideration to how the central bank's costs are passed on to member states.

Costs to member states might arise for three reasons. First, a deterioration of pooled reserves might trigger a contractionary monetary policy by the central bank. We saw above that central bank policy instruments in UMOA have been singularly ineffective. However, an extreme deterioration might force the central bank to instigate an effective contractionary monetary policy. This policy might be aimed at member states whose fiscal policy is perceived to be particularly lax, i.e. ones with higher G_i, or it might require equal monetary contraction in all countries, regardless of past fiscal policy.

Second, a reduction in pooled net foreign assets entails a reduction in the central bank's net interest receipts. This reduction will be passed on in some way to member states, either as a reduction in dividends paid to governments, or as a reduction in 'soft' loans at a low central bank discount rate, or as an increase in the discount rate. These reductions could again apply to all countries equally, or just to 'offending' ones. Third, a decline in pooled reserves might lead to deterioration in the international credit rating of all member states. The deterioration in the rating might depend to some extent on the individual country's contribution to the decline in the reserves, but given the opacity of central bank accounting, the degree of this dependence might be slight.

The possibility of the imposition of a contractionary monetary policy, the different ways in which losses in central bank net receipts might be passed on to member states and the possible deterioration in member states' credit rating suggest that we consider two alternative weighting systems. In the first, costs are borne equally between member states, so $w_i = 1/n$. If however costs are borne in proportion to the size of government debt, then $w_i = G_i/G$. Moreover, if the costs arise mainly from the possibility of monetary contraction, or from higher interest rates, then it is unlikely that the cost function is symmetrical with the benefit function. It is quite likely that $d \geq 1$: a small change can be accommodated quite easily (for example, higher interest rates might be accompanied by higher taxes, with no effect on government spending); a large change requires a major restructuring of the government budget.

We now have two models of reserves. In one, governments maximise:

$$B_i - C_i = a[G_i/s_i]^b - c[(G-h)/ns_i]^d \tag{4.7}$$

In the other, the objective function is:

$$\begin{aligned} B_i - C_i &= a[G_i/s_i]^b - c[(G-h)G_i/Gs_i]^d \\ &= a[G_i/s_i]^b - c[(1-h/G)G_i/s_i]^d \end{aligned} \tag{4.8}$$

If we assume that each country maximises its objective function taking the behaviour of other governments as given, then the corresponding first order conditions are:

$$abG_i^{b-1}/s_i^b = cd(ns_i)^{-d}[(G-h)]^{d-1} \tag{4.9}$$

$$\begin{aligned} abG_i^{b-1}/s_i^b &= (cd/s_i)[(1-h/G)G_i/s_i]^{d-1} \\ &\times [1 - h(G-G_i)/(G)^2] \end{aligned} \tag{4.10}$$

From (4.9), we see that for any two countries:

$$G_i/G_j = (s_i/s_j)^{(d-b)/(1-b)} \tag{4.11}$$

while from (4.10):

$$\begin{aligned} G_i/G_j &= (s_i/s_j)^{(b-d)(d-1)/(b-1)}[[G(G-h)+hG_i] \\ &\div [G(G-h)+hG_j]]^{(d-1)/(b-1)} \end{aligned} \tag{4.12}$$

So as $(G-h)\to 0$, $G_i/G_j \to (s_i/s_j)^{d-1}$, and as $(G-h) \to \pm\infty$, $G_i/G_j \to (s_i/s_j)^{(d-b)(d-1)/(1-b)}$. Not surprisingly, the first case, in which the burden of debt is spread equally across countries regardless of size, favours the larger countries. Since $d > 1 > b > 0$, $G_i/G_j > s_i/s_j$, i.e. the larger countries' debt is more than proportional to their size. In the second case, larger countries are favoured for larger d and for smaller b, i.e. for more convex cost and benefit functions.

In order to measure the cost of individual governments' privately optimising behaviour, we need to find the Pareto optimal levels of government debt in the monetary union. Suppose first of all that the weights w_i are given. Now the different countries' public borrowing levels, G_i, are chosen to maximise total net benefits, $(B-C)$. The Pareto optimum is found from:

$$\begin{aligned} \max(G_1,\ldots,G_n) &\sum(a(G_i/s_i)^b) \\ &- \sum(c[(G-h)w_i/s_i]^d) \end{aligned} \tag{4.13}$$

Note that in each of the n first order conditions the second term (marginal cost) is the same: in considering the welfare effect of a marginal increase in G_i, the extra costs imposed on all countries are taken into account. Marginal benefits are of the form, abG_i^{b-1}/s_i^b. This means that for any two countries:

$$G_i/G_j = (s_i/s_j)^{-b/(1-b)} \tag{4.14}$$

That is, government debt is inversely related to the size parameter. (It is therefore likely that a necessary condition for the feasibility of the Pareto optimum is that side payments from the smaller countries to the larger are possible.) The relationship is independent of the cost function. A necessary condition for the equivalence of the private optimising and Pareto optimal equilibria is that all the countries be of equal size.

If the weights w_i can be varied to minimise total costs for a given level of G, this result is not altered. w_i is then determined by:

$$\min(w_1,\ldots,w_n)\Sigma(c[(G-h)w_i/s_i]^d) \text{ s.t. } \sum w_i = 1$$
$$= \min(w_1,\ldots,w_n)c[(G-h)]^d \sum((w_i/s_i)^d) \text{ s.t. } \sum w_i = 1 \tag{4.15}$$

The solution to this minimisation problem is:

$$w_i = \left[1 + \sum_{j\neq i}((s_j/s_i)^{1/(d-1)})\right]^{-1} \tag{4.16}$$

We can see that the optimal weighting rule is independent of the individual levels of G_i, so equation (4.13) still represents the optimal outcome.

Table 4.3 illustrates these general results. In the numerical examples shown, a/c is set at unity, and the model is solved for selected values of b and d for three countries of different sizes: $s_1 = 1.5$, $s_2 = 1.0$ and $s_3 = 0.5$. The table shows private optimising equilibria (with $w_i = 1/n$) and Pareto optimal equilibria. In Table 4.3 (i and ii), h is arbitrarily large, so that equilibrium G is equal to h (there is no point creating an Operations Account deficit, since the benefits of doing so are so small for such large G_i, and therefore low abG_i^{b-1}/s^b). If the countries were of equal size, both the private optimising equilibrium and the Pareto optimal equilibrium would be at $G_i = 1/3$. However, the asymmetry leads to a divergence between the two equilibria: G_1 (the private optimising equilibrium level of government debt in country 1) rises as $(d-b)/(1-b)$ rises, while G_1^p (the Pareto optimal level) falls as b rises. On the other hand, G_2 and G_3 fall as $(d-b)/(1-b)$ rises, while G_2^p and

Table 4.3 Private optimising equilibria and Pareto optimal equilibria

(i) Equilibrium G_i/h for large values of h, $a/c = 1$; $s_1 = 1.5$, $s_2 = 1.0$, $s_3 = 0.5$

$(d - b)/(1 - b)$	1.0	1.5	2.0	2.5	3.0	3.5	4.0	4.5	5.0
G_1/h		0.500	0.576	0.643	0.701	0.750	0.792	0.827	0.856	0.880
G_2/h		0.333	0.313	0.286	0.254	0.222	0.192	0.163	0.138	0.116
G_3/h		0.167	0.111	0.071	0.045	0.028	0.017	0.010	0.006	0.004

(ii) Pareto optimal G_i/h for large values of h, $a/c = 1$; $s_1 = 1.5$, $s_2 = 1.0$; $s_3 = 0.5$

b	0.1	0.2	0.3	0.4	0.5	0.6	0.7	0.8	0.9
G_1/h		0.315	0.292	0.264	0.228	0.182	0.124	0.060	0.012	0.000
G_2/h		0.330	0.323	0.314	0.298	0.273	0.229	0.156	0.058	0.002
G_3/h		0.355	0.385	0.422	0.474	0.545	0.647	0.784	0.930	0.998

(iii) Selected equilibrium and Pareto optimal G_i for $h = 0$, $a/c = 1$

b	d	G_1	G_2	G_3	G_1^p	G_2^p	G_3^p	G_{EQ}	G_{EQ}^p
0.8	1.8	4.349	0.573	0.018	0.009	0.048	0.763	1.333	0.185
0.8	1.2	11.78	5.237	1.310	0.041	0.206	3.295	5.657	0.210
0.2	1.2	0.826	0.498	0.209	0.169	0.187	0.223	0.500	0.134
0.2	1.8	1.048	0.466	0.117	0.134	0.148	0.176	0.503	0.146

G_3^p rise as b rises. It is impossible for the level of government debt in countries 1 and 3 to be Pareto optimal (private optimising and Pareto optimal equilibrium ranges do not overlap), and therefore it is impossible for the overall equilibrium to be optimal.

In Table 4.3(iii), we see equilibrium values of G_i for $h = 0$. Here, the equilibrium is not Pareto optimal even for countries of equal size, as the last two columns in the table show: the total level of debt is higher than it should be. Moreover, size asymmetry exacerbates the problem: as in the case of a large h, G_1 is too high and G_3 too low; however, the overall level of government debt is also too high, and by a greater magnitude than in the symmetrical case.

We can also see in such a model why a smaller country might be more willing than a larger one to negotiate with the IMF for a loan. In equilibrium, for each country, the marginal cost of present debt equals the marginal benefit, which is abG_i^{b-1}/s_i^b. This means that in the first case, the ratio of marginal costs of two countries, MC_i/MC_j, is $(s_j/s_i)^d$. In the second case, as $(G - h) \to 0$, $MC_i/MC_j \to (s_j/s_i)^{b + (1 - b)(d - 1)}$, and as $(G - h) \to \pm\infty$, $MC_i/MC_j (s_j/s_i)^{b + (d - b)(d - 1)}$. In all cases, the ratio of two countries' marginal costs is inversely proportional to their size, since $d - 1 > b > 0$. Smaller countries tend to have higher marginal costs. The 'price' (in terms perhaps of the strictness of structural adjustment) at which a smaller country will accept a deal with the IMF which reduces its debt is likely to be higher than for a larger country. This explains why Burkina Faso, Niger and Togo have positive net foreign assets as well as net debt with the IMF (in the case of Togo, IMF debt is a larger fraction of GDP than in Côte d'Ivoire and Sénégal).

The final stylised fact to be explained is the increase in the discrepancy between large and small countries after a shock. In order to analyse the evolution of government debt and foreign exchange reserves over time, a dynamic version of the model above can be constructed. In the illustration which follows, we will assume that $w_i = 1/n$, so that first order private optimising conditions for a single time period are of the form given by equation (4.9), with the modification that each country's government expects other countries' government debt this period to be what it was last period, so that with no adjustment costs:

$$ abG_i^*(t)^{b-1}/s^b = (cd/ns_i)^d \left[\left(G_i^*(t) + \sum_{j \neq i} G_j(t-1) - h(t) \right) \right]^{d-1} $$

(4.17)

where G_i^* is privately optimal G_i. However, it is likely that there are adjustment costs for large changes in G_i. Thus, the government sets G_i according to:

$$ G_i(t) = (1 - v)G_i^*(t) + vG_i(t-1) $$

(4.18)

Higher adjustment costs are captured by higher v. Note that $1 \geq v \geq 0$.

In the simulation depicted in Figures 4.6–4.10, $a/c = 1$, $b = 0.8$, $d = 1.2$ and $v = 0.9$. There are three countries in the monetary union. However, the general form of adjustment to equilibrium is similar for most parameter values. Initially, there is a long run equilibrium at $h = 20$; then h falls to zero, initiating a response by the three governments. In Figure 4.6, the countries are of the same size: all $s_i = 1$; in Figures 4.7–4.10, they are of different sizes: $s_1 = 1.5$, $s_2 = 1.0$ and $s_3 = 0.5$.

With the relatively high adjustment costs, it takes more than twenty periods for the countries to reach their new long run equilibrium, which they approach logarithmically. Government debt falls in all cases, although it falls proportionately more in smaller countries, as shown by

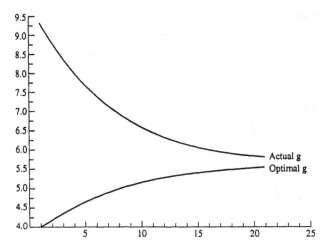

Figure 4.6. Optimal and actual G, all $s = 1$.

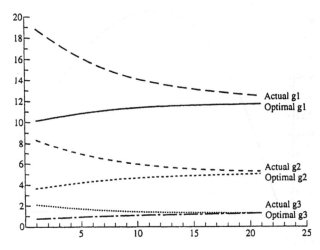

Figure 4.7 Optimal and actual G, $s_1 = 1.5$, $s_2 = 1$, $s_3 = 0.5$.

Figures 4.8 and 4.9, which plot G_1/G_2 and G_1/G_3 in the asymmetrical case. Moreover, there is an 'overshooting' effect in these ratios: as adjustment takes place, there is a time span in which debt is more unequally distributed than at either equilibrium. The reason for this is that in the immediate aftermath of the shock, the proportional gap between actual and optimal G_i is larger in the smaller countries. To see

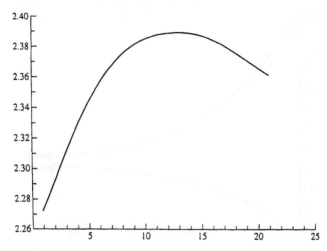

Figure 4.8 G_1/G_2.

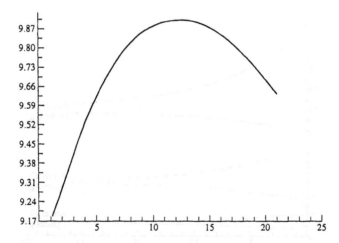

Figure 4.9 G_1/G_3.

this, note that a 10 per cent rise in anticipated G_1 depresses optimal G_3 by proportionately more than a 10 per cent rise in G_3 depresses optimal G_1. If G_1 and G_3 are too high to begin with, country 1's excess will affect country 3 more than country 3's excess affects country 1. As a result, country 3 converges to its long-run equilibrium more quickly than country 1, and G_1/G_3 will be higher than its new equilibrium value while country 1 'catches up'. This is illustrated in Figure 4.10, which plots $(G_i - G_i^*)/G_i$ $(= \alpha)$ for each of the three countries.

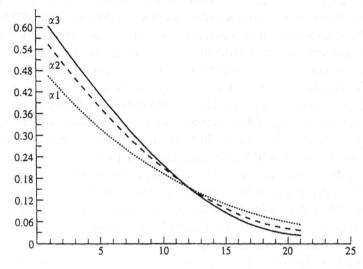

Figure 4.10 Values of α.

The model predicts that with a fall in *h* (a negative shock to private net wealth) in the monetary union, governments will reduce their own debt, but at different rates. Larger countries are tardier in accommodating to the shock, so their balance of payments position will remain poor for longer, and their net foreign asset position will continue to deteriorate as that of smaller countries is recovering. To a certain extent, this is a disequilibrium phenomenon, but some of the discrepancy will persist, and the new equilibrium will embody a more unequal distribution of debt than the old. Referring back to Figures 4.2 and 4.3, we see that this stylisation is generally true of the West African Monetary Union, with Côte d'Ivoire and Sénégal representing the large country case and Burkina Faso, Niger and Togo representing the small country case. The model does not necessarily capture all the determinants of government behaviour in a monetary union, and the case of Bénin (a small country with a persistent deficit) is anomalous. Nevertheless, it does explain the characteristics of the union as a whole.

4.3. Conclusion

For a monetary union to work effectively its constitution must take account not only of the fact that member states' governments are likely to be pursuing conflicting goals, but also of the asymmetries that arise when large and relatively economically powerful countries share financial institutions with smaller, weaker neighbours. The UEMOA has been unsuccessful in mitigating the welfare losses that arise from these asymmetries; it is unlikely to do so in the future without more extensive control of individual governments' economic policy.

The last three chapters have investigated the impact of CFA membership on monetary and fiscal policy and inflation. Chapter 2 indicates that for the average CFA member, long-run monetary growth (and hence inflation) will be lower than otherwise, while Chapter 3 suggests that membership has little impact on short-run fluctuations in monetary aggregates. In this chapter we have seen that for small countries there may be a disadvantage in membership, insofar as they are subsidising some of the public debt of their larger neighbours. If this problem could be solved (for example by fiscal controls more stringent than the 20 per cent rule) then CFA membership would represent a definite advantage, at least from the point of view of monetary policy. As it is, the effect of membership on smaller countries' welfare depends on the monetary value they place on lower long-run inflation.

Appendix 4.1: Operations account deficit payments for the UEMOA

Table 4.A1 below shows how the finance charges paid by the BCEAO evolved over the 1980s, and how explicit dividends and interest rates were adjusted. As the Operations Account moved into debit, finance charges increased substantially, and there was a corresponding fall in dividends. From 1987 onwards, dividends have been zero. Since dividends are always shared equally by all member states, regardless of size, this means that part of the increase in finance costs, at least, has been borne equally by UEMOA members. How the costs associated with the change in the discount rate are measured depends on the measure of the opportunity cost of money. Medhora (1992) prefers the BCEAO *taux divers*, the highest central bank discount rate, which is claimed to represent the true opportunity cost of credit in the union. Using this rate, it can be seen that there has been very little change in the rate of implicit subsidy to member states over the 1980s: the difference between the preferential discount rate and the *taux divers* seldom varies from 4 percentage points. However, if we use an international interest rate, such as the French interbank rate, which has fallen over the 1980s,

Table 4.A1 BCEAO dividends and interest rates

Year	BCEAO finance charges (CFAFbn)	Total divs (CFAFbn)	TEP (%)	TD (%)	FIBR (%)	(i) (%)	(ii) (%)
1979	8.5	6.9	5.5	9.5	9.5	4.0	4.0
1980	8.4	18.0	8.0	12.0	12.2	4.0	4.2
1981	21.8	13.2	8.0	12.0	15.3	4.0	7.3
1982	28.5	12.0	10.0	14.0	14.7	4.0	4.7
1983	38.8	10.8	8.0	12.0	12.6	4.0	4.6
1984	50.4	8.0	8.0	12.0	11.9	4.0	3.9
1985	57.2	7.2	8.0	12.0	10.1	4.0	2.1
1986	51.3	6.6	6.0	9.5	7.8	3.5	1.8
1987	37.7	0.0	6.0	10.0	8.2	4.0	2.2
1988	39.8	0.0	6.0	10.0	7.9	4.0	1.9
1989	46.4	0.0	6.0	10.0	9.3	4.0	3.3
1990	46.5	0.0	9.0	11.5	10.1	2.5	2.1

TEP: preferential BCEAO discount rate; *TD*: *taux divers*; *FIBR*: French interbank rate; (i): $TD - TEP$; (ii): $FIBR - TEP$.

Source: IMF (1991); Medhora (1992).

the implicit subsidy has also fallen. If we take the *taux divers* as a measure of the opportunity cost of credit, then the costs of the deterioration of the Operations Account have been borne equally by UEMOA members, in the form of a fall in dividends. If we use an international interest rate instead, then the implicit subsidy to government borrowing has fallen, and to this extent the costs have been borne in proportion to the size of each members' government debt.

Notes

1 The analysis will exclude Guinea-Bissau, which joined the UEMOA only in 1997; the data used in this chapter relate to the period before Guinea-Bissau's accession.
2 *MON* represents base money, *CTE* central bank net lending to the private sector, *NGD* central bank net lending to government, $E \cdot NFA$ net foreign assets in CFAF and *OAS* is a residual item.

References

BCEAO (1990–91) *Notes d'Information et Statistiques*, Dakar.
IMF (1991) *International Financial Statistics Yearbook*, Washington, DC.
Krumm, K. (1987) 'Adjustment in the Franc Zone: Focus on the real exchange rate', Mimeo, Country Policy Division, World Bank.

84 *Public debt, monetary and fiscal policies*

M'Bet, A. and Niamkey, A. (1993) 'European economic integration and the Franc
  Zone: The future of the CFA Franc after 1996', *AERC Research Paper 19*, Nairobi.
Medhora, R. (1992) 'Seignorage flows in the west African monetary union 1976–89',
  Weltwirtschaftliches Archiv, 128.
UN Economic Commission for Africa (1987) *African Statistical Yearbook*,
  Washington, DC.

5 Asset demand and the monetary transmission mechanism

The case of Côte d'Ivoire*

5.1. Introduction

The last two chapters have dealt with the factors that condition short-term monetary policy in the CFA. However, the impact of a given monetary policy on inflation will depend on the structure of the demand for financial assets. Chapter 2 dealt with the relationship between inflation and money growth in the long run, using cross-section data; in order to complete the picture we need to examine the factors that influence this relationship in the short run, in order to see how a given monetary policy influences short-term movements in prices.

Robust estimation of the short-run relationship will require the adoption of a time-series rather than a cross-section approach to the available data. Adequate time-series data are not available for all CFA countries, and here we estimate the relationship for just one representative CFA member (Côte d'Ivoire). Côte d'Ivoire is one of the largest members of the CFA, and the structure of asset markets in the other major CFA countries is unlikely to differ greatly from the Ivorian case.

One advantage of time-series data is that it allows us to reveal more of the structure of the relationship between money and prices than is possible with a cross-section. Chapter 2 applied a simple, reduced-form money demand function based on a single monetary aggregate, excluding all explanatory variables that were not strictly exogenous. In this chapter we will estimate a model that explicitly disaggregates

*This chapter is based on 'Interest, credit and liquid assets in Côte d'Ivoire', *Journal of African Economies*, **8**: 448–78. By permission of Oxford University Press.

asset demand into different components, that makes the short-run dynamics of the relationship between money, income and prices explicit, and that includes weakly exogenous variables such as the interest rate among the set of regressors.

The time-series employed covers the period 1962–95. We will be concerned with the following questions.

1   Is there – as hypothesised in Chapter 3 – a stable relationship between the stock of narrow money, which the central bank does control, and demand for wider monetary aggregates, which it does not? If such a relationship does not exist (if, for example, narrow and wide money are perfect substitutes, and people are indifferent with respect to the fraction of each in their total financial wealth) then changes in narrow money will not necessarily have any impact on aggregate demand, and so will not necessarily be of any use as a stabilisation policy tool. (But also, shocks to narrow money that result from public borrowing will not necessarily impact on prices, so the high gearing noted in Chapter 3 will not necessarily destabilise prices.)

2   As noted in Chapter 1, the BCEAO has not often been inclined to use its discount rate as a stabilisation policy tool. Would such a policy be effective? How does asset demand respond to changes in the interest rate?

3   There have been two outstanding changes in the Ivorian policy regime in the sample period: a rapid expansion in public investment expenditure in the mid-1970s, followed by a collapse in the mid-1980s; and the CFA franc devaluation in January 1994. How has asset demand responded to these changes?

4   Is asset demand affected by short-term volatility in factor income and asset returns? What does the relationship between volatility and asset demand tell us about the magnitude of the costs that arise from such volatility?

5.2. The asset demand model

The first part of this chapter (Sections 5.2 and 5.3) will deal with questions (2–4) by estimating a real financial asset demand function that excludes narrow money (i.e. currency in circulation). If a stable demand function for such assets exists, we can infer that they are not perfect substitutes for narrow money (otherwise fluctuations and secular trends in narrow money would generate instability in the estimated function). Then we can go on to look at the relationship between the nominal stock of narrow money and the nominal stock of other financial assets (Section 5.4), in order to address question (1).

5.2.1. The asset demand function

The econometric analysis in the first part of the chapter is based on a quarterly regression of the general form:

$$\ln(d/p)_t = \alpha_0(t) + \sum_i \alpha_i \cdot \ln(d/p)_{t-i} + \sum_j [\beta_j \cdot \ln(x)_{t-j}$$

$$+ \gamma_j \cdot \ln(1 + \pi)_{t-j} + \delta_j \cdot \ln(1 + r)_{t-j}$$

$$+ \eta_j \cdot V[\ln(x)]_{t-j} + \theta_j \cdot V[\ln(1 + \pi)]_j] + u_t \qquad (5.1)$$

where $i = 1, \ldots, n$; and $j = 0, \ldots, n$. u_t is a residual. d represents the nominal stock of financial assets held in Côte d'Ivoire, excluding currency, and p represents the Ivorian consumer price index. Measurement of these variables is discussed later. $\alpha_0(t)$ is a deterministic trend (including seasonal components), x is a scale variable: either gross domestic income, *gdy* (i.e. GDP adjusted for changes in the Terms of Trade), or gross domestic expenditure, *gde*. *gde* is more appropriate if transactions demand is the predominant reason for holding d; *gdy* is more appropriate if asset demand predominates. We will consider alternative specifications with each measure. We expect that $\sum_i \beta_i > 0$, i.e. the income elasticity of demand for the asset is positive, at least in the long run.

π is the inflation rate, $\Delta\ln(p)_t$. We expect that $\sum_i \gamma_i < 0$, as higher inflation reduces the real rate of return to financial assets, *ceteris paribus*. r is the nominal interest rate, which will be measured by the central bank discount rate. Since d represents mainly non-interest-bearing assets, we would normally expect in an industrialised economy that $\sum_i \delta_i < 0$: higher rates lead to lower demand. However, this is not necessarily the case in Côte d'Ivoire. In order to see what impact the interest rate has on financial asset demand, we need to look more carefully at the portfolio of assets available to the private sector.

Some limited circumstantial evidence on asset availability comes from data on consumers' capital transactions in the Ivorian Living

Standards Survey, discussed in Deaton (1992). Consumers appear to earn very little capital income from financial assets, suggesting that holdings of interest-bearing financial assets (other than low-interest time deposits) are limited. According to Deaton, physical assets, such as cattle or perennial cash crop plants, are likely to be the major alternative store of wealth.[1]

Such physical assets are not in themselves likely to be close substitutes for bank deposits. However, a distinguishing feature of UEMOA credit policy is the unlimited discounting by the BCEAO of short-term agricultural credit from private sector financial institutions to farmers, to facilitate consumption smoothing over the agricultural cycle, as noted in Chapter 3. The supply of short-run credit is virtually infinitely elastic at the discount rate set by the BCEAO. Holding a bank account and holding physical assets as collateral for agricultural credit are alternative ways of smoothing consumption, and in Chapter 3 there was some evidence that the money stock and agricultural credit are negatively correlated. When the discount rate rises, the optimal response of farmers is not necessarily to reduce borrowing and finance payments by running down liquid financial assets; if short-run credit is costly, farmers might decide to liquidate physical assets and move over to bank deposits as a means of smoothing consumption. For this reason, the demand for non-interest-bearing deposits might depend positively on the discount rate. It is likely then to be the case that it is the central bank discount rate rather than a deposit interest rate which best explains changes in deposit holdings, which is fortuitous, because this is the only rate reported for any length of time.[2] $\sum_i \delta_i$ will be positive if this consumption smoothing argument is correct.

$V[\ln(x)_t]$ and $V[\ln(1+\pi)_t]$ are variability measures reflecting the possibility that demand for financial assets is influenced not only by the level of income/expenditure and inflation, but also by the variability in these series, as indicated in question (4). Randomness in income and the rate of return to assets can in theory influence the desired level of saving, though the a priori signs of these effects are ambiguous (Levhari and Srinivasan, 1969; Rothschild and Stiglitz, 1971; Miller, 1976). We will not use an interest rate variability series in the model because the interest rate is constant for long periods, and falls only twice, in 1984–6 and 1995. A series representing absolute changes in r is highly correlated with one representing actual changes in r. Inclusion of an interest rate variability term in the estimated model did not produce statistically significant or economically interpretable coefficients.

5.2.2. Measurement and illustration of the variables

Quarterly data are available for the variables d/p, π and r for the period 1960–95, and reported in the IMF *International Financial Statistics*. d is measured as time deposits plus demand deposits. p is measured as the consumer price index, and r as the central bank discount rate. No quarterly data are available for the scale variable; moreover, proxies for quarterly production series that might be used for quarterly interpolation of the available annual *gdy* and *gde* data (such as export value figures) are missing from at least the later part of our sample. For this reason the *gdy* and *gde* series used are based solely on the annual figures, using the interpolation suggested in Lisman and Sandee (1964).

The variability series, $V[\ln(z)]$, are calculated as annual moving averages of the absolute change in $\ln(z)$ from one quarter to the next. An alternative measure would be some type of moving standard deviation; however, such measures, while positively correlated with $V[\ln(z)]$, tend to produce large outliers and are not normally distributed across time. There is a marked downward trend in the income and expenditure variability series: lower income growth corresponds to lower income variability; this is less noticeable in the case of inflation.

The variables appearing in equation (5.1) are depicted in Figures 5.1–5.9. These figures reveal the two major changes in Ivorian policy that relate to question (3) above. The first relates to the evolution of gross domestic investment, and therefore to the evolution of GDP. Through the 1970s Côte d'Ivoire had a high rate of investment to GDP, and high GDP growth. Up to 1976, the ratio of GDI to GDP was around 22 per cent; from 1977 to 1980 it was around 29 per cent. Most of the investment was public, and financed by borrowing from abroad, creating an increasing debt burden. By the mid-1980s the Government had accepted World Bank advice to cut borrowing and investment: the debt burden was reduced, but the ratio of GDI to GDP was halved, and GDP growth stopped. Movements in the Terms of Trade reinforced the effect on *gdy* of these changes in public investment. The coffee boom in 1976–7 brought about a 60 per cent increase in the Terms of Trade, coinciding with the peak in public investment spending.

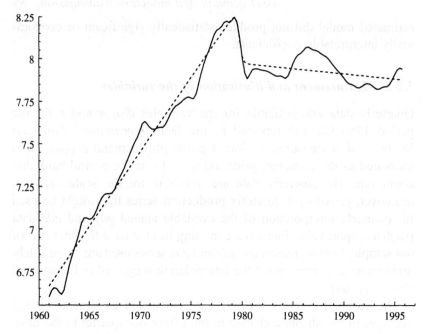

Figure 5.1 ln(*gdy*) with trend.

Figure 5.2 ln(*gde*) with trend.

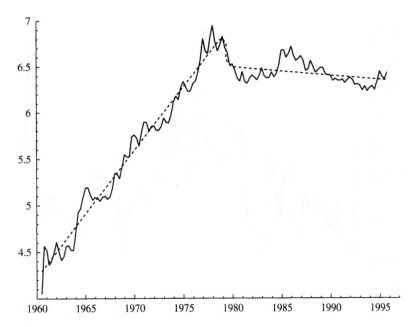

Figure 5.3 ln(*d/p*) with trend.

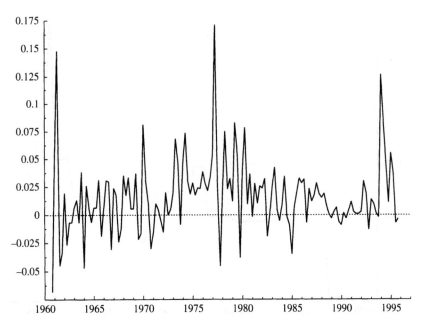

Figure 5.4 Observed ln(1 + π).

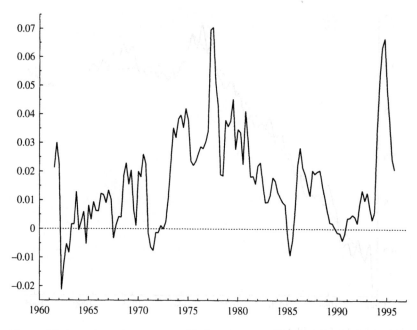

Figure 5.5 Annual moving average of $\ln(1 + \pi)$.

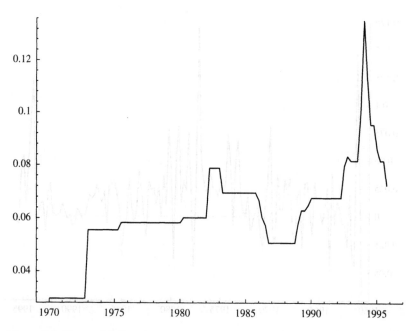

Figure 5.6 Observed $\ln(1 + r)$.

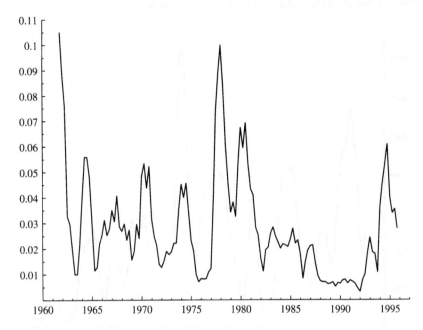

Figure 5.7 $V[\ln(1+\pi)]$.

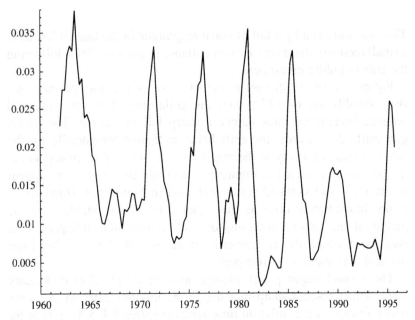

Figure 5.8 $V[\ln(gdy)]$.

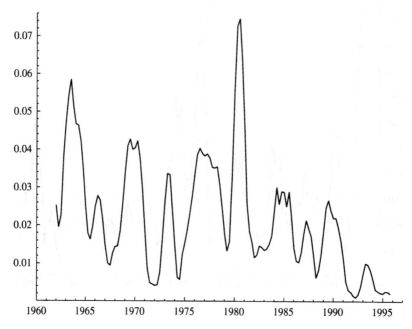

Figure 5.9 $V[\ln(gde)]$.

This was followed by a fall of equal magnitude in the late 1970s; after a small recovery there was another collapse in the late 1980s, following the cuts in public investment.

Figure 5.1 shows the net effect of these two factors on *gdy*. *gdy* rises steadily up to 1979; then the collapsing terms of trade and reduced investment rates induce a sharp fall in income. Thereafter, *gdy* drifts downwards, the drift being mitigated temporarily by the terms of trade recovery in the mid-1980s. A similar pattern appears in the *gde* series depicted in Figure 5.2. Roughly similar patterns appear in the real asset demand series, depicted in Figure 5.3. However, it is not immediately obvious that asset demand was stable over the period of the investment/terms of trade booms and collapses. One issue with which the econometric model will deal is whether asset demand was stable over this period.

The second major policy change was the devaluation in January 1994. This caused a sharp increase in the inflation rate, which is the major feature of the inflation time series (Figures 5.4–5.5), except for the inflation peak in the quarter following the coffee boom. It is also the

major feature in the interest rate series (Figure 5.6), the quarter following the devaluation being the only obvious time when the BCEAO
has used the base rate as a stabilisation device, raising the rate by
5 percentage points in an attempt to avert a collapse in asset demand
due to the high inflation that ensued. Again, we will want to ask
whether the asset demand function is stable over the period of the
policy innovation. We might expect a priori that an asset demand
function that was positive in r and negative in π would not show
substantial change during the devaluation period, unless there was a
marked loss in long-term confidence in the currency. However, a
demand function that was negative in both r and π ought to dip
sharply in 1993–4. The real asset stock series depicted in Figure 5.3
does not dip in this way, which suggests that deposits in this period
are either positive in r or insensitive to both r and π.

5.2.3. *Econometric results (The reader can skip this section without loss of continuity)*

The first stage in estimating equation (5.1) is to establish the order
of integration of each time series. As noted above, the main changes
in direction of *gdy*, *gde* and the real asset stock series correspond to
identifiable changes in government policy and terms of trade. The
test procedure must therefore allow for the possibility of structural
breaks. However, visual inspection of the relevant series indicates
that the shifts in the deterministic components of the series might not
necessarily be instantaneous, so methods involving the imposition or
identification of a discrete break point (such as in Perron, 1989) are
inappropriate. For this reason we test for stationarity using the
method described in Leybourne *et al.* (1995). The first step in this
procedure is to estimate an equation of the form:

$$z_t = a_0 + a_1 \cdot t + \frac{a_2}{[1 + \exp(-b \cdot (t - c))]}$$
$$+ \frac{[a_3 \cdot t]}{[1 + \exp(-b \cdot (t - c))]} + u_t \tag{5.2}$$

by least squares for each variable z. The logistic trend components of
the regression allow for a smooth transition from one deterministic
(trended) mean to another. The parameter b determines the speed of

transition; the parameter c determines the midpoint of this transition. The second step is to test the stationarity of the residual u_t (i.e. of z_t around its nonlinear trend) using an Augmented Dickey–Fuller regression:

$$\Delta u_t = h_0 \cdot u_{t-1} + \sum_i h_i \cdot \Delta u_{t-1} + v_t \qquad (5.3)$$

where $i = 1, \ldots, n$. The lag order n is large enough to ensure that v_t is a serially uncorrelated residual. The null that z_t is difference stationary can be rejected against the alternative of stationarity if h_0 is significantly negative. Leybourne *et al.* (op. cit.) provide critical values for the t-ratio corresponding to h_0 (which are different from those for the ordinary ADF test).

Table 5.1 presents the results of using this test procedure for the dependent variable $\ln(d/p)$ the scale variables $\ln(gdy)$ and $\ln(gde)$. In each case we report the parameters of equation (5.2) and the t-ratio corresponding to h_0 in equation (5.3), denoted t_{LNV}. The fitted trends are illustrated in Figures 5.1–5.5 above. In all cases except that of $\ln(gdy)$ the null of nonstationarity can be rejected at the 1 per cent

Table 5.1 Stationarity test statistics

LNV test statistics			
Coeff.	$\ln(d/p)$	$\ln(gdy)$	$\ln(gde)$
a_0	6.6781^a	8.0895^a	8.2497^a
$a_1 \cdot 0.01$	-0.2303^a	-0.1478^a	-0.33657^a
a_2	-2.4192^a	-1.4928^a	-1.7535^a
a_3	0.0366^a	0.0234^a	0.0264^a
b	-1.9517	-1.6961^b	-1.7288^b
c	76.4^a	77.8^a	78.9^a
t_{LNV}	-5.951^a	-3.686	-5.709^a

ADF test statistics					
Coeff.	$\ln(1+r)$	$V[\ln(gdy)]$	$V[\ln(gde)]$	$V[\ln(1+\pi)]$	$V[\ln(1+\pi)]$
t_{ADF}	-3.459^b	-3.448^b	-4.585^a	-3.373	-3.298^b

Perron test statistics (break in 1977(1))	
Coeff.	$\ln(1+\pi)$
t_P	-6.635^a

a Represents significance at the 1 per cent level.
b Represents significance at the 5 per cent level.

level. Although we cannot reject the null in the case of ln(*gdy*), the similarity of the deterministic component of this series with the others (and in particular with ln(*gde*)) suggests that it is in fact stationary. At worst, treating ln(*gdy*) as stationary will entail estimating an unbalanced regression with a nonstationary variable on the RHS (only); and to treat ln(*gdy*) and ln(*gde*) as being integrated to a different order defies common sense.

Of the other variables, $\ln(1+r)$, $V[\ln(gdy)]$, $V[\ln(gde)]$ and $V[\ln(1+\pi)]$ do not exhibit any obvious structural break; nor is there any particular reason for supposing them to do so. So the order of integration of these series is tested using a standard Augmented Dickey–Fuller procedure, i.e. by testing the null that h_0 is insignificant in the regression:

$$\Delta z_t = a_0 + a_1 \cdot t + h_0 \cdot z_{t-1} + \sum_i h_i \cdot z_{t-i} + v_t \qquad (5.4)$$

using the standard DF critical values (reported in Banerjee *et al.*, 1993). The *t*-ratios corresponding to h_0 are reported in Table 5.1. The null of nonstationarity can be rejected (at least at the 5 per cent level) in all cases except that of $V[\ln(1+\pi)]$. Bearing in mind the caveat of Perron (1988) with regard to nuisance parameters, equation (5.4) is re-estimated with the restriction $a_1 = 0$. With this form of test, the null can be rejected.

Visual inspection of the final series, $\ln(1+\pi)$, indicates the possibility of a structural break in the late 1970s. The break point in this case appears quite definitely to be the coffee boom (see Figures 5.4 and 5.5), so we use a standard Perron test (Perron, 1989), allowing for a break in the coefficients a_0 and a_1 in equation (5.4) in 1977(1). Again the null of nonstationarity can be rejected at the 1 per cent level.

All variables are treated as stationary, and equation (5.1) is estimated by standard least squares methods, without recourse to a cointegration methodology.

Table 5.2 The four classes of model

	Scale variable	All variables detrended	Periodisation
Class A	ln(*gdy*)	yes	quarterly
Class B	ln(*gdy*)	yes	annual
Class C	ln(*gdy*)	no	quarterly
Class D	ln(*gde*)	yes	quarterly

Given the maintained hypothesis that there are nonlinear trends in the deterministic components of some of the series of interest, including the alternative dependent variables, the ideal procedure for estimating equation (5.1) would be to construct a multivariate equation with a nonlinear trend component. However, given the large number of variables in the equation, it is infeasible to attempt to locate the maximum of the corresponding log-likelihood function. Two alternative approaches are to detrend all variables before estimation, or to detrend only $\{\ln(gde), \ln(gdy)\}$ and also include the fitted trend for the scale variable (which will give us the correct model if we are correct in assuming that the trend in the dependent variable arises entirely as a result of the trend in the scale variable). It turns out that the two approaches give virtually identical results. Most of the tables below report the results of using the first approach; however, we also report the results of using the second approach to estimate our final (preferred) version of equation (5.1).

As indicated in the introductory chapter to this volume, there are no strong a priori grounds for preferring one of the alternative scale variables to the other. We begin with the results of models that use *gdy* as the scale variable, leaving the results of *gde* models for later. Table 5.2 delineates four classes of model, to which the subsequent tables refer. These four classes do not cover all of the possible permutations, and other permutations are discussed without being reported. We must also make a decision with respect to the lag order, n. This choice is made using standard information criteria: a lag order of two beats all higher lag orders on the Schwartz and Hannon–Quinn Criteria and on Final Prediction Error (Table 5.3). Zero- and first-order lag models exhibit residual autocorrelation, so Table 5.4 reports the parameters of the Class A model with two lags. This equation produces significant long-run coefficients on the variables $\ln(gdy)$ (1.59), $\ln(1 + \pi)$ (-2.59) and $\ln(1 + r)$ (6.18); the $V[\ln(1 + \pi)]$ terms are jointly significant, but the coefficients on lags of this variable have reversed signs and the long-run effect is statistically insignificant, suggesting that there is a significant short-run effect.

Interpreting the dynamics of the asset demand equation is difficult because all lags of all explanatory variables except $V[\ln(1 + \pi)]$ are insignificant. This suggests that omission of these lags would result in increased model parsimony, and Table 5.5 indicates that this supposition is supported by standard model selection criteria. Under the alternative specification there is no significant change in the

Table 5.3 Model selection criteria for class A and D models

Lag order	Schwartz	Hannon–Q	FPE
Class A			
2	− 5.38575	− 5.65534	0.00292
4	− 5.00647	− 5.43431	0.00329
6	− 4.69521	− 5.28449	0.00349
8	− 4.38232	− 5.13634	0.00375
Class D			
2	− 5.22794	− 5.49753	0.00342
4	− 4.72705	− 5.11600	0.00463
6	− 4.55430	− 5.10430	0.00427
8	− 4.30371	− 5.01810	0.00429

long-run coefficients on $\ln(gdy)$, $\ln(1 + \pi)$ and $\ln(1 + r)$, which fall to 1.44, −2.03 and 4.18 respectively. There is also a positive long-run coefficient on $V[\ln(gdy)]$ (3.01), which is significant at the 10 per cent level. The impact coefficients on the explanatory variables are much smaller: only 31 per cent of the long-run effect of a change in each explanatory variable is registered immediately, and it takes five quarters for the first 90 per cent of the effect to be realised.

A rough indicator of the relative importance of each explanatory variable is its long-run coefficient multiplied by the ratio of its sample standard deviation to that of $\ln(d/p)$.[3] These figures are $\ln(gdy)$: 0.87; $\ln(1 + \pi)$: 0.50; $\ln(1 + r)$: 0.41; $V[\ln(gdy)]$: 0.07. Income, inflation and the interest rate all have a substantial impact on demand for real financial assets. Although the interest elasticity of asset demand is twice that of the inflation elasticity, inflation is much more variable than the interest rate, and a one standard deviation (s.d.) increase in inflation has a slightly larger impact on d/p than a one s.d. increase in the interest rate. Income variability has a somewhat smaller impact, which is positive: i.e. more uncertainty with regard to income leads to a higher financial asset demand, suggesting that at least part of the reason for holding bank deposits is a precautionary motive.

The coefficients on lags of $V[\ln(1 + \pi)]$ are more difficult to interpret. The sign reversals suggest a term in $\Delta^2 V[\ln(1 + \pi)]_t$, and if this variable is used to replace the inflation variability terms in Table 5.5 its estimated coefficient is −0.76, significant at the 5 per cent level. It is not surprising that higher inflation volatility should reduce the demand for financial assets, but it is puzzling that it should be

Table 5.4 Model A1: 1962(3) to 1995(4)[a]

Variable	Coeff.	Std. err.	t-value	HCSE	Inst.
Constant	0.02927	0.01347	2.173	0.01465	0.07
$\ln(d/p)_{-1}$	0.85903	0.09234	9.303	0.09467	0.22
$\ln(d/p)_{-2}$	−0.19650	0.08562	−2.295	0.08177	0.04
$\ln(gdy)$	0.19542	0.38862	0.503	0.39460	0.03
$\ln(gdy)_{-1}$	0.31708	0.68873	0.460	0.70175	0.03
$\ln(gdy)_{-2}$	0.02558	0.41170	0.062	0.39862	0.04
$\ln(1+\pi)$	−0.61823	0.19401	−3.187	0.21096	0.04
$\ln(1+\pi)_{-1}$	−0.18708	0.20176	−0.927	0.23062	0.11
$\ln(1+\pi)_{-2}$	−0.06924	0.19788	−0.350	0.22314	0.07
$\ln(1+r)$	0.58597	0.94362	0.621	0.95060	0.28
$\ln(1+r)_{-1}$	0.86318	1.26270	0.684	0.98146	0.27
$\ln(1+r)_{-2}$	0.63646	0.95493	0.666	0.70876	0.41
$V[\ln(gdy)]$	2.31320	1.51000	1.532	1.76970	0.04
$V[\ln(gdy)]_{-1}$	−1.92050	2.40120	−0.800	2.84180	0.04
$V[\ln(gdy)]_{-2}$	0.66278	1.52000	0.436	1.76060	0.08
$V[\ln(1+\pi)]$	−0.59701	0.55494	−1.076	0.56580	0.03
$V[\ln(1+\pi)]_{-1}$	1.22370	0.77365	1.582	0.81189	0.04
$V[\ln(1+\pi)]_{-2}$	−0.90544	0.50945	−1.777	0.48020	0.06
$Q(1)$	0.02493	0.01447	1.723	0.01422	0.09
$Q(2)$	−0.05629	0.01717	−3.279	0.01682	0.16
$Q(3)$	−0.05896	0.01361	−4.332	0.01420	0.35

$R^2 = 0.8290$ Adjusted $R^2 = 0.3678$ $\sigma = 0.05022$ VIT $= 0.23127$ JIT $= 3.96988$
SC $= -5.38575$ HQ $= -5.65534$ FPE $= 0.00292$

Lag order	LM Autocorrelation test	LM ARCH test
1	$F(1, 112) = 2.0454$	$F(1, 111) = 0.0000$
4	$F(4, 109) = 0.7540$	$F(4, 105) = 0.1248$
8	$F(8, 105) = 1.1369$	$F(8, 97) = 0.9364$

Solved long run equation

Variable	Coeff.	Std. err.
Constant	0.087	0.044
$\ln(gdy)$	1.594	0.306
$\ln(1+\pi)$	−2.591	1.116
$\ln(1+r)$	6.180	2.385
$V[\ln(gdy)]$	3.128	2.007
$V[\ln(1+\pi)]$	−0.826	0.939

a 'Std. err.' represents standard errors without correction for heteroskedasticity; 'HCSE' represents corrected standard errors. 'Inst.' is Hansen's parameter instability statistic. 'JIT' is joint parameter instability statistic, 'VIT' is variance instability statistic, 'SC' is the Schwartz Criterion, 'HQ' the Hannon–Quinn Criterion and 'FPE' the Final Prediction Error.

Table 5.5 Model A2: 1962(3) to 1995(4)

Variable	Coeff.	Std. err.	t-value	HCSE	Inst.
Constant	0.02597	0.01252	2.074	0.01335	0.09
$\ln(d/p)_{-1}$	0.90616	0.08310	10.905	0.08602	0.24
$\ln(d/p)_{-2}$	−0.21743	0.07747	−2.807	0.07607	0.04
$\ln(gdy)$	0.44828	0.09587	4.676	0.09085	0.03
$\ln(1+\pi)$	−0.63078	0.18721	−3.369	0.20965	0.04
$\ln(1+r)$	1.29980	0.56184	2.313	0.50950	0.25
$V[\ln(gdy)]$	0.93743	0.55049	1.703	0.56660	0.03
$V[\ln(1+\pi)]$	−0.65808	0.53216	−1.237	0.56133	0.03
$V[\ln(1+\pi)]_{-1}$	1.55030	0.73990	2.095	0.79657	0.03
$V[\ln(1+\pi)]_{-2}$	−1.00700	0.48586	−2.073	0.45476	0.04
Q(1)	0.02443	0.01378	1.773	0.01360	0.12
Q(2)	−0.05840	0.01582	−3.692	0.01475	0.14
Q(3)	−0.06165	0.01247	−4.943	0.01294	0.45

$R^2 = 0.8215$ Adjusted $R^2 = 0.3402$ $\sigma = 0.04957$ VIT $= 0.25594$ JIT $= 3.20493$
SC $= -5.63551$ HQ $= -5.80240$ FPE $= 0.00270$

Chow tests: 1991(1)-end: F(20, 101) $= 0.8958$; 1978(1)-end: F(72, 50) $= 0.8732$

Lag order	LM autocorrelation test	LM ARCH test
8	F(8, 113) $= 1.3837$	F(8, 105) $= 1.3332$
4	F(4, 117) $= 1.0585$	F(4, 113) $= 0.1276$
1	F(1, 120) $= 3.0679$	F(1, 119) $= 0.2791$

Solved long run equation

Variable	Coeff.	Std. err.
Constant	0.083	0.045
$\ln(gdy)$	1.440	0.286
$\ln(1+\pi)$	−2.027	0.730
$\ln(1+r)$	4.176	2.059
$V[\ln(gdy)]$	3.012	1.802
$V[\ln(1+\pi)]$	−0.369	0.884

the rate of acceleration of this variable, rather than its level, which is significant.

It is important to establish that income and inflation are at least weakly exogenous to d/p. For this reason, Tables 5.6–5.7 report models of income and inflation which are used in testing for weak exogeneity in the way described by Engle and Hendry (1993). The inflation model uses quarterly data; the income model uses annual data. Table 5.7 shows the inflation model: present inflation depends on lagged inflation and the lagged interest rate. Adding the residual from this equation to the asset demand equation constitutes a test of

Table 5.6 Exogeneity test statistics: $\ln(1 + \pi)$

$\ln(1 + \pi)$ *model: 1962 (4) to 1995 (4)*

Variable	Coeff.	Std. err.	t-value	HCSE	Inst.
Constant	−0.00020	0.00224	−0.089	0.00226	0.05
$\ln(1 + \pi)_{-2}$	−0.23656	0.08206	−2.883	0.09162	0.11
$\ln(1 + \pi)_{-4}$	0.17392	0.08111	2.144	0.07315	0.09
$\ln(1 + r)_{-1}$	0.94598	0.21724	4.355	0.22828	0.31

$R^2 = 0.2039$ Adjusted $R^2 = 0.4080$ $\sigma = 0.02578$ VIT $= 0.08402$ JIT $= 0.72556$
SC $= -7.19943$ HQ $= -7.25104$ FPE $= 0.00068$

Lag order	LM autocorrelation test	LM ARCH test
8	$F_{(8, 121)} = 0.71358$	$F_{(8, 105)} = 0.44030$
4	$F_{(4, 125)} = 0.41702$	$F_{(4, 113)} = 0.28333$
6	$F_{(1, 128)} = 0.43521$	$F_{(1, 119)} = 0.24146$

$\ln(1 + \pi)$ exogeneity test: $t = 1.278$

weak exogeneity. As Table 5.6 shows, the *t*-ratio on the residual is insignificant, so the null of inflation exogeneity cannot be rejected.

Table 5.7 reports the annual models of income and asset demand used to test income exogeneity. Model selection criteria indicate the parsimony of a zero-lag annual model of $\ln(d/p)$ (which is consistent with a quarterly model in which the highest lag order is two). Adding the residual from the income equation to this model does not generate a significant coefficient, so we cannot reject the hypothesis that $\ln(gdy)$ is weakly exogenous. The elasticities of the estimated asset demand equation are similar to those for the long-run in the quarterly model, though (except for $V[\ln(gdy)]$) somewhat smaller.

One key area of interest is the stability of the asset demand equation over periods in which there has been a large change in macroeconomic conditions, in particular over the income growth slowdown after the coffee price boom, and over the 1994 devaluation. We therefore constructed Chow Test statistics for models estimated over sub-samples up to (i) 1977(4) and (ii) 1990(4), forecasting over the remainder of the sample period (up to 1995(4)). In neither case is there the slightest indication of parameter instability. This is confirmed by the Hansen parameter instability statistics shown in Tables 5.4–5.7. Figure 5.10 shows the forecasts in case (ii), for 1991(1) to 1995(4). In only two periods are the forecasts close to two standard errors from actual $\ln(d/p)$: actual asset demand is higher than predicted

Table 5.7 Exogeneity test statistics: ln(gdy)

Class B model: Selection criteria

Lag order	Schwartz	Hannon–Q	FPE
0	−5.58853	−5.74442	0.00298
1	−5.30265	−5.62030	0.00320
2	−4.69842	−5.18415	0.00502

Model B: 1965 to 1995

Variable	Coeff.	Std. err.	t-value	HCSE	Inst.
Constant	−0.00433	0.00918	−0.472	0.00870	0.19
ln(gdy)	1.06720	0.16879	6.322	0.16571	0.40
ln($(1+\pi)_{-3}$)	−1.37290	0.72601	−1.891	0.64445	0.13
ln($(1+r)$)	3.69910	1.08200	3.419	0.70580	0.47
V[ln(gdy)]	4.40380	1.32830	3.315	0.81988	0.13

$R^2 = 0.6640$ Adjusted $R^2 = 0.6455$ $\sigma = 0.05063$ VIT 0.02512   JIT 1.29505
SC = −5.58853   HQ = −5.74442   FPE = 0.00298

Lag order	LM autocorrelation test	LM ARCH test
1	$F(1, 25) = 0.88924$	$F(1, 24) = 2.2655$
2	$F(2, 24) = 0.45342$	$F(2, 22) = 2.8241$

ln(gdy) model: 1965 to 1995

Variable	Coeff.	Std. err.	t-value	HCSE	Inst.
Constant	0.00548	0.00705	0.778	0.00689	0.11
ln(gdy)$_{-1}$	0.57038	0.10976	5.197	0.12731	0.04
ln($(1+\pi)_{-2}$)	−1.37690	0.58198	−2.366	0.59139	0.18
ln($(1+r)_{-3}$)	3.89640	0.88396	4.408	0.77093	0.08

$R^2 = 0.67774$ Adjusted $R^2 = 0.51284$ $\sigma = 0.03864$ VIT 0.21946   JIT 0.66843
SC = −6.20183   HQ = −6.32655   FPE = 0.00169

Lag order	LM autocorrelation test	LM ARCH test
2	$F(2, 25) = 1.4074$	$F(2, 23) = 1.5188$
1	$F(1, 26) = 1.8666$	$F(1, 25) = 2.6841$

ln(gdy) exogeneity test: $t = -0.738$

in 1993(3) and lower than predicted in 1993(4). These periods coincide with the suspension of the external convertibility of the CFA franc in August 1993, the main event triggering the currency attack that led to the devaluation (Azam, 1997). Sight deposits were not affected by the suspension, so it is likely that people would wish to convert from cash to deposits in the Fall of 1993, explaining the forecast error for 1993(3). The following quarter was dominated by the ensuing expectation of imminent devaluation, at which time it is likely that people would have an increased desire for the most liquid

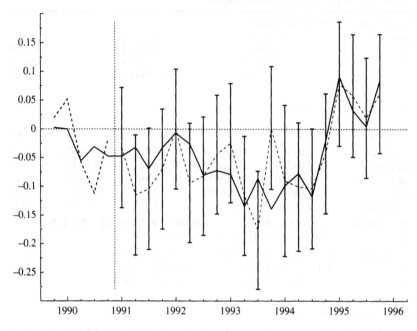

Figure 5.10 Actual ln(d/p) (solid line) with forecasts (dashed line) $\pm$ 2 std. err.

form of the currency and substitute out of deposits, explaining the forecast error for 1993(4).

These results also come out of a model (Class C) in which only ln(gdy) is detrended, and the fitted income trend is included as an extra explanatory variable. Tables 5.8 and 5.9 report the basic results for this model, and correspond to Tables 5.4 and 5.5. The estimated coefficients in Tables 5.8 and 5.9 are virtually identical to those in Tables 5.4 and 5.5. Moreover, the estimated coefficient on the income trend, ln(gdy)§, is very close to that on detrended income. Variations in income around its trend do not affect asset demand differently from trend changes.

Tables 5.10 and 5.11 report the model (Class D), which uses *gde* as a scale variable instead of *gdy*. This model is estimated with a lag order of two: as Table 5.3 indicates, higher order lags result in poorer performance according to standard model selection criteria. A number of factors suggest that the Class D model is inappropriate: (i) it loses out to the Class A model on the criteria used in Table 5.4; (ii) V[ln(gde)] is always an insignificant explanatory

Table 5.8 Model C1: 1962(3) to 1995(4)

Variable	Coeff.	Std. err.	t-value	HCSE	Inst.
Constant	−1.91980	0.39609	−4.847	0.37014	0.03
Trend	0.00034	0.00022	1.543	0.00023	0.04
$\ln(d/P)_{-1}$	0.89183	0.09492	9.396	0.08381	0.04
$\ln(d/p)_{-2}$	−0.23248	0.08134	−2.858	0.07063	0.04
$\ln(gdy)^{\S}$	0.51694	0.09648	5.358	0.09337	0.03
$\ln(gdy)$	0.21752	0.39448	0.551	0.40767	0.04
$\ln(gdy)_{-1}$	0.29552	0.68836	0.429	0.69101	0.04
$\ln(gdy)_{-2}$	0.05001	0.40924	0.122	0.37586	0.04
$\ln(1+\pi)$	−0.75592	0.19373	−3.902	0.20777	0.05
$\ln(1+\pi)_{-1}$	−0.30331	0.20365	−1.489	0.20826	0.11
$\ln(1+\pi)_{-2}$	−0.15617	0.20136	−0.776	0.24286	0.06
$\ln(1+r)$	0.69602	0.94082	0.740	1.06420	0.26
$\ln(1+r)_{-1}$	1.01280	1.25630	0.806	1.04260	0.26
$\ln(1+r)_{-2}$	0.61083	0.95563	0.639	0.71044	0.41
$V[\ln(gdy)]$	2.75540	1.50430	1.832	1.64960	0.07
$V[\ln(gdy)]_{-1}$	−2.97070	2.38840	−1.244	2.49670	0.05
$V[\ln(gdy)]_{-2}$	1.40980	1.51790	0.929	1.62110	0.07
$V[\ln(1+\pi)]$	−0.64419	0.56177	−1.147	0.65335	0.06
$V[\ln(1+\pi)]_{-1}$	1.34170	0.77075	1.741	0.88811	0.09
$V[\ln(1+\pi)]_{-2}$	−0.94311	0.51795	−1.821	0.52309	0.13
Q(1)	0.02283	0.01433	1.594	0.01456	0.09
Q(2)	−0.05804	0.01719	−3.376	0.01611	0.19
Q(3)	−0.05898	0.01361	−4.335	0.01419	0.36

$R^2 = 0.9945$ Adjusted $R^2 = 0.4556$ $\sigma = 0.04993$ VIT $= 0.15568$ JIT $= 3.74830$
SC $= -5.34186$ HQ $= -5.63713$ FPE $= 0.00292$

Lag order	LM autocorrelation test	LM ARCH test
1	$F(1, 110) = 0.56457$	$F(1, 109) = 1.54750$
4	$F(4, 107) = 0.33316$	$F(4, 103) = 0.41239$
8	$F(8, 103) = 0.85617$	$F(8, 95) = 0.51298$

Solved long run equation

Variable	Coeff.	Std. err.
Constant	−5.6360	0.4084
Trend	0.0010	0.0006
$\ln(gdy)^{\S}$	1.5180	0.0564
$\ln(gdy)$	1.6530	0.3000
$\ln(1+\pi)$	−3.5680	1.1800
$\ln(1+r)$	6.8090	2.3660
$V[\ln(gdy)]$	3.5060	1.9890
$V[\ln(1+\pi)]$	−0.7210	1.0140

Table 5.9 Model C2: 1962(3) to 1995(4)

Variable	Coeff.	Std. err.	t-value	HCSE	Inst.
Constant	−1.78760	0.34964	−5.113	0.33203	0.03
Trend	0.00028	0.00021	1.335	0.00021	0.04
$\ln(d/p)_{-1}$	0.95333	0.08255	11.549	0.06908	0.03
$\ln(d/p)_{-2}$	−0.26513	0.07433	−3.567	0.06451	0.03
$\ln(gdy)^{\S}$	0.47781	0.08399	5.689	0.08224	0.03
$\ln(gdy)$	0.46538	0.09384	4.959	0.08103	0.04
$\ln(1+\pi)$	−0.73622	0.18567	−3.965	0.20939	0.05
$\ln(1+r)$	1.38460	0.56096	2.468	0.51899	0.15
$V[\ln(gdy)]$	0.97794	0.55440	1.764	0.55653	0.04
$V[\ln(1+\pi)]$	−0.82751	0.53362	−1.551	0.66040	0.04
$V[\ln(1+\pi)]_{-1}$	1.72590	0.74053	2.331	0.91642	0.06
$V[\ln(1+\pi)]_{-2}$	−1.09460	0.49262	−2.222	0.52479	0.10
Q(1)	0.02362	0.01379	1.713	0.01335	0.11
Q(2)	−0.06145	0.01593	−3.857	0.01411	0.15
Q(3)	−0.06339	0.01248	−5.080	0.01258	0.40

$R^2 = 0.9944$ Adjusted $R^2 = 0.4225$ $\sigma = 0.04959$ VIT = 0.14942   JIT = 2.83551
SC = −5.58055   HQ = −5.77218   FPE = 0.00273

Lag order	LM autocorrelation test	LM ARCH test
8	$F(8, 112) = 0.86043$	$F(8, 104) = 0.79728$
4	$F(4, 116) = 0.80539$	$F(4, 112) = 0.32533$
1	$F(1, 119) = 2.33030$	$F(1, 118) = 0.87978$

Solved long run equation

Variable	Coeff.	Std. err.
Constant	−5.7330	0.4197
Trend	0.0009	0.0006
$\ln(gdy)^{\S}$	1.5320	0.0581
$\ln(gdy)$	1.4930	0.2805
$\ln(1+\pi)$	−2.3610	0.7227
$\ln(1+r)$	4.4410	2.0550
$V[\ln(gdy)]$	3.1370	1.8080
$V[\ln(1+\pi)]$	−0.6292	0.9099

variable; (iii) the *t*-ratio for the long-run coefficient on $\ln(gde)$ is lower than that for the coefficient on $\ln(gdy)$ in the Class A model. We do not attempt a formal encompassing test because the difference between *gde* and *gdy* is aggregate saving, and the change in the dependent variable, *d/p*, is identically equal to one component of aggregate saving.

Table 5.10 Model D1: 1962(3) to 1995(4)

Variable	Coeff.	Std. err.	t-value	HCSE	Inst.
Constant	0.02980	0.01455	2.048	0.01627	0.03
$\ln(d/p)_{-1}$	0.99884	0.09177	10.884	0.08772	0.11
$\ln(d/p)_{-2}$	−0.19297	0.09093	−2.122	0.08912	0.26
$\ln(gde)$	0.07057	0.47008	0.150	0.53031	0.09
$\ln(gde)_{-1}$	0.47972	0.79079	0.607	0.94833	0.08
$\ln(gde)_{-2}$	−0.46708	0.44716	−1.045	0.52556	0.07
$\ln(1+\pi)$	−0.59972	0.21240	−2.823	0.23433	0.11
$\ln(1+\pi)_{-1}$	−0.10959	0.21928	−0.500	0.25557	0.17
$\ln(1+\pi)_{-2}$	0.03995	0.21765	0.184	0.25278	0.04
$\ln(1+r)$	−0.28468	0.99727	−0.285	1.06770	0.01
$\ln(1+r)_{-1}$	0.65126	1.36430	0.477	1.06920	0.03
$\ln(1+r)_{-2}$	0.37765	1.04790	0.360	0.80098	0.05
$V[\ln(gde)]$	−0.53589	1.42280	−0.377	1.71990	0.05
$V[\ln(gde)]_{-1}$	−0.09378	2.39950	−0.039	2.94190	0.07
$V[\ln(gde)]_{-2}$	0.73611	1.40810	0.523	1.62880	0.15
$V[\ln(1+\pi)]$	−0.09563	0.61151	−0.156	0.62680	0.07
$V[\ln(1+\pi)]_{-1}$	1.11620	0.83463	1.337	0.92488	0.07
$V[\ln(1+\pi)]_{-2}$	−1.10690	0.54130	−2.045	0.51949	0.09
$Q(1)$	02270	0.01563	1.452	0.01587	0.07
$Q(2)$	−0.06687	0.01831	−3.653	0.01849	0.19
$Q(3)$	−0.06494	0.01466	−4.430	0.01533	0.31

$R^2 = 0.79974$ Adjusted $R^2 = 0.25971$ $\sigma = 0.05434$ VIT $= 0.15696$
JIT $= 3.47386$ SC $= -5.22790$ HQ $= -5.49753$ FPE $= 0.00342$

Lag order	LM autocorrelation test	LM arch Test
1	$F(1, 112) = 2.61860$	$F(1, 111) = 0.30548$
4	$F(4, 109) = 0.98047$	$F(4, 105) = 0.26465$
8	$F(8, 105) = 1.32120$	$F(8, 97) = 1.50010$

Solved long run equation

Variable	Coeff.	Std. err.
Constant	0.1535	0.0926
$\ln(gde)$	0.4286	0.7234
$\ln(1+\pi)$	−3.4480	2.2740
$\ln(1+r)$	3.8340	4.7290
$V[\ln(gde)]$	0.5483	2.5490
$V[\ln(1+\pi)]$	−0.4445	1.8130

Although there are some small variations in the estimated parameters over the four model classes, there is little substantial difference in the economic implications of each. The next section summarises the general stylised facts that are common to all specifications.

Table 5.11 Model D2: 1962(3) to 1995(4)

Variable	Coeff.	Std. err.	t-value	HCSE	Inst.
Constant	0.03430	0.01338	2.564	0.01507	0.05
$\ln(d/p)_{-1}$	1.03830	0.08436	12.308	0.08605	0.14
$\ln(d/p)_{-2}$	−0.24404	0.08480	−2.878	0.09112	0.32
$\ln(gde)$	0.19659	0.10366	1.896	0.09819	0.16
$\ln(1+\pi)$	−0.58161	0.20442	−2.845	0.23455	0.09
$\ln(1+r)$	0.76568	0.63700	1.202	0.61637	0.03
$V[\ln(gde)]$	0.08028	0.36269	0.221	0.32162	0.14
$V[\ln(1+\pi)]$	−0.31860	0.57335	−0.556	0.63070	0.06
$V[\ln(1+\pi)]_{-1}$	1.41670	0.80169	1.767	0.89044	0.06
$V[\ln(1+\pi)]_{-2}$	−1.22880	0.51366	−2.392	0.49029	0.08
Q(1)	0.01814	0.01497	1.212	0.01573	0.08
Q(2)	−0.07433	0.01682	−4.419	0.01565	0.15
Q(3)	−0.06714	0.01354	−4.958	0.01365	0.38

$R^2 = 0.7865$ Adjusted $R^2 = 0.2202$ $\sigma = 0.05401$ VIT $= 0.13593$ JIT $= 2.25114$
SC $= -5.46616$ HQ $= -5.63224$ FPE $= 0.00320$

Lag order	LM autocorrelation test	LM ARCH test
8	$F(8, 114) = 1.00940$	$F(8, 106) = 0.84523$
4	$F(4, 118) = 1.69180$	$F(4, 114) = 0.13247$
1	$F(1, 121) = 0.49916$	$F(1, 120) = 0.00053$

Solved long run equation

Variable	Coeff.	Std. err.
Constant	0.1667	0.0854
$\ln(gde)$	0.9554	0.4939
$\ln(1+\pi)$	−2.8260	1.2940
$\ln(1+r)$	3.7210	3.4740
$V[\ln(gde)]$	0.3901	1.7690
$V\ln[(1+\pi)]$	−0.6350	1.4370

5.3.4. The asset demand function: Stylised facts

In the light of the econometric results in Section 5.3.3, we can now address questions (2–4) in Section 5.1.

Question 2 Across all econometric specifications of equation (5.1) there is a robust relationship between real deposit demand and the base interest rate. The interest elasticity is large and positive. An increase in the interest rate will lead to an immediate increase in real deposit demand; if there is a stable relationship between the narrow money stock and deposits then, for a given money stock, an increase in the base interest rate will have a deflationary effect as excess demand for money leads to lower expenditure. Conversely, the impact on prices of a shock to narrow money (for example, one generated by a shock to public borrowing from the BCEAO) could be offset by adjustment of the base rate. Given the fact that the BCEAO has not been able completely to insulate the evolution of base money from shocks to public borrowing (Chapter 3), there is a rationale for a more active interest rate policy than is apparent in Figure 5.6 above.

Question 3 It appears that the deposit demand function has been stable over a long period of time. Large changes in income (both secular and cyclical) have not altered the income elasticity of deposit demand. Consequently, econometric models of the financial sector do have some predictive power. The asset demand function did become temporarily unstable in the months around the devaluation in January 1994, but this instability was not permanent.

Question 4 There is some evidence that higher income volatility increases deposit demand, suggesting that at least some deposits have a precautionary or income-smoothing function. To the extent that agents respond to volatility by increasing their deposit holdings (and therefore forgoing consumption), the marginal increase in deposit demand that results from an increase in volatility represents a measure of the social cost of that increase, in terms of current consumption units. There also appears to be some effect on asset demand of an increase in inflation volatility, but the unusual dynamics of this effect make it difficult to interpret economically.

Some of the observations above are conditional on the existence of a stable relationship between deposit demand and the narrow money stock. Such a relationship has still to be established, and this will be the focus of the next section.

5.4. The relationship between different monetary aggregates

In this section we address question (1) in the introduction: Is there a stable relationship between a narrow monetary aggregate that appears on the central bank balance sheet (over which it has complete control) and the wider monetary aggregate that appears on the LHS of equation (5.1)?

A preliminary *caveat* that needs to be acknowledged is that real Ivorian currency holding cannot be measured with precision. Although it is possible to measure currency outside banks issued by the BCEAO–Abidjan (the Ivorian currency-in-circulation figures reported in the BCEAO *Notes d'Information et Statistiques* and copied into the IMF *International Financial Statistics*), this currency does not all remain in the country. Some is exported by migrant workers of other UEMOA members, mostly from Burkina, Mali and Togo (where it is legal tender) and some is retained outside the CFA, as part of hard currency holdings (mostly in Nigeria). The monetary authorities do make some attempt to track the '*billets déplacés*', but their calculations are rough, and not reported on a regular quarterly basis. The rest of this chapter will use the figures for currency issued in Côte d'Ivoire as a proxy for currency held there.

Before examining the relationship between wide and narrow aggregates further, it is important to remember that the money base appearing in previous chapters (*MON*) has two components: currency in circulation (*m*) and currency reserves of private banks. In this chapter we will consider the link between currency in circulation and deposits. It turns out that *MON* and *m* have rather different time-series properties, as indicated in Table 5.12. Table 5.12 corresponds to Table 5.1, but reports tests for the stationarity of ln(*MON/p*) and ln(*m/p*) around a smooth transition. (As can be seen from Figure 3.4 in Chapter 3, narrow monetary aggregates apparently have a similar time-series pattern to deposits and GDP, so it makes sense to do this.) It is not possible to reject the null that ln(*MON/p*) is I(1), even at the 10 per cent level, but it is possible to reject the same null for ln(*m/p*) at the 1 per cent level. Currency in circulation

Table 5.12 Stationarity test statistics

Coeff.	ln(MON/p)	ln(m/p)
a_0	4.7488	4.7571
$a_1 \cdot 0.01$	1.7599	1.4950
a_2	1.5605	1.3991
a_3	−0.0221	−0.0194
b	43.435	40.783
c	74.700	72.375
t_{LNV}	−3.1990	−5.3740

appears to be stationary but banks' currency reserves do not. There is no contradiction in treating base money (*MON*) as an I(1) variable in Chapter 3 and then treating currency in circulation (*m*) as an I(0) variable in this chapter. Here we are concerned with just one (stationary) component of the narrow money aggregate over which the BCEAO has control.[4]

Visual inspection of a time series for the ratio of *d* to *m* (Figure 5.11) indicates that its unconditional mean is certainly not constant. There is a nonlinear trend in the ratio that mirrors the trend in income and expenditure. However, it might still be the case that there is a constant mean conditional on income, the pattern in Figure 5.11 arising because the income elasticity of demand for *d* is larger than the income elasticity of demand for *m*: for a given income level, people would like to maintain a constant ratio between their cash and deposit holdings. So for a given income level we can expect the ratio to be constant (or at least to have a low variance, relative to the variance of the total money stock), and BCEAO adjustment of *m* will be an effective monetary policy tool.

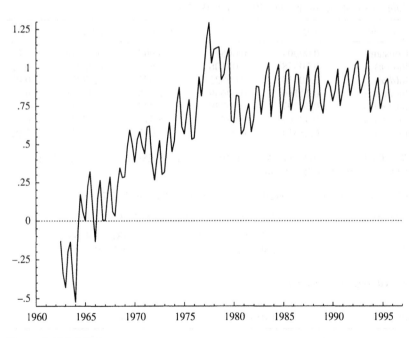

Figure 5.11 ln(*d*/*m*).

In order to test this conjecture, we estimate a model of the ratio depicted in Figure 5.10:

$$\ln(d/m)_t = \alpha_0(t) + \sum_i \alpha_i \cdot \ln(d/m)_{t-i} + \sum_j [\beta_j \cdot \ln(gdy)_{t-j}$$
$$+ \gamma_j \cdot \ln(1+\pi)_{t-j} + \delta_j \cdot \ln(1+r)_{t-j}$$
$$+ \eta_j \cdot V[\ln(gdy)]_{t-j} + \theta_j \cdot V[\ln(1+\pi)]_j] + u_t \qquad (5.5)$$

All variables are defined as in equation (5.1). No RHS variable except $\ln(gdy)_t$ is statistically significant when $\ln(d/m)$ and the RHS variables are detrended. Standard model selection criteria indicate the exclusion of all RHS variables except $\ln(gdy)_t$ and a lag order of five for the dependent variable. The results of estimating such a model are reported in Table 5.13.

Table 5.13 indicates that the long-run income elasticity of the ratio of deposits to currency is insignificantly different from unity, i.e. the ratio is proportional to income in the long run. With standard Chow Test statistics, it is not possible to reject the null of parameter constancy. However, the Hansen parameter instability test statistics

Table 5.13 Model of $\ln(d/m)$: 1963(4) to 1995(4)

Variable	Coeff.	Std. err.	t-value	HCSE	Inst.
Constant	−0.00004	0.00580	−0.007	0.00576	0.04
$\ln(d/m)_{-1}$	−0.70358	0.08106	−8.679	0.08911	0.12
$\ln(d/m)_{-2}$	0.00710	0.09825	0.072	0.09755	0.08
$\ln(d/m)_{-3}$	0.11166	0.09659	1.156	0.09358	0.10
$\ln(d/m)_{-4}$	−0.36297	0.09739	−3.727	0.09639	0.04
$\ln(d/m)_{-5}$	0.42267	0.07958	5.311	0.07938	0.32
$\ln(gdy)$	0.28514	0.09390	3.037	0.10020	1.02[a]

$R^2 = 0.63165$ $\sigma = 0.0655$ VIT $= 0.19016$ JIT $= 2.28966$[a]   SC $= -5.24416$
HQ $= -5.33629$ FPE $= 0.00452$

Chow tests: 1991(1)-end: $F(20, 102) = 1.2185$; 1978(1)-end: $F(72, 50) = 1.2957$

Lag order	LM autocorrelation test	LM ARCH test
1	$F(1, 49) = 0.39085$	$F(1, 48) = 3.48680$
4	$F(4, 46) = 2.60630$[a]	$F(4, 42) = 0.69013$

Solved long run equation

Variable	Coeff.	Std. err.
$\ln(gdy)$	1.0300	0.2071

a Represents significance at the 5 per cent level.

indicate that the income elasticity is not constant over the sample period. This result is confirmed by recursive estimation of the (short-run) income elasticity, illustrated in Figure 5.12. The elasticity is stable up to 1982; then it declines rapidly. Tables 5.14 and 5.15

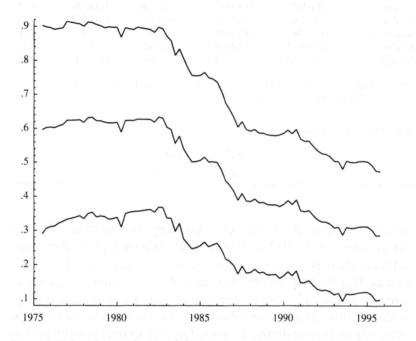

Figure 5.12 Recursive estimates of short-run income elasticity of $(d/m) \pm 2$ std. err.

Table 5.14 Model of $\ln(d/m)$: 1963(4) to 1982(4)

Variable	Coeff.	Std. err.	t-value	HCSE	Inst.
Constant	−0.00623	0.00689	−0.904	0.00640	0.13
$\ln(d/m)_{-1}$	−0.71832	0.09754	−7.365	0.12107	0.04
$\ln(d/m)_{-2}$	0.08164	0.12119	0.674	0.09828	0.02
$\ln(d/m)_{-3}$	0.14601	0.11906	1.226	0.10900	0.03
$\ln(d/m)_{-4}$	−0.42073	0.11972	−3.514	0.14704	0.07
$\ln(d/m)_{-5}$	0.50542	0.09163	5.516	0.10241	0.04
$\ln(gdy)$	0.62998	0.13132	4.797	0.15488	0.02

$R^2 = 0.7868$ $\sigma = 0.0596$ VIT $= 0.45706$ JIT $= 1.09044$ SC $= -5.34123$
HQ $= -5.46907$ FPE $= 0.00387$

Solved long run equation

Variable	Coeff.	Std. err.
$\ln(gdy)$	1.0610	0.1939

Table 5.15 Model of ln(*d/m*): 1983(1) to 1995(4)

Variable	Coeff.	Std. err.	t-value	HCSE	Inst.
Constant	−0.00510	0.00973	−0.524	0.01034	0.49*
ln(*d/m*)$_{-1}$	0.33088	0.14817	2.233	0.14389	0.07
ln(*d/m*)$_{-2}$	0.04693	0.14867	0.316	0.14331	0.08
ln(*d/m*)$_{-3}$	−0.01786	0.14841	−0.120	0.16114	0.04
ln(*d/m*)$_{-4}$	0.36461	0.14851	2.455	0.13412	0.26
ln(*d/m*)$_{-5}$	−0.10442	0.14919	−0.700	0.16208	0.12
ln(*gdy*)	0.07194	0.12755	0.564	0.11108	0.10

$R^2 = 0.2542$ $\sigma = 0.0632$ VIT $= 0.09079$ JIT $= 1.22434$ SC $= -5.13431$
HQ $= -5.29628$ FPE $= 0.00454$

Solved long run equation

Variable	Coeff.	Std. err.
ln(*gdy*)	0.1894	0.3428

therefore present the results of estimating the equation over two sub-samples: 1963–1982 and 1982–1995. Within each of these sub-samples, there is no evidence of parameter instability. The tables indicate that the long-run income elasticity of the ratio of deposits to currency is insignificantly different from unity up to 1982, and insignificantly different from zero afterwards. In other words, the ratio was increasing in income during the period of high income growth, but has been independent of income since. In other words, up to 1982 income elasticity of demand for deposits was significantly higher than the income elasticity of demand for currency; in the subsequent period, however, there has been no significant difference.

So, controlling for the time-varying income elasticity and for the dynamics of asset demand, is the ratio of deposit holdings to currency holdings approximately constant? The standard errors (σ) reported in Tables 5.14 and 5.15 imply that the conditional variance of ln(*d/m*) is about 0.3–0.4 per cent;[5] this is about one quarter of the value of the variance of ln(*d/p*) around its nonlinear trend (1.29 per cent). The ratio of the corresponding standard deviations is about one half. In other words, the ratio of *d* to *m* is substantially less variable than the real value of *d*; however, the variability in the ratio is not trivially small. So, if the BCEAO increases the quantity of currency issued then this will on average lead to an excess supply of money (broadly defined) and higher prices, but there is a substantial amount of uncertainty about the magnitude of the effect.[6] There are two corollaries to this observation. First, m could be used as a monetary policy tool, but it is likely to be a rather blunt one. Second, if m is adjusted not as part of a stabilisation policy but in order to accommodate higher public borrowing then the impact on inflation is uncertain. Accommodating public borrowing in this way is quite risky.

5.5. Conclusion

We have been able to estimate a deposit demand equation for one of the largest CFA members, Côte d'Ivoire, and have found stable and theory-consistent parameters. Bank deposits depend positively on income (with a long run elasticity of around 1.4) and negatively on inflation (with a long run elasticity of around 2.0). These figures indicate slightly more sensitivity to income and slightly less to inflation than in some recent studies of anglophone African economies, for example Adam (1992). A more striking difference from anglophone Africa is the large positive interest rate elasticity (around 4.2 in the long run). A likely explanation for this positive relationship is that Ivorians wanting to smooth consumption have an alternative to holding bank deposits, namely to hold physical assets and take out short-term loans. An increase in the cost of loans induces a switch to bank deposits as the main facility for smoothing consumption. This is a consequence of the special rules in the UEMOA regarding the provision of short-term agricultural credit.

The deposit demand relationship is stable over two major changes in the economic environment: the slowdown in growth at the end of the 1970s and the CFA Franc devaluation in 1994. There is no evidence that the domestic private sector has reduced its total financial asset holding because of a loss of confidence in the currency; the only noticeable change in deposit holdings which is attributable to the devaluation was a temporary increase in mid-1993 and a temporary reduction at the end of the year, presumably as consumers brought forward the timing of purchases of goods and services. Because of the positive relationship between deposits and the interest rate, the temporary increase in the central bank discount rate accompanying the devaluation and matching the consequent inflation, which was presumably intended to prevent capital flight, also had the effect of stabilising demand for liquid assets.

There is also some evidence for a positive relationship between deposits and income variability, although the effect is rather less important than that of changes in inflation and the interest rate. Within the relatively stable monetary system of the CFA, financial assets are used for precautionary saving. No existing study of an anglophone African economy investigates the potential significance of income variability; it would not be surprising if this variable were less important in a more unstable financial system. This is not a cause for complacency on the part of the monetary authorities. If devaluations became a frequent occurrence, confidence might very well be damaged. There is already some evidence that the single devaluation induced a switch to more liquid assets, with an increase in the ratio of demand to time deposits which reversed a long run trend. Frequent devaluations might well retard progress towards a more developed financial system with a larger share of wealth held in the form of more illiquid financial assets.

We have also found a systematic positive relationship between the quantity of currency in circulation (m) and the quantity of bank deposits (d). The conditional variance in the ratio of d to m is about a quarter of the variance of d. This means that shocks to m will on average lead to shocks to wider monetary aggregates and, for a given level of real money demand, to prices. However, the size of the conditional variance suggests that this mechanism incorporates a large stochastic component, so that the consequences of monetary shocks for inflation will always be uncertain. So there is a rationale for minimising the variance of the money base and conducting monetary stabilisation through adjustment of the interest rate.

Notes

1 Land has not been scarce in many areas over the sample period (Deaton, 1992), so it is unlikely that land is held as a store of wealth. Nor is there evidence of large holdings of non-Franc currency.
2 It is also possible that deposit holding depends on the rate of change of the relative price of an aggregate of those commodities used as a store of wealth. However, the range of assets available (which varies across regions: cattle are more likely to be used in the northern savannah and trees in the south) makes it difficult to construct an aggregate price series. We could find neither aggregate nor individual price series that were significant explanatory variables in an asset demand model.
3 Note that these standard deviations are of detrended variables.
4 However, we are implicitly assuming that the central bank can control commercial banks' currency reserves if need be, so that control over *MON* entails control over *m*.
5 From Tables 14, $\sigma^2 = 0.0036$, and from Table 5.15, $\sigma^2 = 0.0040$.
6 *Caveat*: some of this uncertainty may arise because of the measurement error associated with the *billets déplacés*.

References

Adam, C. (1992) 'On the dynamic specification of money demand in Kenya', *Journal of African Economies*, **1**(2), 233–70.

Azam, J-P. (1997) 'Public debt and the exchange rate in the CFA Franc Zone', *Journal of African Economies*, **6**: 54–84.

Banerjee, A., Dolado, J., Galbraith, J. and Hendry, D. (1993) *Co-integration, Error-Correction, and the Econometric Analysis of Non-stationary Data*, Oxford University Press, Oxford.

Deaton, A. (1992) 'Saving and income smoothing in Côte d'Ivoire', *Journal of African Economies*, **1**(1), 1–24.

Engle, R. and Hendry, D. (1993) 'Testing superexogeneity and invariance in regression models', *Journal of Econometrics*, **56**, 117–39.

Levhari, D. and Srinivasan, T. (1969) 'Optimal savings under uncertainty', *Review of Economic Studies*, **36**: 153–63.

Leybourne, S., Newbold, P. and Vougas, D. (1995) 'Unit roots and smooth transitions', Mimeo, University of Nottingham.

Lisman, J. and Sandee, J. (1964) 'Derivation of quarterly figures from annual data', *Journal of the Royal Statistical Society (Series C)*, **13**: 87–90.

Miller, B. (1976) 'The effect on optimal consumption of increased uncertainty in labor income in the multiperiod case', *Journal of Economic Theory*, **13**: 154–67.

Perron, P. (1988) 'Trends and random walks in macroeconomic time series: further evidence from a new approach', *Journal of Economic Dynamics and Control*, **12**: 297–332.

Perron, P. (1989) 'The great crash, the oil shock and the unit root hypothesis', *Econometrica*, **57**: 1361–402.

Plane, P. (1988) 'Performances comparées en matière de stabilité des prix', in Guillaumont, P. and Guillaumont, S. (eds) *Stratégies de Développement Conparées'*, Economica, Paris.

Rothschild, M. and Stiglitz, J. (1971) 'Increasing risk II: Its economic consequences', *Journal of Economic Theory*, **3**: 66–84.

World Bank (1992) *World Tables*, World Bank, Washington DC.

6 Tests of capital market integration between the CFA and France

In Chapter 1 we raised the possibility that the institutions of the CFA with respect to currency convertibility, transferability and exchange harmonisation might promote the integration of capital markets, both within the CFA and between the CFA and France. The next three chapters pursue this idea. In this chapter, we will investigate ways of testing for the degree of capital market integration, and then in Chapters 7 and 8 we will investigate in more detail the determinants of investment performance in CFA countries.

6.1. Alternative tests of capital market integration

In this chapter we will not be directly concerned with measuring the magnitude of international capital flows. Whether a country enjoys a large inflow of financial capital or a high level of foreign investment is a different issue from whether it is free of impediments to the movement of capital, since freedom of movement could just as easily lead to capital flight as to an inflow of resources. To test whether CFA institutions remove barriers to foreign investment, we need a modelling framework within which hypotheses about the degree of capital market integration can be tested.

There already exists a large literature on capital market integration between Western economies. These generally employ some kind of 'asset pricing' model. A sophisticated example is Jorion and Schwartz (1986). However, these models are very data-demanding: they require detailed information on rates of return on domestic and foreign stock exchanges. Such information is not available for African economies, so this approach is not used here.

Another approach is to examine whether there are any significant links between domestic investment and domestic saving. If an economy's capital market is integrated with the international market, domestic investment should, it is hypothesised, be entirely independent of domestic saving. Domestic firms will borrow on the World capital market and domestic investors will invest on the World market. Each will face an international interest rate. At the opposite extreme, if firms have no access to international sources of capital, and investors cannot save abroad, investment will identically equal savings, as in the ISLM model. An example of this approach is Blanchard (1983). However, this methodology is suspect. For example, independence of savings and investment depends not just on tradability of capital, but also on tradability of goods. If there is a domestic industry consuming capital and producing an internationally nontraded good, then domestic output, and therefore domestic investment, will depend on domestic consumption, which is likely to be correlated with savings. In order to make use of the idea of looking for a link between investment and savings, it is necessary to produce a complete investment function, including all determinants of investment for which savings might be a proxy.

In particular, domestic investment may depend not just on the degree of capital market integration with Europe, but also on other factors in which we are interested, for example, relative price stability. Using the savings-investment approach, we cannot examine capital market integration without an extensive treatment of these other factors. For this reason, this approach is left to later chapters. However, even the savings-investment approach is quite data-demanding, and cannot be applied to some of the CFA members where data are poorest. For these, some other technique must be found.

A third approach, which avoids many of the complexities of the first two, has been suggested by Obstfeld (1986), and used by others (see for example Artus, 1987). This focuses on a comparison of real interest rates between different countries, using data on consumption, prices and nominal exchange rates.

6.2. The theoretical background to the Obstfeld model

Obstfeld's idea is to test capital market integration by comparing interest rates. If there is complete integration, then interest rates should not vary significantly from country to country. If both domestic and foreign agents trade a particular asset on a single market, then both groups should buy and sell the asset at a common price (one market entails one price). If there is a common market for all assets in the two countries, then all nominal interest rates will be the same, even if real interest rates differ because of different rates of inflation.

The major problem in applying this idea in an empirical model is that data on domestic market interest rates, other than the basic bank lending rate, are often difficult to find, so that computation of an aggregate nominal interest rate is impossible. One would first have to collect data on the returns to various securities, and then use accurate weights to construct an aggregate interest rate. (The type of security prevalent in one country is not always the same as that prevalent in another, so direct comparison of 'similar' securities in different countries is unlikely to be an option.) One answer to this problem is to use a more indirect method to compute national interest rates, using data on consumption that is more readily available.

Figure 6.1 illustrates the basic idea. It shows an indifference curve for a typical consumer, reflecting preferences between consumption in the present, $C(0)$, and consumption in the future, $C(1)$. Given a real interest rate R, the slope of the budget line is $-1/(1+R)$. Supposing that R is such that the constraint is budget line a in the figure, a utility-maximising consumer would consume at point a, where the indifference curve is tangential to the budget line implied by the interest rate, consuming $C(0)_a$ this period and $C(1)_a$ next period. If the interest rate rises, so that *ex post* the constraint is represented by budget lines with the same slope as budget line b, then the pure substitution effect will take the consumer to point b, with less consumed now ($C(0)_b$) and more in the future ($C(1)_b$). In general, if we know the shape of the indifference curve and we know $C(0)$ and $C(1)$ then, assuming that the budget constraint has not shifted between the two periods, we can infer the level of the real interest rate, since the slope of the indifference curve in equilibrium is the same as the slope of the budget line, which is $1/(1+R)$. If we also know the value of the domestic rate of inflation then we can infer the value of the nominal interest rate.

In order to make use of this idea, we need to tackle a number of analytical problems. How do we deal with the possibility of different shaped indifference curves? How do we know when the budget constraint has shifted? The Obstfeld approach to these problems is

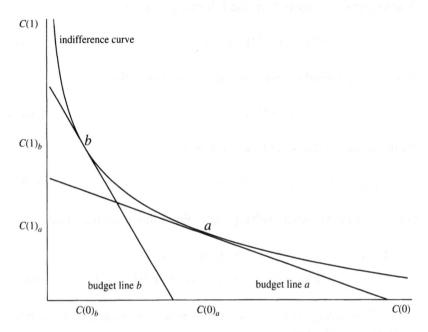

Figure 6.1 Indifference curve for a typical consumer reflecting preferences between consumption in the present, $C(0)$, and consumption in the future, $C(1)$.

given in the following formal model. Suppose that the following assumptions hold: (i) domestic residents habitually consume a basket of goods which has a price $P(t)$ and foreigners habitually consume a basket of goods which has a price $P^*(t)$; (ii) everyone maximises the expected utility according to the equation:

$$\max V_t = \mathrm{E}\left[\sum_{\tau=t} b^{\tau-t}U(C_t)\right] \tag{6.1}$$

where C_t is consumption at t and $\mathrm{E}[\,]$ is an expectations operator. b is a constant denoting the subjective rate of time preference.

Suppose that the real return in $(t+1)$ to a non-risky domestic asset bought at t is R_{t+1} for domestic residents and R_{t+1}^* for foreigners. If domestic residents buy it, then in equilibrium, their expected return should be such that:

$$\mathrm{E}[R_{t+1} \cdot b \cdot U'(C_{t+1})/U'(C_t)] = 1 \tag{6.2}$$

If foreigners can buy it, then the following equation should hold:

$$E[R_{t+1}^* \cdot b \cdot U'(C_{t+1})/U'(C_t)] = 1 \qquad (6.3)$$

Now if the nominal interest rate on the asset is i_t, then:

$$E[R_{t+1}] = E[(1 + i_t) \cdot P_t/P_{t+1}] \qquad (6.4)$$

for domestic residents, and for foreigners

$$E[R_{t+1}^*] = E[(1 + i_t) \cdot e_t \cdot P_t^*/(e_{t+1} \cdot P_{t+1}^*)] \qquad (6.5)$$

where e_t is the nominal exchange rate. From this it follows that:

$$
\begin{aligned}
(1 + i_t)^{-1} &= E[(P_t/P_{t+1}) \cdot b \cdot U'(C_{t+1})/U'(C_t)] \\
&= E[(e_t \cdot P_t^*/(e_{t+1} \cdot P_{t+1}^*)) \cdot b \cdot U'(C_{t+1}^*)/U'(C_t^*)] \quad (6.6)
\end{aligned}
$$

where C^* is foreign consumption *per capita*. Assuming that the utility function takes the form:

$$U = C_t^{1-\Omega}/(1 - \Omega) \qquad (6.7)$$

where Ω is a measure of risk aversion in consumption, it follows with constant income that:

$$(P_t/P_{t+1}) \cdot (C_t/C_{t+1})^\Omega - [e_t \cdot P_t^*/(e_{t+1} \cdot P_{t+1}^*)] \cdot (C_t^*/C_{t+1}^*)^\Omega = 0 \qquad (6.8)$$

when expectations are fulfilled. Denote the LHS of equation (6.8) by z_t. With Rational Expectations it follows that:

$$z_t = u_t \qquad (6.9)$$

where u_t is a stochastic error term. z_t will differ from zero only randomly, as agents' mis-predictions of prices and the exchange rate are entirely random. Moreover, with Rational Expectations, the only changes in consumers' income which will affect the budget constraint are random, unpredictable changes, which will again move z_t away from zero in an entirely random way; so the model can be used even when changes in income are observed. It does, however, rely very heavily on the assumption of Rational Expectations, a point to which we will return later.

A test of capital market integration, under the above assumptions, is to estimate:

$$z_t = \alpha + \sum_n \beta_n \cdot z_{t-n} + \sum_n \delta_n' X_{t-n} + u_t \qquad (6.10)$$

where X_t represents a vector of parameters and α a constant. No significant coefficients should emerge.[1] Obstfeld himself assumes that no other variable will be significant, and imposes a priori the restriction $\delta_n = (0, \dots, 0)$. In the next section, we will follow Obstfeld in imposing this restriction, and in a later section, we will see if relaxation of the restriction makes any difference.

6.3. Empirical evidence: The basic Obstfeld model

Before the Obstfeld technique is applied to the CFA, a few observations are in order. The model is specifically a test of whether foreign investors have the same access to domestic assets as domestic residents. There is also the question of whether domestic residents have access to foreign bonds. However, this does not directly affect domestic investment opportunities, and in the CFA, where $e_t/e_{t+1} = 1$ when the foreign country is France (except in January 1994), the two tests are identical. (Of course, it might be claimed that this is a weakness of the model.) Also, the test as it stands does not admit any degrees of capital market integration, just showing whether we can reject the hypothesis of 100 per cent integration or not. However, since work on European markets (Obstfeld, 1986; Artus, 1987) shows that the hypothesis of complete integration cannot be rejected for many pairs of developed countries, what we have is a test of whether CFA financial markets are, with respect to ease of capital movement, of a European standard.[2] Also, even if the hypothesis of capital market integration is rejected, we are left with a model of z_t which may shed light on domestic capital markets.

It is also quite possible, amongst the poorer CFA members, that capital markets of different regions of the country are not integrated. While it is not necessary that everyone have a bank account for a country to have an integrated financial system (in many areas, for example, there are informal moneylenders who intermediate between farmers in remote villages and the bank in the nearest town), the absence of a developed banking system is likely to make segmentation of financial markets more likely. If markets are segmented, and those consumers without access to urban financial facilities make up a considerable percentage of the population, the null hypothesis will be rejected. So what we have is a test of whether financial markets are both integrated with foreign markets and available to the majority of domestic consumers. This is an appropriate test to make: it is of little use for a small enclave of a country to have financial markets integrated with markets abroad, but not with the rest of the country.

It is also important to remember that there is still one parameter in the model that is unobservable: Ω. It is therefore necessary to estimate z_t equations for a number of different values of Ω. Following the existing literature, we will select a range of different values between 0.5 and 25.0. It is highly unlikely that people are either more or less averse to risk than this. In fact, one can reasonably expect Ω to take a value of 2–3 (Obstfeld, 1986).

It should be noted that the choice of a reported variable to proxy the theoretical C_t is not trivial. This is the real value of the consumption of a typical person in the economy. Thus, public consumption should probably not be included in the measure of C_t: expenditure on executive Mercedes may enter into private utility functions, but expenditure on the Army is unlikely to do so. Private consumption alone is used in the tests below. Reported real private consumption in national accounts is unreliable, as it is often used as a balancing item for the components of real GDP. Thus, it is necessary to take nominal consumption, and deflate by the reported consumer price index used as a proxy for $P(t)$. This is not entirely satisfactory – for example, expenditure patterns of wealthy European residents of a country may differ markedly from that of poorer nationals, and CPIs for different groups are not always available. However, we can find no better alternative. The private agent is taken to be an individual person, not a household. The latter may be theoretically superior: two-year-olds do not have the same level or pattern of consumption as adults; neither are they likely to optimise an intertemporal utility function. However, while estimates of the sizes of total populations are readily available for the construction of a *per capita* series, more detailed demographic information is often not.

Table 6.1 reports tests of capital market integration using the basic Obstfeld framework, i.e. tests for the significance of the α and

Table 6.1 Tests of capital market integration using the basic model: $z(t) = \alpha + \Sigma_n \beta_n z(t-n) + u(t)$

Value of Ω	0.5	0.75	1.0	1.5	2.0	3.0	5.0	7.0	12.0	25.0
				Probability (%)						
Burkina Faso										
n = 1 to 4										
$z(t-n)$	75	86	91	81	67	56	55	61	75	92
α	44	46	46	46	43	36	26	20	14	13
n = 1 to 2										
$z(t-n)$	37	49	55	58	58	57	58	64	82	100
α	23	28	32	34	34	32	25	21	17	17
n = 0, *t* =	1.74	1.73	1.68	1.61	1.61	1.69	1.95	2.18	2.45	1.99
Cameroon										
n = 1 to 4										
$z(t-n)$	77	55	47	39	35	31	26	27	29	48
α	21	40	58	84	97	70	37	22	11	11
n = 1 to 2										
$z(t-n)$	22	12	9	7	6	6	5	5	6	22
α	35	58	73	95	88	63	31	15	3	1
n = 0, *t* =	0.57	0.46	0.34	0.17	0.04	0.18	0.56	0.90	0.60	2.38
Centrafrique										
n = 1 to 4										
$z(t-n)$	78	66	64	65	68	74	81	86	95	99
α	95	63	45	32	26	23	21	21	23	29
n = 1 to 2										
$z(t-n)$	56	53	53	53	52	51	48	49	64	93
α	91	56	40	27	21	14	9	8	10	24
n = 0, *t* =	0.50	0.88	1.09	1.33	1.49	1.69	1.95	2.06	1.95	1.29
Congo										
n = 1 to 4										
$z(t-n)$	28	23	20	17	15	14	13	13	28	87
α	7	4	3	2	2	1	2	3	6	16
n = 1 to 2										
$z(t-n)$	16	19	21	22	22	21	21	25	41	76
α	11	11	11	8	6	4	2	1	2	10
n = 0, *t* =	1.25	1.28	1.32	1.43	1.55	1.78	2.12	2.31	2.32	1.65

Table 6.1 continued

Value of Ω	0.5	0.75	1.0	1.5	2.0	3.0	5.0	7.0	12.0	25.0
					Probability (%)					

Côte d'Ivoire

$n = 1$ to 4

$z(t-n)$	27	20	18	23	32	49	68	76	85	95
α	73	54	43	35	33	34	34	34	33	28

$n = 1$ to 2

$z(t-n)$	18	11	8	8	11	21	40	52	68	90
α	58	45	38	31	27	22	17	15	12	9
$n = 0$, $t =$	1.08	1.62	2.06	2.67	3.01	3.32	3.49	3.52	3.46	3.08

Gabon

$n = 1$ to 4

$z(t-n)$	76	28	10	3	2	3	5	7	12	25
α	97	77	53	26	17	13	16	21	34	66

$n = 1$ to 2

$z(t-n)$	81	38	19	9	7	7	10	15	30	66
α	69	42	24	9	5	2	1	1	2	9
$n = 0$, $t =$	0.55	0.78	0.92	1.10	1.23	1.43	1.69	1.84	1.90	1.58

Niger

$n = 1$ to 4

$z(t-n)$	87	90	90	92	94	98	100	100	100	100
α	35	25	21	19	21	23	26	26	28	32

$n = 1$ to 2

$z(t-n)$	76	67	58	60	67	81	100	100	100	96
α	4	2	2	2	3	5	9	12	20	30
$n = 0$, $t =$	3.01	3.37	3.39	3.23	3.08	2.88	2.58	2.30	1.70	1.10

Sénégal

$n = 1$ to 4

$z(t-n)$	90	49	54	79	85	88	91	92	91	89
α	48	53	67	77	72	59	42	31	15	9

$n = 1$ to 2

$z(t-n)$	72	59	75	99	95	79	65	61	59	70
α	29	15	11	10	10	9	8	6	5	6
$n = 0$, $t =$	1.76	2.36	2.64	2.79	2.81	2.81	2.88	2.96	2.99	2.41

Table 6.1 continued

Value of Ω	0.5	0.75	1.0	1.5	2.0	3.0	5.0	7.0	12.0	25.0
					Probability (%)					
Ghana										
$n=1$ to 4										
$z(t-n)$	90	83	74	50	53	71	73	59	39	83
α	42	33	18	19	26	35	36	31	23	28
$n=1$ to 2										
$z(t-n)$	58	65	40	50	74	96	64	37	19	50
α	45	11	8	4	5	12	24	31	34	26
$n=0$, $t=$	0.81	3.61	1.51	1.94	2.16	2.36	2.52	2.57	2.46	1.87
Nigeria										
$n=1$ to 4										
$z(t-n)$	7	9	11	18	31	62	89	85	53	77
α	80	44	29	30	37	35	21	14	8	14
$n=1$ to 2										
$z(t-n)$	1	4	10	27	44	61	61	50	43	80
α	71	62	55	42	31	15	7	6	11	28
$n=0$, $t=$	0.22	0.40	0.59	0.94	1.27	1.83	2.50	2.64	2.15	1.30

β_n in equation (6.10), and excluding all variables from the regression except lags of z_t. z_t is constructed for eight CFA countries for which data are available. These are, in the BCEAO region: Burkina Faso, Côte d'Ivoire, Niger and Sénégal; in the BEAC region: Cameroon, Centrafrique, Congo Republic and Gabon. By way of an extra-zonal comparison, the same test is applied to Ghana and Nigeria. In all cases, the foreign country used in constructing z_t is France. The annual data set runs from 1967 to 1987. Thus, the earliest observation for C_t/C_{t+1} is in 1968. Data on consumer price indices and nominal exchange rates for France, Ghana and Nigeria come from the International Financial Statistics Yearbook (various editions). Data on population and consumption come from the World Bank World Tables (1987, 1990). z_t is not persistently away from zero for any of the countries. However, deviations from zero are smallest in the two most industrialised countries (and the largest in terms of GNP): Cameroon and Côte d'Ivoire. With the average deviation in Niger several times larger than that in Côte d'Ivoire, it is unlikely that the former enjoys capital market integration, even if the more developed, Ivorian economy does.

The results in the table show confidence limits in percentage points for an F-test for the joint significance of α and the z_{t-n}, where $n = $ (i) 1–4, or (ii) 1–2. So a figure of ten or less shows that the parameter is significant at 10 per cent. The t-ratio on α in the equation $z_t = \alpha + u_t$ is also given (for this model, the sample size is twenty). For Burkina Faso, Centrafrique, Congo Republic, Côte d'Ivoire, Niger, Sénégal, Ghana and Nigeria, the z_{t-n} are insignificant, but the α significant for Ω of more than about 1.5 when the insignificant variables are omitted. For Cameroon and Gabon, lags of z_t are significant. On the basis of this model, the hypothesis of capital market integration is rejected at most values of W for most countries, both CFA members and others, and even for those countries, Cameroon and Côte d'Ivoire, in which deviations of z_t from zero have been relatively small.

However, the a priori restriction that $\delta_n = (0, \ldots, 0)$ is a serious deficiency in this model: it does not really allow for testing of the assumption of Rational Expectations. If expectations are not rational, then trends in income could affect changes in consumption from one period to the next, as people revise their estimation of lifetime income (for example, if expectations are in some way 'adaptive'). The fact that lags of z_t are important in explaining z_t in oil exporters, where the income shocks over the sample period were the greatest, is perhaps an indication that there are significant income terms here which are being omitted. The lags may be important because past z_t is correlated with past income, which is also important in explaining present z_t.

An increase in income would increase consumption and so the apparent (but not actual) real interest rate. Since z_t is inversely related to C_{t+1}/C_t, the coefficient on the term for change in income should be negative. Moreover, if z_t does not follow a random walk, other variables may be significant, even if α or z_{t-n} are not. Significance of these variables would lead to the rejection of the hypothesis of full integration. Also, if the capital market integration hypothesis is rejected, these variables may shed some light onto the determinants of domestic interest rates. It is necessary then to augment the Obstfeld model in order to provide a more reliable test of capital market integration.

6.4. Empirical evidence: The augmented Obstfeld model

In order to construct a more robust test of the hypothesis that interest rates in the CFA are not significantly different from those in France, real income terms must be included, along with variables which might influence z_t if financial markets are not in fact integrated. On theoretical grounds, we can think of a number of factors which will influence z_t if the null is false: (1) both factor income (terms of trade-adjusted real GDP) and non-factor income (for example, borrowing from abroad), for reasons discussed above; (2) the degree of domestic financial integration; (3) risk – the riskier it is to lend to a country, the lower lending is likely to be to that country; (4) in the absence of complete integration, the domestic demand for funds will also affect relative interest rates.

The tests reported in Tables 6.2–6.10 are therefore based on estimates of equation (6.10) that include the following variables, all derived from World Bank World Tables.[3]

(1) *A real per capita factor income term, Y.* The nominal series used to construct this term is nominal GDP at factor cost in the National Accounts statistics. As a measure of private nominal disposable income, this will be reasonably accurate as long as average tax rates (on which data are limited) remain more or less constant. The GDP deflator is used to construct a real income series, and adjustment is made for terms of trade changes: a rise in the terms of trade will increase domestic residents' purchasing power, even if their GDP at constant prices remains the same.[4] As the dependant

Table 6.2 Augmented results (Burkina Faso)

	Value for Ω					
	1.0	1.5	2.0	3.0	5.0	7.0
R^2 (1)	0.148	0.104	0.093	0.098	0.123	0.163
$z(t-2)$	x	x	x	x	x	x
$M/Y(t-1)$	x	x	x	x	x	x
$D/Y(t)$	x	x	x	x	x	x
$D/Y(t-1)$	x	x	x	x	x	x
D1981	x	x	x	x	x	x
D1985	x	x	x	x	x	x
CONST	x	x	x	x	x	x
R^2 (2)	0.959	0.958	0.937	0.905	0.881	0.876

Table 6.3 Augmented results (Cameroon)

	Value for Ω					
	1.0	1.5	2.0	3.0	5.0	7.0
R^2 (1)	0.154	0.119	0.110	0.112	0.140	0.180
$z(t-2)$	x	x	x	x	x	x
$M/Y(t)$	x	x	x	x	x	x
$M/Y(t-1)$	x	x	x	x	x	x
$\Delta P_I/P_I^*(t)$	x	x	x	x	x	x
CONST	x	x	x	x	x	x
R^2 (2)	0.887	0.899	0.880	0.841	0.773	0.709

Table 6.4 Augmented results (Centrafrique)

	Value for Ω					
	1.0	1.5	2.0	3.0	5.0	7.0
R^2 (1)	0.202	0.235	0.257	0.286	0.322	0.339
$z(t-1)$	x	x	x	x	x	x
$z(t-2)$	x	x	x	x	x	x
$M/Y(t)$	x	x	x	x	x	x
$M/Y(t-1)$	x	x	x	x	x	x
$M/Y(t-2)$	x	x	x	x	x	x
$D/Y(t)$	x	x	x	x	x	x
$D/Y(t-1)$	x	x	x	x	x	x
$D/Y(t-2)$	x	x	x	x	x	x
CONST	x	x	x	x	x	x
R^2 (2)	0.864	0.903	0.921	0.937	0.930	0.907

Table 6.5 Augmented results (Congo)

	Value for Ω					
	1.0	1.5	2.0	3.0	5.0	7.0
R^2 (1)	0.111	0.110	0.118	0.142	0.190	0.222
$z(t-1)$	x	x	x	x	x	x
$M/Y(t)$	x	x	x	x	x	x
$M/Y(t-1)$	x	x	x	x	x	x
$M/Y(t-2)$	x	x	x	x	x	x
$D/Y(t)$	x	x	x	x	x	x
$D/Y(t-2)$	x	x	x	x	x	x
D1981-2	x	x	x	x	x	x
CONST	x	x	x	x	x	x
R^2 (2)	0.940	0.956	0.959	0.956	0.972	0.959

Table 6.6 Augmented results (Côte d'Ivoire)

	Value for Ω					
	1.0	1.5	2.0	3.0	5.0	7.0
R^2 (1)	0.171	0.267	0.333	0.405	0.462	0.487
$M/Y(t)$	x	x	x	x	x	x
$M/Y(t-1)$	x	x	x	x	x	x
$M/Y(t-2)$	x	x	x	x	x	x
$D/Y(t)$	x	x	x	x	x	x
$D/Y(t-1)$	x	x	x			
$D/Y(t-2)$	x	x	x	x	x	x
$P/P^*(t)$	x	x	x			
$P/P^*(t-1)$	x	x	x	x	x	x
$P/P^*(t-2)$	x	x	x	x	x	x
CONST	x	x	x	x	x	x
R^2 (2)	0.941	0.960	0.947	0.869	0.824	0.801

Table 6.7 Augmented results (Niger)

	Value for Ω					
	1.0	1.5	2.0	3.0	5.0	7.0
R^2 (1)	0.436	0.384	0.351	0.314	0.274	0.242
$z(t-1)$	x	x	x	x	x	x
$M/Y(t)$	x	x	x	x	x	x
$M/Y(t-2)$	x	x	x	x	x	x
$D/Y(t)$	x	x	x	x	x	x
$P/P^*(t)$	x	x	x	x	x	x
$P/P^*(t-2)$	x	x	x	x	x	x
$|\Delta P_1/P_1^*|(t)$	x	x	x	x	x	x
CONST	x	x	x	x	x	x
R^2 (2)	0.893	0.889	0.871	0.848	0.820	0.789

variable is constructed with C_{t-1}/C_t, so the income term used is Y_t/Y_{t-1}. As discussed above, we would expect the coefficient on the income term to be negative.

(2) *The ratio of total foreign debt to GDP, D/Y, with lags.* In the absence of capital market integration, this might be important for two reasons. First, if there is a risk of default on foreign commitments then the domestic interest rate may vary positively with the stock of debt: a higher ratio being associated with a higher risk and therefore a lower supply of credit to the domestic economy. With the introduction of risk, we are moving away from the classical paradigm

Table 6.8 Augmented results (Sénégal)

	Value for Ω					
	1.0	1.5	2.0	3.0	5.0	7.0
R^2 (1)	0.404	0.427	0.422	0.412	0.412	0.417
$z(t-1)$	x	x	x	x	x	
$M/Y(t-1)$	x	x	x	x	x	x
$D/Y(t-1)$	x	x	x	x	x	x
$P/P^*(t)$	x	x	x	x	x	x
$P/P^*(t-1)$			x			
$P/P^*(t-2)$	x	x	x	x	x	x
$|\Delta P|(t)$	x	x	x	x	x	x
$|\Delta P|(t-1)$		x	x	x	x	x
D1984	x	x	x	x	x	x
CONST	x	x	x	x	x	x
R^2 (2)	0.800	0.930	0.977	0.973	0.962	0.947

Table 6.9 Augmented results (Ghana)

	Value for Ω					
	1.0	1.5	2.0	3.0	5.0	7.0
R^2 (1)	0.433	0.432	0.380	0.286	0.170	0.112
$z(t-1)$			x	x	x	x
$z(t-2)$		x		x		x
$M/Y(t)$			x	x	x	x
$D/Y(t)$	x	x	x	x	x	x
$D/Y(t-1)$	x	x				
$|\Delta P|(t)$	x	x	x			
D1981	x		x	x	x	
D1985				x		
CONST	x		x		x	x
R^2 (2)	0.808	0.910	0.968	0.979	0.861	0.806

of the basic Obstfeld model. Second, negotiation of more international credit (a higher $\Delta D/Y$) may lower domestic interest rates as the supply of credit for investment increases, producing a negative correlation. Again, if the credit is for consumption purposes, $\Delta D/Y$ may represent disposable private income, increasing domestic consumption and so the apparent real interest rate as calculated above.

   (3) *The liquidity ratio, M/Y.* This is defined as the ratio of M_2 in World Tables to nominal GDP. In general, it is the most industrialised

Table 6.10 Augmented results (Nigeria)

	Value for Ω					
	1.0	1.5	2.0	3.0	5.0	7.0
R^2 (1)	0.187	0.273	0.339	0.418	0.438	0.379
$z(t-1)$					x	x
$M/Y(t)$		x	x	x		
$M/Y(t-1)$					x	x
$M/Y(t-2)$					x	x
$D/Y(t)$		x	x	x	x	x
$D/Y(t-1)$	x	x	x	x	x	x
$P/P^*(t)$	x	x	x			
$P/P^*(t-1)$	x				x	
$P/P^*(t-2)$					x	x
CONST	x	x	x	x	x	
R^2 (2)	0.931	0.949	0.931	0.852	0.914	0.884

members of the CFA (those with the highest *per capita* GNP, such as Cameroon, Côte d'Ivoire and Gabon) that have the highest ratios. A high ratio could reflect a high degree of domestic financial market integration, and a relatively well developed financial system.

(4) *The ratio of the domestic industrial value added deflator to that of France, P_I/P_I^* (1980 = 1).* This may work as a measure of the return to investment activities at home compared to the return abroad. If P_I/P_I^* is higher, the demand for funds in the domestic economy may well be higher too. Thus the domestic interest rate may rise with respect to the foreign interest rate, so the coefficient on P_I/P_I^* will be negative.[5]

(5) *The absolute value of the first difference of (4),* $|\Delta P_I/P_I^*|$. A polynomial lag of $|\Delta P_I/P_I^*|$ is a measure of the variability of returns to domestic investment activities relative to those abroad. (It is assumed that the returns to investment in France are relatively stable, so that an increase in $|\Delta P_I/P_I^*|$ reflects an increase in the riskiness of domestic investment. A high variability may deter investment, reduce the demand for funds, and so the real interest rate, so the coefficient on $|\Delta P_I/P_I^*|$ ought to be positive.

Before proceeding to estimation of the augmented equations, a number of remarks are in order. First of all, the purpose of the estimation is to see if the null hypothesis of capital market integration can be rejected. In this respect, the reason for the inclusion of the income term in the equations is different from the reason for the inclusion of the other terms. The significance of the coefficients in the basic model in the previous section was not enough to ensure rejection, since inclusion of an income term might render them insignificant. In this case, the hypothesis is not rejected, since the significant income terms show to what extent z_t is an inaccurate indicator of the real interest rate gap. The true gap has still not been shown to differ systematically from zero.

Second, if, in addition to the income terms, other variables prove to be significant, then, unless it can be shown that these terms are in some way reflecting changes in private disposable income (which is possible for D/Y, but not for the others), the null hypothesis is rejected. In this case, even taking into account real income effects, the real interest rate gap has been shown to differ predictably from zero.

The purpose of the estimation is not to construct an accurate forecasting model of the behaviour of z_t over time. In fact, the data are not really sufficient for this more demanding task, which would involve a general-to-specific reduction procedure, beginning with the inclusion of all possibly significant variables (including ones not mentioned above) with all possibly significant lags, and comparing different functional forms. There are not enough degrees of freedom for this with only about twenty observations. It is enough for our purposes to show that the addition of some variable or other to the equation,

$$z_t = \sum_n \eta_n \cdot [Y_{t-n}/Y_{t-n-1}] \tag{6.11}$$

is significant. This is enough for rejection of the null hypothesis.

Strictly, our null hypothesis is that all coefficients other than those on the income terms are zero. The correct test statistics for this hypothesis is:[6]

$$[SSE(1) - SSE(2)][n - k]/rSSE(2) \sim F_{r,[n-k]} \tag{6.12}$$

where $SSE(1)$ is the sum square error under the null, $SSE(2)$ is the sum square error when coefficients on the extra explanatory variables are allowed to be non-zero, r is the number of restricted coefficients under the null, n is the sample size and k the number of regressors. The smaller SSE(2) relative to SSE(1) (i.e. the larger the corresponding R^2), the more likely the hypothesis is to be rejected.

If other variables are to be added to equation (6.11), then there are not enough degrees of freedom for four lags, as was possible in the basic model. In this section, we restrict ourselves to two. So Tables 6.2–6.10 show the improvement in goodness of fit gained by adding the set of extra explanatory variables to the equation:

$$z_t = \eta_0 \cdot Y_t/Y_{t-1} + \eta_1 \cdot Y_{t-1}/Y_{t-2} + \eta_2 \cdot Y_{t-2}/Y_{t-3} \qquad (6.13)$$

If all lags of variables (2–5) are included, then we do not have a very powerful test; there are so many extra variables that any random selection of an equal number of variables is likely to increase R^2 substantially, and therefore the chances of making Type II errors with respect to our null are high. However, it is possible for each country to find small subsets of (2–5) which substantially increase R^2. These are the variables indicated in the tables by a cross. Note that lags of z_t and the constant may also be included in the set of extra explanatory variables. In certain cases, dummy variables are also included: in Burkina Faso, Ghana and Sénégal for the effects of drought in the 1980s, capturing possibly changes in perceived permanent income which *per capita* GNP series do not pick up, and in Congo for the oil price shock of 1981 (Congo is an oil exporter, so the oil price shock will have changed the return to Congolese investment). R^2 (1) is the R^2 statistic for equation (6.13), and R^2 (2) is that produced after the addition of the extra variables.

In all cases, the increase in R^2 is significant at least 5 per cent. The hypothesis that there is free flow of financial capital between France and CFA members can be rejected as strongly as it can in the case of anglophone Ghana and Nigeria. Liquidity ratios and foreign debt ratios are important factors in explaining the wedge between French and African interest rates; in a number of countries (Niger, Sénégal, Ghana), relative price stability is also an important explanatory factor.

6.5. Conclusion

An examination of the history of CFA institutions in Chapter 1 suggested that there might be a number of impediments to the free flow of funds between member countries. This chapter has shown that such impediments are indeed restricting the flow of funds. The econometric technique we have chosen rejects the hypothesis of complete capital market integration between France and the CFA.

However, in order to measure degrees of integration, another technique must be used. In the next chapter, we will investigate more fully the interaction between savings and investment, and how this is affected by CFA membership. It may be possible to estimate an investment function for some countries, and see to what extent investment depends on saving. A complete model of investment ought also to include other variables reflecting the ways in which the CFA might differ from other African countries, for example, some measure of relative price stability. Already, we have seen that inclusion of price stability terms help to explain the variance in real interest rates between France and a number of CFA members. However, this will not be possible in all of the countries included in the study here: detailed industrial data do not exist for countries like Burkina Faso.

Notes

1 One rejoinder here might be that even if all coefficients did turn out to be insignificant, we would still have to demonstrate that the reason for this was *not* that all the data were inaccurate, in order to claim that there was capital market integration. However, we note that (i) non-rejection of the null does not strictly justify the assertion that there is integration, anyway; (ii) in all cases, it turns out that the null can be rejected.
2 However, given the criticisms of Obstfeld's assumptions discussed below, the results on European capital markets should be regarded as only preliminary.
3 There is not enough data to construct this model for Gabon, so the tables show the results for only nine countries.
4 Terms of trade adjustment figures are quoted in World Bank World Tables.
5 Although a priori it may equally well be the case that a higher ratio reflects relative uncompetitiveness and a resulting low demand for funds.
6 See for example Kmenta (1986), pp. 247–8.

References

Artus, P. (1987) 'Efficiencé et cloisonnement du marché des changes et des marches financières en France 1970–1986', *Banque de France Cahiers Economiques et Monétaires*, 31.

Blanchard, O. (1983) 'Debt and current account deficit in Brazil' in Armella, P. (ed.), *Financial Policies and the World Capital Market*, Washington, DC: NBER.

Jorion, P. and Schwartz, E. (1986) 'Integration versus segmentation in the Canadian stock market', *Journal of Finance*, 41, 603–14.

Kmenta, J. (1986) *Elements of Econometrics*, London: Macmillan.

Obstfeld, M. (1986) 'Capital mobility in the world economy: Theory and measurement', *Carnegie Rochester Conference Series on Public Policy*, 24, 55–103.

7 Savings, investment and CFA membership

Time-series evidence from a comparison of Côte d'Ivoire with Kenya*

7.1. Introduction

In the previous chapter, we saw that there is not complete financial market integration between the CFA and France (and by extension, the rest of the Europe). However, there remains the possibility that the 'degree' of integration is greater within the CFA than outside it. It might be the case that a fraction of investors in the CFA have access to international capital markets, and face an infinitely elastic loanable funds supply curve. Other investors (and consumers) might not have access to these international capital markets, and must borrow and lend on an autarkic domestic financial market with a domestically determined interest rate. Given the extent of financial repression in the typical domestic African capital market, even in the CFA, these investors are likely to be constrained by an exogenous level of savings, net of public sector investment. But at least some part of aggregate private sector investment will be determined by the world interest rate and the risk-discounted marginal rate of return to physical capital. It is unlikely to be possible to distinguish a priori which investors are constrained, but the relative sizes of the elasticities of aggregate private sector investment with respect to savings on the one hand and rate-of-return variables on the other ought to provide some information about the relative sizes of the two groups. In particular, it will be possible to compare elasticities estimated in CFA countries with those estimated in other African economies. If the CFA delivers a greater degree of capital market integration (in the sense that a larger fraction of investors

*This chapter is based on 'Determinants of investment in Kenya and Côte d'Ivoire', *Journal of African Economies*, **2**: 299–328. By permission of Oxford University Press.

have access to international capital markets) then savings ought to be a quantitatively less important determinant of private sector investment in the CFA, and rate-of-return variables quantitatively more important, compared with the experience of non-CFA Africa.

In addition to the effect of restricted access to international financial capital, we ought also to consider the effect of restricted access to international currency. Outside the CFA, some firms might be prevented from investing as much as they would like because of foreign exchange restrictions. The rationing of foreign currency by African governments who enforce a domestic price of forex below the world price is less endemic now than in the 1980s and early 1990s, but in many parts of Africa there is still a parallel domestic foreign currency market, suggesting that the official market does not clear at the official exchange rate. The absence of such foreign exchange restrictions in the CFA (except at times of extreme crisis, as in the 1994 devaluation episode) might well be a more important characteristic than any access it could provide to foreign capital markets. CFA membership represents a pre-commitment to a liberal foreign exchange regime as well as one to monetary stability and low inflation, and this might promote private sector investment.

In addition, the monetary stability engendered by the CFA (see Chapter 2) could in itself promote private sector investment. If there are fewer and smaller nominal shocks inside the CFA, then the real returns to investment could well be less variable (unless all goods and asset prices adjust instantaneously to their long-run equilibrium values). So a comprehensive assessment of the impact of the Franc zone on investment should also include an estimate of the degree of variability faced by investors in different countries, and the magnitude of the impact of such variability on investment.

In this chapter we will investigate all three of these potential channels for an impact of CFA membership on investment. The next section will elaborate the modelling framework to be used. This framework is much more data-demanding than that of the previous chapter, so this chapter has a much narrower geographical focus. We will restrict ourselves to a comparison of just two countries: one CFA member (Côte d'Ivoire) and one non-CFA member (Kenya). As noted in Chapter 3 these two countries are economically quite similar, except for the differences in their financial institutions. In Chapter 8 we will expand the geographical focus in order to see to what extent the stylized facts uncovered here have a wider application. Given the data limitations when the geographical range is extended, Chapter 8 will take a more reduced-form approach and will employ cross-section data. In this chapter we will use time-series data that permits us to uncover more of the structure in the mechanisms that drive private sector investment.

7.2. Theoretical background

7.2.1. Existing models of investment in LDCs

The most popular empirical models of investment in the development literature fall into one of two categories. Papers such as Root and Ahmed (1979), Schneider and Frey (1985) and Guillaumont (1988) present the results of cross-country regressions, where the rate of investment – usually either gross domestic investment or direct foreign investment – is explained by variables which are meant to capture factors affecting both the expected rate of return to investment (for example the ICOR or measures of political stability) and factors which may constrain the supply of funds for investment (such as the availability of foreign exchange, often proxied by export earnings).[1] Seldom is any thought given to the structure of the equations estimated, or to the instrumenting of explanatory variables which are unlikely to be independent.

A second group of articles (that has been briefly mentioned in Chapter 6 and includes Blanchard, 1983) uses time series analysis to examine links between gross domestic investment and gross domestic savings. The methodology of these papers derives from a study of developed countries by Feldstein and Horioka (1980).[2] Investment – usually expressed as a fraction of GDP – is regressed on savings. A coefficient not significantly different from unity is taken to mean that the economy is financially 'closed', i.e. it has no access to international capital markets, so that domestic investment is constrained to equal domestic savings. However, this approach has a number of limitations. It is possible that savings and investment will be highly correlated even when there is perfect integration into international capital markets. For example, a negative trade shock might reduce income and so saving, and also reduce the returns to investment. In other words, a simple regression of investment on savings might suffer from omitted variables bias. Moreover, even if there is perfect capital market integration, it would not be surprising if the capital account, net of foreign aid inflows, were to be zero in the long run, as the economy tended towards Balance of Payments equilibrium. In order to use savings and investment figures to investigate the openness of capital markets, we need to distinguish between the short-run and the long-run, and to identify the direction of causality. More attention to the structure of the equations being estimated is required.

7.2.2. Constructing a comprehensive model of savings and investment

A comprehensive model of investment should take into account the possible links between saving and investment, and should also allow for other variables to enter into the model. However, attention needs to be paid to the structure of the investment model. First of all, it should provide an account of how the economy moves from a short run in which the long run zero capital account condition does not bind, to the long run in which it does. The model will embody a long-run relationship between savings and investment reflecting this constraint:

$$I = I^* = S + AID \tag{7.1}$$

where I is gross investment, I^* its long-run equilibrium level, S savings and AID foreign aid inflows. With financial repression, I will be the dependent variable with respect to the loans market (although this does not entail that S will be an independent variable in the estimated equations). That this relationship holds is to be tested empirically: it is possible that there is no tendency towards Balance of Payments equilibrium within the sample period.

An important modification to this equation needs to be made when there is a possibility of foreign exchange rationing in the domestic economy. When foreign exchange is rationed (as is possibly the case in Kenya in the sample period we will be using) some domestic investors may not have access to the currency necessary to buy imported capital equipment. In the extreme case, where forex availability is the binding constraint for all investors, then the $I = S + AID$ constraint will no longer feature in the dynamic investment model: I will depend on forex availability, and it will be S which adjusts to long-run equilibrium. The long-run constraint in a simple exposition of the intermediate case, with some investors constrained by forex and some by savings, will not differ from the case of no forex rationing. Those investors who are not forex constrained will face a financial constraint of $S + AID$ less investment by forex constrained investors, which amounts to a constraint on total investment of $I = S + AID$. However, this assumes that there is perfect capital market integration within the domestic economy, so that net saving in forex constrained sectors can finance net borrowing in unconstrained sectors. (For example, if the private sector is forex constrained and the government sector is not, it may or may not be possible for the government to mobilise private saving for its own purposes.) Otherwise, the long-run constraint will involve both a savings and a forex term:

$$I = I^*(S + AID, FOREX) \tag{7.2}$$

Ideally, the $(S + AID)$ term would represent funds available to just those investors who are not rationed in foreign exchange, while *FOREX* would represent the foreign exchange holdings just of those investors who are so rationed. However, without knowing a priori which investors fall into which category, it is not possible to carry out a sensible disaggregation of these two terms. In the model below, total savings, aid and forex are used to proxy the ideal measures. The accuracy of this proxy will depend on the extent to which savings and forex in each sector remain proportional to aggregate savings and forex.

How is such a constraint to be built into a dynamic model of investment? If the investment, saving and forex series are integrated to order 1, then the appropriate dependent variable in the investment function will need to be expressed as a first difference, in order to ensure stationarity. For example, in a log-linear model, the dependent variable would be $\Delta\ln(I_t)$. In this case, the long run constraint can be built in as an 'error correction' term[3] in an equation of the form:

$$\Delta\ln(I_t) = -\alpha \cdot [\ln(I_{t-1}) - \ln(I^*_{t-1})] + \cdots \tag{7.3}$$

The coefficient α measures the speed with which investment converges on its long-run equilibrium level, I^*. Other terms on the RHS of the equation will reflect the determinants of investment in the short-run, which may include $(S + AID)$ and *FOREX*, but need not do so. In an economy that has no access to international capital and is financially repressed or in one that is forex-constrained, the rate of return to physical investment will not enter equation (7.3). If, however, some investors are not constrained then rate-of-return variables will enter the equation.

In constructing a short-run investment model, we will restrict our attention to private capital formation in Côte d'Ivoire and Kenya where private investment makes up roughly 75 per cent of the total. Government investment is left unmodelled and appears just in the long-run constraint, which can be expressed as:

$$\Delta \ln(I_{Pt}) = -\alpha \cdot [\ln(I_{Pt-1} + I_{Gt-1}) - \ln(I_{t-1}^*)] + \cdots \tag{7.4}$$

where I_P is private investment, I_G is government investment, and $I_P + I_G = I$.

Variables to be included in the short-run model will reflect the different possible ways in which investment might be determined. Assuming no forex rationing in a completely financially closed economy the only variable needed (for a constant level of government investment) will be $\Delta \ln(S_t + AID_t)$, which ought to have a coefficient of unity, since investment must always equal savings plus aid. However, in a completely financially open economy, the coefficient should be zero, since there is no savings-investment constraint. With perfect capital markets, the determinants of investment will be those determining its rate of return and, with uncertain returns, the accompanying risk.

The simplest way of relating the level of investment to its rate of return is to consider a risk-neutral, profit-maximising firm facing an infinitely elastic supply of loanable funds,[4] which has the problem:

$$\max \int_{\tau=t}^{\tau=T} [p_\tau \cdot Q(K_\tau) - p_{I\tau} \cdot I_{P\tau}] \exp(-i\tau) d\tau$$

$$\text{subject to} : dK_t = I_{Pt} - hK_t \tag{7.5}$$

over a time horizon $[t,T]$, where p_t is the expected output price at t, p_{It} the expected capital goods price, $Q(\ )$ output, i the interest rate, K_t the private capital stock and h its rate of depreciation. Solving this problem for $dK = \omega = 0$, where ω is the rate of change of the Lagrangian multiplier, yields an equilibrium investment function:

$$I_{Pt} = f(p_t, \ldots, p_T, p_{It}, \ldots, p_{IT}, i, I_{Pt-1}) \tag{7.6}$$

Equation (7.6) poses us with a number of problems. First of all, it does not typically have a tractable functional form. Empirical estimation will be feasible only with the imposition of some a priori restrictions on f( ), since the data sets to be used are quite small. In the model below, we will impose constant elasticities on the arguments of f( ). With more data, the validity of this restriction could be tested. The second problem is in providing an account of how expectations of future prices are formed. With rational expectations expected prices will equal actual prices plus a random error term. With adaptive expectations, expectations will be based on lagged prices. Given the high degree of uncertainty and high information costs that are likely to face an African investor, the latter approach is taken in the model below. Again, with more data, this is an assumption that could be tested.

There are at least three ways in which equation (7.6) is likely to be over-restrictive. First, there is unlikely to be a single production function driving all investment activity: some production processes are more capital-intensive than others. The movement of variable factors of production between capital intensive and non-capital intensive activities is likely to affect the return to investment. If, for example, labour is shifted away from a highly capital-intensive sector and into one that uses negligible capital, because of a relative output price change, then the aggregate marginal physical product of capital will fall, which may reduce investment. In this case, it will not be simply the aggregate output price that matters, but the price of capital-intensive output relative to that of other output. So an empirical investment equation needs to treat p as a relative price term.

Second, equation (7.6) was derived assuming that investment activities are risk-free. In our model, we also introduce the possibility of a relationship between the uncertainty of returns to capital and investment. Two choices must be made: (1) to select the variable on which the measure of risk is to be based, and (2) having selected this variable, to choose an appropriate transformation which measures its volatility. These choices will be discussed in the next section.

Third, we ought to test whether the volume of concessional loans has any impact on domestic investment. Concessional loans make up an important part of foreign investment finance for many developing countries. These are loans tied to particular investment projects made at low interest rates, as part of the foreign aid packages of donor countries. It might be argued that these loans have little to do with the profitability of individual projects, and more to do with the politics of the donor country. If such loans dominate investment finance, including concessional loans in the model will render insignificant any variable reflecting the rate of return to investment. If this scenario is incorrect, the coefficient on the concessional loans term will be insignificant. In intermediate cases, where some investment activity is constrained by such loans, but some investors do genuinely have access to international capital markets, both will be significant explanatory variables.

These observations lead to an empirical investment equation that nests both the rate-of-return variables and the Balance of Payments constraint. Assuming that investment is not constrained by forex shortages, we have:

$$\Delta \ln(I_{Pt}) = \beta_0 + \beta_1 \cdot \Delta \ln(I_{Pt-1}) + \sum_i \gamma_i \cdot \Delta \ln(p_{t-i})$$
$$+ \sum_i \delta_i \cdot \Delta \ln(p_{It-i}) + \sum_i \zeta_i \cdot \Delta \ln(1 + i_{t-i})$$
$$+ \sum_i \eta_i \cdot VAR_{t-i} + \sum_i \theta_i \cdot \Delta \ln(S + AID)_{t-i}$$
$$+ \sum_i \lambda_i \cdot \Delta \ln(I_{Gt-i}) + \sum_i \nu_i \cdot \Delta \ln(CONC_{t-i})$$
$$- \alpha \cdot [\ln(I_{Pt-1} + I_{Gt-1}) - \ln(I^*_{t-1})] \qquad (7.7)$$

where VAR is the chosen measure of risk, $CONC$ is concessional aid and, in this case, $I^*_t = (S + AID)_t$. In the case of financial repression and a completely financially closed economy, all coefficients will be equal to zero except θ_1 and λ_1. In a completely financially open economy, these coefficients will be equal to zero, and the rate-of-return variables will determine private sector investment; though if $\alpha > 0$ there is some long-run Balance of Payments constraint. In an economy that is neither completely financially open nor completely financially closed, both domestic savings and rate-of-return variables will be significant. The size of the coefficient on the savings term will reflect the degree of openness: a smaller coefficient implies a more open economy. With some forex rationing (as perhaps in the case of Kenya), we will need to modify $I^*()$ and include $\Delta \ln(FOREX_t)$ as an explanatory variable:

$$\Delta \ln(I_{Pt}) = \beta_0 + \beta_1 \cdot \Delta \ln(I_{Pt-1}) + \sum_i \gamma_i \cdot \Delta \ln(p_{t-i})$$

$$+ \sum_i \delta_i \cdot \Delta \ln(p_{lt-i}) + \sum_i \zeta_i \cdot \Delta \ln(1 + i_{t-i})$$

$$+ \sum_i \eta_i \cdot VAR_{t-i} + \sum_i \theta_i \cdot \Delta \ln(S + AID)_{t-i}$$

$$+ \sum_i \kappa_i \cdot \Delta \ln(FOREX_{t-i}) + \sum_i \lambda_i \cdot \Delta \ln(I_{Gt-i})$$

$$+ \sum_i \nu_i \cdot \Delta \ln(CONC_{t-i}) - \alpha \cdot [\ln(I_{Pt-1} + I_{Gt-1})$$

$$- \ln(I_{t-1}^*)] \qquad (7.8)$$

where now $I_t^* = I^*((S + AID)_t, FOREX_t)$.

The contemporaneous savings term in equations (7.7) and (7.8) needs to be instrumented if we do not want to assume a priori that savings are independent of investment demand. So we also need a model of savings. The success of error correction models of consumption in Western economies[5] suggests that a similar model of savings might be applied to the countries to be studied here. The form of such a model is guided by the restriction that in the stationary state, people will be consuming and saving constant fractions of their income, so we have:

$$S = n \cdot INC \qquad (7.9)$$

Note that this is strictly a model of private savings behaviour. For our investment model, we need a model of aggregate savings, since this is the variable that is used to capture the magnitude of financial openness of the domestic economy. In the extreme case of complete Ricardian equivalence, the distinction is unnecessary, since private agents perceive any government saving as temporary, and dissave an equal amount in anticipation of future budget deficits, which will increase private disposable income. However, this extreme case relies on the assumption of perfect capital markets and no uncertainty, conditions unlikely to be fulfilled in the countries that we will be looking at. Nevertheless, if private agents do offset some of the current budget deficit/surplus, perceiving a long-run budget balancing constraint, then a model of private savings may work reasonably well as a model of aggregate savings.

One useful relaxation of equation (7.9) is to allow the marginal propensity to save to vary, so:

$$S = nINC^{\sigma} \tag{7.10}$$

If savings are disturbed from their long-run equilibrium level, then adjustment back to equilibrium is described by:

$$S_t = S_{t-1}^{\tau} \cdot [n \cdot INC^{\sigma}]^{(1-\tau)} \tag{7.11}$$

If $\tau = 0$, then people attain their long-run equilibrium immediately; otherwise adjustment takes some time, and savings converge logarithmically to their equilibrium level. If income is away from its long-run equilibrium level, then the time path of savings is described by:

$$S_t = n \cdot S_{t-1}^{\tau} \cdot \{n \cdot [INC_t^{\mu} \cdot INC_{t-1}^{(1-\mu)}]^{\sigma}\}^{(1-\tau)} \tag{7.12}$$

This approach endows consumers with some degree of myopia: savings depending on just past and present income, regardless of where long-run equilibrium is. Using logarithms, equation (7.12) becomes:

$$\ln(S_t) = \tau \cdot \ln(S_{t-1}) + (1 - \tau) \cdot \sigma \cdot [\mu \cdot \ln(INC_t) + (1 - \mu)$$
$$\cdot \ln(INC_{t-1})] + (1 - \tau) \cdot \ln(n) \tag{7.13}$$

which, if savings are integrated $I(1)$, can be estimated as:

$$\Delta \ln(S_t) = (1 - \tau) \cdot \sigma \cdot \mu \cdot \Delta \ln(INC_t) - (1 - \tau)$$
$$\cdot [\ln(S_{t-1}) - \sigma \cdot \ln(INC_{t-1}) - \ln(n)] \tag{7.14}$$

Three further modifications of the savings function might be empirically important. First, the long-run savings propensity n might depend on the real interest rate, i.e. the difference between the nominal interest rate and the rate of inflation. Moreover, the nominal interest rate and the rate of inflation might not have identical elasticities. OECD consumption functions often include an inflation term with a negative short-run coefficient.[6] A possible explanation for this is that changes in the rate of inflation are typically unexpected: so in the short-run, a rise in inflation will mean that people's money balances for transactions purposes will be worth less than intended. So real consumption will be lower than intended. In this case, there will be a positive short-run coefficient on inflation in the savings function.

Secondly, the savings propensity might depend on the level of foreign aid. Foreign aid is typically tied to investment activities: it is a gift that is given on the condition that it is not consumed. If aid increases, an optimising response on the part of the recipients is to save less out of current income and consume more. We may then find that savings are a negative function of aid.

Thirdly, it is possible that lags of the explanatory variables will be empirically important, if there is some lag in the decision-making process.

Combining these three extensions, the savings equation will take the form:

$$
\Delta \ln(S_t) = \sum_i \phi_i \cdot \Delta(S_{t-i-1}) + \sum_i \xi_i \cdot \Delta \ln(INC_{t-i}) + \sum_i \psi_i
$$
$$
\cdot \Delta \ln(1 + r_{t-i}) + \sum_i \chi_i \cdot \Delta \ln(1 + \pi_{-t-i})
$$
$$
+ \sum_i \rho_i \cdot \Delta \ln(AID_{t-i}) - \delta \cdot [\ln(S_{t-1}) - \xi \cdot \ln(INC_{t-1})
$$
$$
+ \psi \ln(1 + r_{t-1}) + \chi \cdot \ln(1 + \pi_{-t-1})
$$
$$
+ \rho \cdot \ln(AID_{t-1}) - \ln(n)] \tag{7.15}
$$

where r is the real domestic return on savings and π is the consumer price inflation rate. r need not be the same as the international opportunity cost of capital finance, i, in equations (7.7) and (7.8). Equations (7.7) and (7.15) form the model to be estimated for Côte d'Ivoire; equations (7.8) and (7.15) form the model to be estimated for Kenya.

Although the structure of the equations is the same for both countries, the results might differ in number of ways. These differences reflect the differing financial institutions of the two countries. Côte d'Ivoire's membership of UEMOA might affect investment determination in the following ways.

(1) The convertibility of the CFA Franc ensures that domestic agents will never be rationed in foreign exchange. The domestic currency is fully convertible, and is not economically distinct from the currency of the country's major trading partner. The *FOREX* term will not appear on the RHS of the investment equations.

(2) This convertibility, along with the institutional framework that links the UEMOA financial system with that of France, may encourage capital market integration. It might be easier for Ivorians to borrow from and lend abroad than if Côte d'Ivoire maintained independent financial institutions. Guaranteed convertibility reduces the risks involved in lending to Ivorians – there is no risk that they will unable to acquire the foreign exchange to repay the loan – and this may stimulate the creation of financial links. If this is the case, we ought to observe a smaller coefficient on the $\Delta\ln(S + AID)$ terms in the investment equation.

(3) Low inflation may mean that future prices are easier to anticipate, so there is less risk involved in investment. A fixed exchange rate may make the prices of imported capital goods or of import-competing industrial output less variable. In the case of Kenya and Côte d'Ivoire, it remains to be seen whether the appropriate measure of *VAR*, the variability of returns to investment, registers less volatility in the UEMOA member.

7.3. The estimated model

7.3.1. Choice and definition of explanatory variables

The data we will use are drawn from National Accounts, aid and trade statistics for the two countries, as reported in World Bank (1987, 1991), IMF (1991), OECD (1970–89), UNECA (1973, 1980, 1986), UNCTAD (1979–90), BCEAO (1987, 1990) and Kenya Central Bureau of Statistics (1970–88). These sources provide annual observations for 1966–89 in Côte d'Ivoire and for 1966–88 in Kenya. The variables chosen are as follows.[7]

(1) *Investment and capital prices (I, I_P, I_G, p_I)* National Accounts statistics report real and nominal gross domestic investment and fixed capital formation. Real GDI is used for the variable I in Section 7.2. Real and nominal capital formation figures are used to derive a capital price series, p_I. (Note that what we need is a real capital goods price, so p_I is the capital formation deflator expressed as a fraction of the GDP deflator.) Kenyan statistics disaggregate capital formation by public and private sector, providing series for I_G and I_P. In Côte d'Ivoire, government investment only is reported, so I_P must be calculated as a residual. This is probably the weakest part of the construction of the investment series.

(2) *Savings (S)*   Nominal gross domestic savings are reported in National Accounts statistics. An appropriate deflator needs to be found to express savings in real terms. Here, there is a conflict between the deflator which would be appropriate when considering the impact of saving on investment – in this case, it would be appropriate to use a capital price series, measuring the real value of savings in terms of the capital goods they could be used to buy – and that which would be appropriate when constructing a behavioural model of savings. The value of the savings to savers is the opportunity cost of the consumption foregone, so a consumer price deflator ought to be used. They differ to the extent that (i) capital goods prices vary relative to the price of output and (ii) consumer prices vary relative to output prices, i.e. to the extent that indirect taxes vary over time. A compromise approach is to use an output price series. In the equations below, the GDP deflator is used as a proxy for aggregate output prices. In fact, the results are insensitive to the deflators used here, since the rate of growth of prices is much less variable than the rate of growth of nominal savings.

(3) *Income (INC)*   National Accounts statistics report real GDP and terms of trade adjustment figures (an improvement in the terms of trade results in an increase in income for a given GDP). The sum of these components is taken as real domestic income.

(4) *Aid (AID)*   OECD tables report total annual grants to each country from multilateral and unilateral sources, in US Dollars. This is the source of the *AID* series used in the model. The World Bank exchange conversion factor is used to convert this into domestic currency units. This figure is deflated in the same way as the savings series.[8]

(5) *Concessional loans (CONC)*   UNCTAD defines a concessional loan as one where there is a grant element of at least 25 per cent. The grant element is derived by calculating the financial value of the loan (the value of the principal plus interest payments at a 'competitive' rate of interest, taken to be 10 per cent) and subtracting the total discounted value of the actual required repayments. The point of this definition is that the loans so defined are not 'commercial', and could not be acquired on competitive international markets. The definition is arbitrary insofar as the figures of 25 per cent and 10 per cent are arbitrary. If it is these loans plus savings plus aid that determine domestic investment, then one would not be justified in claiming that the domestic economy had access to international capital markets. UNCTAD tables report the US Dollar value of concessional loans, which are converted into real domestic currency values in the same way as AID.

(6) *Foreign exchange availability (FOREX)* IMF tables report the US$ value of foreign exchange holdings in Kenya, which are converted into real domestic currency values in the same way as *AID*.

(7) *Interest rates and inflation (i, r, π)* There are two relevant interest rates, the one that appears in the savings function, and the one that appears in the investment function. In the savings function, we need a measure of the real return to savings. The available proxy for the nominal rate of return is the bank deposit interest rate. (The only other domestic interest rate reported for the whole of the sample is the central bank discount rate.) r is measured as the difference between this rate and the inflation rate. The consumer price index is used for the calculation of inflation rates, since what we are trying to capture is the opportunity cost of deferred consumption.

Choosing an international interest rate, i, for the investment function is more problematic. Capital flows are not disaggregated by country of origin (indeed, some flows are from multinational agencies, and so they do not have a country of origin), so it is not possible to construct a weighted average of foreign national lending rates. However, it is likely that France predominates in capital flows to Côte d'Ivoire, so a French rate (the lending rate reported in IMF tables) is used in this case. For Kenya, it is assumed that capital flows from the US predominate, so a US rate is used.

(8) *Output price (p)* The first proxies for the output price tried were industrial and (more narrowly) manufacturing production deflators. However, these turned out to be insignificant in the estimated equations. Using the reciprocal of the terms of trade turns out to work much better, and this is the variable used in the equations below. In Côte d'Ivoire and Kenya exports are dominated by agricultural commodities and imports by manufactured commodities. If agricultural activities are less capital intensive than manufacturing activities, then the negative relationship between the terms of trade and investment can be interpreted as a relative price effect, as discussed in Section 7.2.

(9) *The variability of returns to investment (VAR)* Insofar as the output price, the price of capital goods and the interest rate which firms face all influence the returns to investment, the variability of any one of them might affect investment. However, transformations of the p and i series turn out never to be significant in the estimated equations. What do turn out to be significant are variability measures based on p_I. There are many ways of constructing a variability measure, the most straightforward of which is to calculate a moving variance or standard

152 Savings, investment and CFA membership

deviation of the series. However, the distribution of such a measure is typically far from normal: it creates a number of large outliers in the right hand tail. This means that it performs poorly as an explanatory variable. More satisfactory is to use a polynomial lag of the absolute value of the first difference of the series: this is typically approximately normally distributed, but positively correlated with the moving standard deviation. $|\Delta p_I|$ and $|\Delta \ln(p_I)|$ turn out to be significant explanatory variables. In the reported equations, the latter has been used, although the choice makes little difference to the results. The choice of this measure of variability is particularly interesting with respect to the CFA/non-CFA comparison, since the average value of *VAR* in Côte d'Ivoire is 0.053, lower than in Kenya, where it is 0.076. In the next chapter, we will see that this difference extends to a wider range of CFA and non-CFA countries. In this chapter, it remains to be seen whether Côte d'Ivoire has benefited from the lower level of variability.

7.3.2. The estimated equations

In order to estimate the savings and investment functions efficiently, we must first ascertain the order of integration of the series of interest. The sample sizes we are dealing with are very small, so it is not possible to reject the null hypothesis of non-stationarity for any variable using the standard Dickey–Fuller or Phillips–Perron test statistics; but in such a small sample these tests have very low power, and we will not base any inference on them here. (In previous chapters we have dealt with larger, quarterly samples of Ivorian macroeconomic data, but inference about the moments of an annual series cannot be based on evidence about the moments of the corresponding quarterly series.) Here, we will base our inference on the Durbin–Watson (DW) stationarity statistics.[9] If the DW statistics for the first difference of a time series is close to two, but the statistics for the series itself is much lower, this suggests that the series is integrated to order one. Table 7.1 shows the DW statistics for the variables of interest and their first differences. It shows that the large drop in the statistic between Δx_t and x_t occurs for all the variables except *VAR*. This indicates that it would be sensible to treat the variables (excluding *VAR*) as I(1), although it is to be stressed that this choice is not based on a formal statistical test, due to the inadequacy of the data.[10]

Table 7.1 Durbin–Watson stationarity tests[a]

	Côte d'Ivoire	Kenya
$\ln(I_P)$	1.439	1.138
$\Delta\ln(I_P)$	2.764 (−0.4)	2.215 (3.9)
$\ln(S)$	0.441	0.273
$\Delta\ln(S)$	1.518 (1.0)	2.073 (5.9)
$\ln(INC)$	0.089	0.077
$\Delta\ln(INC)$	2.185 (4.0)	1.798 (4.4)
$\ln(1+\pi)$	1.586	1.616
$\Delta\ln(1+\pi)$	2.717 (−0.2)	2.908 (0.2)
$\ln(1+r)$	0.177	0.078
$\Delta\ln(1+r)$	2.385 (0.2)	0.905 (0.3)
$\ln(P_I)$	1.064	0.140
$\Delta\ln(P_I)$	2.388 (1.1)	2.082 (2.6)
$\ln(p)$	0.991	1.356
$\Delta\ln(p)$	1.886 (−1.7)	2.771 (−0.8)
VAR	1.367 (5.3)	1.996 (7.6)
ΔVAR	2.121	2.581
$\ln(FOREX)$		1.361
$\Delta\ln(FOREX)$		1.997 (3.8)

a   Mean values of stationary series (in %) are reported in parentheses.

Given that the dependent variables are I(1), the modelling procedure described in Section 7.1 can be implemented. First of all, it is necessary to derive a long-run relationship between investment, savings and (in the case of Kenya) forex; and between savings, income and interest rates. Again, the small size of the sample constrains our choice of estimator. We will proceed on the assumption that there is at most a single cointegrating vector for each set of variables, and use the approach of Kramers *et al.* (1992). The parameters in the error-correction terms in equations (7.7) and (7.8) are estimated by constructing dynamic regressions of the form:

$$a(\text{L})\ln(I_t) = b_1(\text{L})\ln(S_t + AID_t)$$
$$+ b_2(\text{L})\ln(FOREX_t) + u_t \qquad (7.16)$$

where $a(\text{L})$, $b_1(\text{L})$ and $b_2(\text{L})$ are lag operators and in Côte d'Ivoire $b_2(\text{L})$ is excluded. (The Schwartz Criterion indicates a lag order of one in these regressions.) The error-correction term parameters are constructed as $b_i(0)/[1 - a(0)]$. These parameters are reported in Table 7.2, along with the *t*-test for cointegration of Banerjee *et al.* (1992). The same method is used to estimate the parameters of the error-correction

Table 7.2 Estimated cointegrating vectors

Country	Long-run equation	Cointegration t-ratio
Kenya	$\ln(I) = 0.205 \cdot \ln(S + AID) + 0.303 \cdot \ln(FOREX)$	-5.390
Kenya	$\ln(S) = 1.084 \cdot \ln(INC) + 0.199 \cdot \ln(1 + r)$	-12.25
Côte d'Iv.	$\ln(I) = 0.978 \cdot \ln(S + AID)$	-1.926
Côte d'Iv.	$\ln(S) = 0.583 \cdot \ln(INC) + 0.713 \cdot (1 + \pi) - 0.245 \cdot \ln(AID)$	-5.892

term in equation (7.15):

$$a(L) \ln(S_t) = b_1(L) \ln(INC_t) + b_2(L) \ln(1 + r_t)$$
$$+ b_3(L) \ln(1 + \pi_{-t}) + b_4(L) \ln(AID_t) \qquad (7.17)$$

However, in this case the dynamic regression must be restricted before the null of no cointegration can be rejected. $b_2(L)$ is omitted in the case of Côte d'Ivoire and $b_3(L)$ and $b_4(L)$ in the case of Kenya. (Here the Schwartz Criterion indicates a lag order of two.) These estimates are also reported in Table 7.2. Having estimated these long-run relationships, error-correction terms are created so as to estimate equations (7.7), (7.8) and (7.15) directly. These estimates are reported in Tables 7.3–7.6; the error-correction terms are denoted *ecm*. The results for each country are discussed in turn.

7.3.3. Results for Kenya

In the savings function for Kenya reported in Table 7.2 the coefficient on $\ln(INC)$ is very close to (and insignificantly different from) unity: savings are proportional to income. The corresponding dynamic equation for $\Delta \ln(S_t)$ that is reported in Table 7.3 is the result of imposing restrictions on an estimate of equation (7.15) with a lag order of two. This equation implies that the short-run income elasticity is significantly higher than the long-run elasticity of unity. This result is similar to those in empirical consumption functions estimated for OECD countries,[11] where the short-run income elasticity of consumption is less than unity. The explanation of these results is that consumers take time to adjust consumption levels in response to a change in income, and so in the short-run, the change in consumption following a change in income is less than proportional. Note also that there are positive short-run coefficients on the inflation terms, $\Delta \ln(1 + \pi_t)$ and $\Delta \ln(1 + \pi_{t-1})$; this is also consistent with existing models of consumption, as discussed above. The model passes a selection of test criteria reported in Table 7.2. The Chow test reported is based on a sub-sample that omits the final four observations. It shows that there is no significant parameter instability.

Table 7.3 Kenyan dynamic savings function[a]. Dependent variable: $\Delta\ln(S)$; sample: 1969–88

Variable	Coefficient	Std. error	HCSE	t-ratio	Partial r^2
$\Delta\ln(S)_{-1}$	−1.5032181	0.16801	0.17304	−8.94732	0.8792
$\Delta\ln(S)_{-2}$	0.3471263	0.14391	0.11936	2.41216	0.3460
$\Delta\ln(INC)$	1.4266629	0.25163	0.20056	5.66958	0.7450
$\Delta\ln(INC)_{-1}$	2.2096405	0.24048	0.19167	9.18841	0.8847
$\Delta\ln(1+r)_{-1}$	−0.2178956	0.07814	0.07432	−2.78870	0.4142
$\Delta\ln(1+\pi)$	0.7604462	0.16719	0.13122	4.54853	0.6529
$\Delta L(1+\pi)_{-1}$	0.6183084	0.22394	0.18692	2.76107	0.4093
ecm_{-2}	−2.3153555	0.26627	0.31501	−8.69560	0.8730
intercept	−0.0373668	0.01913	0.01831	−1.95362	0.2576

$R^2 = 0.9840843$ $\sigma = 0.0341140$
LM test for autocorrelation: $F(1,10) = 2.06$ [0.1818]
LM ARCH test: $F(1,9) = 0.01$ [0.9342]
χ^2 normality test: $\chi^2(2) = 1.118$
Chow test: $F(4,7) = 0.41$ [0.7963]

a 'HCSE' represents standard errors corrected for heteroskedasticity (but in the investment equation not the variance in the estimate of S) and 'std. error' uncorrected standard errors.

Table 7.4 Kenyan dynamic investment function[a]. Dependent variable: $\Delta\ln(I_P)$; sample: 1968–88

Variable	Coefficient	Std. error	HCSE	t-ratio	Partial r^2
$\Delta\ln(I_P)_{-1}$	−0.4414059	0.10497	0.12566	−4.20515	0.5763
$\Delta\ln(S+AID)_{-1}$	1.1043379	0.15191	0.19586	7.26980	0.8026
$\Delta\ln(p)$	1.1598589	0.18671	0.25604	6.21197	0.7480
$\Delta\ln(p)_{-1}$	1.0873778	0.20300	0.26762	5.35660	0.6882
VAR_{-1}	−2.0807781	0.50905	0.60089	−4.08757	0.5624
$\Delta\ln(CONC)_{-1}$	0.6190909	0.17160	0.29849	3.60780	0.5003
ecm_{-1}	−0.8882447	0.13416	0.13260	−6.62061	0.7713
intercept	0.0630873	0.04228	0.05227	1.49218	0.1462

$R^2 = 0.9486149$ $\sigma = 0.0656220$
LM test for autocorrelation: $F(1,12) = 0.69$ [0.4230]
LM ARCH test: $F(1,11) = 0.05$ [0.8354]
χ^2 normality test: $\chi^2(2) = 0.475$
Chow test: $F(4,9) = 1.08$ [0.4224]

a 'HCSE' represents standard errors corrected for heteroskedasticity (but in the investment equation not the variance in the estimate of S) and 'std. error' uncorrected standard errors.

The savings series fitted in Table 7.3 is then used to model investment. This model is reported in Table 7.4, and embodies the long-run cointegrating relationship for investment reported in Table 7.2. Since I_P is approximately equal to both $(S + AID)$ and *FOREX* over the sample period, the estimated long-run elasticities (0.2 and 0.3 respectively) can also be interpreted as the marginal change in investment for a change in savings/forex. The low long-run savings coefficient reflects the fact that it is not true of all investors that the long-run binding constraint is savings: for some the binding constraint is foreign exchange availability.

We can arrive at a measure of the cost of the forex constraint by comparing the actual equilibrium level of investment in Kenya (based on Table 7.2) with the hypothetical equilibrium level, based on a long-run solution with $I_P = S + AID - I_G$. Since S, *FOREX* and I_G are evolving over time, the actual and hypothetical equilibrium levels of investment are evolving over time, too. The ratio of actual to hypothetical equilibrium investment is given below:

1972	82%
1976	71%
1980	79%
1984	55%
1988	53%

That is, the costs in terms of total private investment are substantial, and increased over the 1980s.

In the dynamic equation the significant explanatory variables are: $\Delta\ln(S + AID)$, $\Delta\ln(CONC)$, $\Delta\ln(FOREX)$, $\Delta\ln(p)$, *VAR* and the error-correction term. Note that the coefficient on the error correction term is not significantly different from unity: the economy adjusts very quickly to its long-run equilibrium level. The coefficient on the savings term is not significantly different from unity, either. That is, a rise in savings will, *ceteris paribus*, lead to a proportional rise in investment in the short run. Investment is not independent of savings, and therefore the hypothesis of perfect financial market integration is rejected for Kenya. However, investment does not depend entirely on domestic funds. Investment is influenced both by variables affecting the demand for investment goods (p and *VAR*) – suggesting that some agents have access to foreign financial markets – and by concessional aid flows. The picture of Kenya is therefore very mixed: some investors depend on domestic funds, or on foreign concessional loans. However, others appear to have access to foreign capital markets.

Of particular interest is the magnitude of the impact of the uncertainty term, *VAR*, on investment. The average value of *VAR* in Kenya is 0.076. The coefficient on *VAR* is 2.00. This implies an average value of I_{Pt}/I_{Pt-1} that is 86 per cent of the level which it would have been with zero *VAR*. The maximum value of *VAR* is 0.179, and the minimum 0.020, implying maximal and minimal values of I_{Pt}/I_{Pt-1} equal to 70 per cent and 96 per cent of their hypothetical level with zero VAR. It remains to be seen how this compares with the CFA member, Côte d'Ivoire.

7.3.4. Results for Côte d'Ivoire

The dynamic Ivorian savings function is reported in Table 7.5. The error correction term is constructed in the same way as for Kenya, based on the coefficients in Table 7.2. In this case, savings are cointegrated with income, inflation and the level of foreign aid. There is a positive long-run coefficient on inflation (in Kenya, the positive coefficient was only a short-run phenomenon). This suggests that agents never fully adjust their expectations when the rate of change of prices increases. There is also a negative coefficient on the foreign aid term: when aid increases, less is saved than would otherwise be the case, as anticipated above. As in Kenya, the dynamic savings equation suggests that short-run income coefficient is significantly larger than the long-run coefficient. The savings regression in Table 7.5 passes the selection of test criteria.

Table 7.5 Ivorian dynamic savings function. Dependent variable: $\Delta\ln(S)$; sample: 1968–89

Variable	Coefficient	Std. error	HCSE	t-ratio	Partial r^2
$\Delta\ln(INC)$	2.0138846	0.20387	0.17009	9.87852	0.8516
$\Delta L(1+\pi)$	0.5406232	0.10888	0.07702	4.96515	0.5919
$\Delta L(1+\pi)_{-1}$	-0.1939459	0.11594	0.07525	-1.67285	0.1413
ecm_{-1}	-0.7797683	0.12234	0.12735	-6.37393	0.7050
intercept	-0.0045122	0.01730	0.02070	-0.26081	0.0040

$R^2 = 0.8934822$ $\sigma = 0.0603754$
LM test for autocorrelation: $F(1,16) = 2.41$ [0.1403]
ARCH test: $F(1,15) = 0.02$ [0.8766]
χ^2 normality test: $\chi^2(2) = 0.227$
Chow test: $F(4,13) = 0.67$ [0 .6220]

Table 7.6 Ivorian dynamic investment function. Dependent variable: $\Delta\ln(I_P)$; sample: 1969–89

Variable	Coefficient	Std. error	HCSE	t-ratio	Partial r^2
$\Delta\ln(S+AID)$	0.9902080	0.26000	0.24905	3.80849	0.5687
$\Delta\ln(p)$	1.1402681	0.27701	0.24921	4.11635	0.6064
$\Delta\ln(p)_{-1}$	0.8238430	0.15986	0.13502	5.15352	0.7071
$\Delta\ln(p_I)$	−2.2808830	0.25545	0.28425	−8.92884	0.8788
VAR	−1.5278046	0.38700	0.33979	−3.94782	0.5862
VAR_{-1}	−1.3721441	0.48036	0.25990	−2.85648	0.4259
$\Delta\ln(I_P/I_G)_{-1}$	−0.3432550	0.05322	0.03476	6.45025	0.7909
$MA\Delta^2\ln(CONC)$	0.9408934	0.18192	0.17160	5.17180	0.7086
ecm_{-1}	−0.4221832	0.06593	0.06221	−6.40394	0.7885
intercept	0.1870796	0.04722	0.03059	3.96190	0.5880

$R^2 = 0.9669156$ $\sigma = 0.0918720$
LM test for autocorrelation: $F(1,10) = 0.58$ [0.4643]
LM ARCH test: $F(1,9) = 0.01$ [0.9211]
χ^2normality test: $\chi^2(2) = 0.696$
Chow test: $F(4,7) = 1.75$ [0.2427]

We now proceed to estimation of the dynamic Ivorian investment function (Table 7.6). This function incorporates the error-correction term reported in Table 7.2, in which the estimated coefficient on $\ln(S+AID)$ is 0.98, which is not significantly different from unity. In the reported equation for $\Delta\ln(I_{Pt})$ insignificant variables have been omitted so as to minimise the Schwartz Criterion, and linear restrictions have been imposed to create the variables $MA\Delta^2\ln(CONC)$, a two-period moving average of $\Delta^2\ln(CONC)$, and $\Delta\ln(I_P/I_G)$.[12] Other significant variables are: p, p_I, VAR, $(S+AID)$ and the error-correction term. As in the case of Kenya, the coefficient on the savings term is not significantly different from unity: a fall in savings leads to a proportional fall in investment both in the short run and in the long run. So there is no evidence that Côte d'Ivoire's membership of the CFA has led to a greater degree of integration with foreign capital markets. The results for Côte d'Ivoire are similar to those for Kenya in other ways: the significant explanatory variables reflect the importance of both concessional aid and of the rate-of-return to investment, suggesting that some Ivorian investors have access to foreign financial markets. However, the route by which concessional aid affects investment seems to be more indirect than in Kenya. Investment is higher just when concessional aid is increasing more rapidly. It may be that the speed at which donors are prepared to increase concessional aid to Côte d'Ivoire reflects (or indicates to investors) the return to, and therefore the level of, investment.

If we calculate the impact of the variability term, VAR, on investment in the same way as for Kenya, we find that at the average level of VAR, I_{Pt}/I_{Pt-1} is 86 per cent of its hypothetical level with $VAR = 0$. For the maximum VAR, this figure is 58 per cent, and for the minimum, 99 per cent. That is, the impact of VAR on investment has been roughly the same as in Kenya, despite the higher level of VAR there. This is because the coefficients on VAR are larger in Côte d'Ivoire. The potential benefit from lower variability has been offset by the greater sensitivity of Ivorian investors.

7.4. Conclusion

It has been possible to construct an econometric model that explains the evolution of private investment in two African countries – one inside the CFA and one outside – over a twenty-year period. The results strongly reject the extreme hypotheses of completely open and completely closed domestic capital markets in either country: domestic funds, aid and concessional loans do affect the growth of investment, but these are not the only factors. Variables reflecting the rate of return to investment are also important. That these demand-side factors are significant suggests that some investors are able to borrow on international capital markets. In particular, the rate of growth of investment can be impaired by an increase in the variability of capital goods prices.

We considered three possible advantages of CFA membership: greater financial openness, an absence of foreign exchange rationing and more stable prices. The results for Kenya and Côte d'Ivoire suggest that the CFA has not led to greater financial openness. However, the absence of foreign exchange rationing is an important advantage: Kenyan investment has been seriously impaired due to the lack of foreign exchange. In this respect, CFA membership confers important advantages over other countries whose governments cannot credibly commit to a liberal foreign exchange regime. With regard to price stability, the results are more ambiguous. Although prices are less variable in Côte d'Ivoire than in Kenya, Ivorian investment has not benefited, due to the greater sensitivity of Ivorian investors to risk.

The time-series data available for Kenya and Côte d'Ivoire are not available for very many other African countries, so it is not possible to see to what extent these results are more generally applicable.

However, with respect to financial openness it is unlikely that many other African countries, inside or outside the CFA, are more financially open than these two relatively industrialised countries. With respect to forex rationing, Kenya appears to have been less severely constrained than many of its anglophone neighbours, if the black market exchange rate premia in *Pick's Currency Yearbook* are anything to go by. So the associated advantages of CFA membership are likely to be as least as large as those estimated in this chapter. With respect to price stability, there are some data for other African countries that allow us to use alternative estimation techniques in order to determine the extent to which the stylised facts emerging from this chapter are more widely applicable. This will be the subject of the next chapter.

Notes

1 An interesting time series version of this type of model is Matin and Wasow (1992).
2 See Bayoumi (1990) for a genealogy of these models.
3 Note that in this case, the error-correction term is not to be understood as reflecting a particular behavioural model: it simply reflects how quickly investment converges on its long-run equilibrium.
4 See Precious (1987) for a more detailed exposition of this model.
5 See for example Bovenberg and Evans (1990).
6 See for example Davidson *et al.* (1978).
7 Mean sample values of stationary explanatory variables are shown in Table 7.1.
8 Since we do not have to model *AID* (it is assumed to be exogenous), it would *ceteris paribus* be better to use the import price deflator (aid can be used only to buy imports). However, compatability with the savings series is required, and since savings are much larger than aid, it is appropriate to use the deflator most appropriate for savings alone.
9 For each variable x_t, the DW statistic is defined as $[\sum_t \Delta x_t]/[\sum_t (x_t - E(x_t))^2]$.
10 The DW for I_P is quite high, but this result is very sensitive to the sample size. The high value of the statistic is due to a very low level of I_P in 1984; the DW for the sample, 1967–83 is much lower. Given this, it is prudent to treat I_P as an I(1) variable.
11 See for example Davidson *et al.* (1978).
12 Interpretation of this last term should be treated with caution, as I_P has been calculated as a residual. But if private investors have a larger share of domestic financial funds in period $t-1$, perhaps because the government has underestimated the quantity of funds available, then in period t the government will require a greater share. So for a given S private investment will have to fall.

References

Banque Centrale des Etats de l'Afrique de l'Ouest (1987, 1990) *Notes d'Information et Statistiques*, Dakar.

Bayoumi, T. (1990) 'Savings – Investment correlations', *IMF Staff Papers*, **37**: 360–87.

Bovenberg, A. and Evans, O. (1990) 'National and personal saving in the US', *IMF Staff Papers*, **37**: 636–69.

Central Bureau of Statistics, Ministry of Finance and Planning, Kenya (1970–88) *Economic Survey*, Nairobi.

Davidson, J., Hendry, D., Srba, F. and Yeo, S. (1978) 'Interpreting econometric evidence: The behaviour of consumers' expenditure in the UK', *Economic Journal*, **88**: 661–92.

Feldstein, M. and Horioka, C. (1980) 'Domestic saving and international capital flows', *Economic Journal*, **90**: 314–29.

International Monetary Fund (1975–90) *International Financial Statistics*, Washington, DC.

Matin, K. and Wasow, B. (1992) 'Adjustment and private investment in Kenya', *World Bank Policy Research Working Paper 878*.

Organisation for Economic Co-operation and Development (1969–88) *Geographical Distribution of Financial Flows*, Paris.

Root, F. and Ahmed, A. (1979) 'Empirical determinants of manufacturing direct foreign investment in developing countries', *Economic Development and Cultural Change*, **27**: 751–67.

United Nations Economic Commission for Africa (1973, 1980, 1987) *African Statistical Yearbook*, Washington, DC.

United Nations Commission for Trade and Development (1979–90) *Handbook of International Trade and Development Statistics*, Washington, DC.

World Bank (1987, 1991) *World Tables*, Johns Hopkins: Washington, DC.

8 CFA membership and the role of relative price stability in investment performance

In the last chapter, we saw that in certain CFA countries investment is affected by the instability of capital goods prices, this instability reflecting the variability of returns to investment. It is not possible to investigate the time-series relationship between investment and variability of returns in all African countries, since in many countries the data is wanting. However, it is possible to study the link between investment and variability using cross-country data, and so to widen the scope of our investigation. The factors that explain differences in rates of investment between countries are not necessarily the same as those that explain differences in one country over time; but we can ask whether the variability of returns is important in both cases. Guillaumont (1988) finds that the unconditional mean of the investment-GDP ratio is higher in the CFA than in other African countries. If we find that variability is lower in the CFA, then we have one explanation for why investment in the CFA is higher.

This is not the end of the story, however. It remains to be shown why variability is lower in some countries than in others. Attention has often been drawn to the fact that CFA members have a nominal exchange rate that is fixed with respect to a major western economy (see Chapter 1). However, a fixed nominal exchange rate does not entail fixed relative prices (a fixed 'real' exchange rate), whether these are consumer goods prices or capital goods prices. For any domestic price of an internationally traded commodity, p, and equivalent foreign price, p^*, the relative price will be p/ep^*, where e is the nominal exchange rate.[1] p^* is likely to be exogenous from the point of view of a small domestic economy, but there is no a priori reason why p should not be determined by the 'law of one price', $p/ep^* = 1$. In this case, the process that determines e has no effect on the relative price, which is constant at unity. Again, if p is not flexible, then having a fixed e is unlikely to lead to greater relative price stability when p^* is variable. There are cases in which a fixed e corresponds to stability of p/ep^*, e.g. when both p and p^* vary little, but a floating e is likely to be highly volatile. However, it remains to be shown that this is the case that corresponds to the experience of African economies.

On the other hand, there are reasons why the law of one price should not hold, even with flexible domestic prices. Tariffs and quotas will drive a wedge between p and ep^*, and the goods may not be a perfect substitute for any internationally traded commodity. In these cases, it would be interesting to know whether the commercial and financial institutions of the CFA have some effect on the determination of domestic prices, if only in limiting domestic governments' ability to impose tariffs and quotas. If membership of the CFA does indeed lead to lower relative price instability, and in particular to lower variability of relative returns to investment, we will need to investigate which of the Zone's institutions is responsible for this effect.

8.1. Determinants of investment in Africa

In the first part of this chapter, we will investigate a cross-country model of gross domestic investment, using data from the World Bank World Tables (1989–90) and World Debt Tables (1989).[2] There are a number of existing cross-country models of investment in the literature, which employ a wide range of variables to explain differences in investment between countries.[3] The model below is in the same style as these, using explanatory variables that have been significant in previous studies, and in addition, an index of the variability of returns to investment. Although there is some similarity between explanations for time-series variation in investment performance and explanations for cross-sectional variation, there are also many differences: some determinants of investment vary substantially only over time, or only between countries. For this reason, the regression equation presented in this chapter will be somewhat different in structure from those of the previous chapter.

The dependent variable in the equations is a measure of gross domestic investment, calculated for each country as an average for the period 1970–87. (This period is chosen because 1970 is the first year for which comprehensive debt tables exist, and 1987 is the last in which investment is recorded in all countries in the sample.) It is possible to express gross domestic investment as a fraction of GDP – the 'investment ratio', I/Y (I and Y measured in US Dollars, as reported in World Bank World Tables[4]), or as a fraction of total population – '*per capita* investment', *IPC*. Note that the investment ratio is an average of I/Y for each year, rather than the ratio of total gross investment for the period to total income, though substituting the latter for the former does not significantly alter the results. We consider both I/Y and *IPC* below; the two measures turn out to produce comparable results.

The following variables appear on the RHS of the equations:

(i) *The ratio of the Dollar value of exports to GNP* (X/Y)   A higher X/Y will mean more foreign exchange, and so more funds available for the importation of capital goods. (Here, there is an implicit acknowledgement of the existence of foreign exchange rationing, although this is never made explicit in existing studies: if a country's currency is fully convertible, then the share of forex-earning activities in total production will not affect the ability of firms to buy capital goods.) X/Y is calculated as an average for the period 1970–87.

(ii) *The Dollar value of total debt as a fraction of GNP* (D/Y)   This variable too indicates the availability of funds for investment, this time in the form of foreign lending. The higher the level of foreign lending, the more funds are available for investment. (This assumes that a constant fraction of foreign lending is being allocated to investment activities.) Note that total debt is a stock of credit, not a flow, so it is inappropriate to calculate an average D/Y for the sample period. Since debt in 1970 is negligible for all countries, D in 1987 represents the sum of past flows. Dividing D by 18 would therefore produce a figure for average annual flow. However, scaling of D by an arbitrary constant does not affect the statistical model, so D in 1987 is used as the explanatory variable, divided by average Y for the period.

(iii) *Dollar* per capita *GNP* (GNPPC)   If higher output levels are correlated with higher investment (this relationship depends on the value of the ICOR), then the appropriate dependant variable is *IPC*. If higher income *per capita* entails a higher I/Y, as a wealthier community allocates more of present income to investment, then the appropriate dependant variable is I/Y.

(iv) *The ratio of extractive industries output to agricultural output* (M/A)   In countries where this is high, with a heavy reliance on the extractive sector, investment may be higher just because their natural resources favour activities that are very capital-intensive. This is true independently of the size of the manufacturing sector, which may be endogenous. The ratio is calculated as the constant price value of extractive industries output as a fraction of the constant price value of agricultural output, in order to produce an index of relative quantities.

(v) *The variability of returns to investment*   This variable is analogous to the one used in the time-series equations in the previous chapter. The interpretation is the same: in countries where variability is higher, the prices which trigger entry into investment activities will be higher, and actual investment correspondingly lower, because of the hysteresis effects already discussed. The calculation of the variable is also analogous. For each year of the sample period, a 'foreign capital price' eP_I^* is constructed for each African country outside the CFA. This is a weighted average of the gross domestic investment deflator in each of the country's trading partners, measured in domestic currency. The weights are based on each partner's share in the country's non-primary imports, this being a proxy for its share in export of physical or financial capital to the country. The weights are calculated from the UN Yearbook of International Trade Statistics (1988). The domestic investment deflator, P_I, is divided by eP_I^*, and expressed as an index with $1980 = 1$. The measure of variability, VAR, is the average of $|\Delta P_I / eP_I^*|$ between 1971 and 1987. The weights are listed in Table 8.1. For the CFA the weight given to France is 100 per cent, reflecting the dominance of France in the CFA financial system. Note again that P_I represents the marginal return to investment – *qua* the marginal Tobin's Q – under certain conditions (see Chapter 7). These conditions may or may not be fulfilled. Even if the conditions are not fulfilled, P_I represents a major component of investment profitability, and so ought to be important in investment determination.

This model does not have the elaborate structure of the time-series models of earlier chapters, simply explaining differences in investment between countries by a number of general economic indicators for which data are readily available for a wide selection of Sub-Saharan African economies. It would be extremely rash to

Table 8.1 Trade weights used to calculate P_1^*

Country	B	D	E	F	I	J	NL	P	SA	SW	US	UK
Botswana									1.00			
Burundi	0.41	0.21		0.23		0.16						
Ghana		0.22									0.28	0.50
Guinea-Bis.			0.19			0.13	0.54		0.14			
Kenya		0.20				0.23					0.16	0.42
Liberia												
Madagascar		0.20		0.80								
Malawi		0.07				0.10			0.55			0.28
Mauritania			0.16	0.84								
Mauritius				0.30					0.38			0.32
Nigeria		0.21		0.13		0.21					0.17	0.29
Sierra Leone		0.35									0.26	0.39
Somalia				0.13	0.59						0.16	0.13
Sudan		0.31			0.16						0.17	0.36
Tanzania		0.30				0.30						0.40
Zaire	0.58	0.19									0.23	
Zambia		0.11							0.31		0.14	0.44
Zimbabwe		0.12				0.10			0.49		0.12	0.17

Key: *B* = Belgium, *D* = Germany, *E* = Spain, *F* = France, *I* = Italy, *J* = Japan, *NL* = Netherlands, *P* = Portugal, *SA* = South Africa, *SW* = Sweden, *US* = United States, *UK* = United Kingdom.

interpret the coefficients as investment elasticities (in, for example, using the parameters estimated to calculate hypothetical levels of investment for a country for different hypothetical values of the explanatory variables). However, between them, these variables are able to explain most of the variation in investment from country to country.

There is no obvious functional form for this type of estimation. In order to see whether non-linearity makes a difference, and whether a logarithmic model is more appropriate than a model in simple levels, the following approach is used. The model is estimated in four basic forms, using either I/Y or *IPC*, and either a quadratic or a log-quadratic equation.

We might reasonably be worried about the exogeneity of two of the explanatory variables, *GNPPC* and D/Y, which may depend on the level of investment rather than vice versa. However, in all countries privately funded debt actually makes up a small proportion of total debt. Most lending is from governments and multinational agencies, such as the World Bank and the IMF. It is reasonable to suppose that such international borrowing is supply-constrained: at the interest rates at which the lending takes place, debtor governments would like to engage in more net borrowing (if this were not so, the multinational agencies would not be able to impose extra conditions on the governments, for instance, structural adjustment programmes). The CFA Operations Accounts are an exception, but they are coming to make up an increasingly small fraction of total CFA debt, and eleven CFA members are now engaged in structural adjustment programmes. The magnitude of borrowing depends on the IMF's supply curve. The maintained hypothesis is that this supply curve is independent of the other explanatory variables.

There is no obvious solution to the problem of endogeneity of *GNPPC*: it is difficult for example to find instruments adequate for estimating *GNPPC* across countries. However, since *GNPPC* is sometimes an important explanatory variable, it is included in the equations below; it is recognised that ensuring the independence of the *GNPPC* term would be an improvement on the models below. The relative price variability term is also treated as independent. As we will see later, relative price variability does depend on a number of government policy choices, but it is unlikely to be affected by the other variables in the equations here.

Tables 8.2–8.5 present the results of the estimation, with the unrestricted general form of each equation, and a final model from which insignificant variables have been omitted so as to minimise the Schwartz Criterion. In certain cases, dummy variables are included for Niger and Sudan, since these countries tend to represent outliers that make the error terms non-spherical.

Using *IPC* produces a better fit than using *I/Y*, although most of the variability in *I/Y* across countries can also be explained. The two variables which are of universal importance in the models are *D/Y* and *VAR*. Again, there is support for the hypothesis that variability in the returns to investment reduce levels of investment, with significant negative coefficients on *VAR* in all models: countries with a higher *VAR* tend to have lower investment rates. *GNPPC* and *M/A* account for much of the variation in *per capita* investment between countries; the ratio of exports to GDP is more important in explaining the cross-country variation in the investment ratio. Note that this type of cross-country model does not produce parameters which are country-specific, and it is not appropriate for the calculation of investment elasticities: the parameters of the model should not be used to predict what investment in Mali would have been, had Malian *M/A* for the

Table 8.2 Cross-country equation 1: I/Y

Variable	Model (1)		Model (2)	
	Coefficient	HCSE	Coefficient	HCSE
Constant	0.896	0.271	0.924	0.095[a]
X/Y	−0.134	0.199		
$(X/Y)^2$	0.131	0.063	0.102	0.027[a]
D/Y	0.117	0.207		
$(D/Y)^2$	0.052	0.060	0.090	0.029[a]
VAR	−0.103	0.475	−0.189	0.066[a]
VAR^2	−0.032	0.192		
M/A	0.011	0.066		
$(M/A)^2$	0.002	0.009		
R^2		0.794		0.777
σ		0.174		0.162
$X^2(2)$ normality		1.56		1.89
SC		−2.824		−3.323

a Significant at 1%.
HCSE Heteroskedasticity-consistent standard error.
SC Schwartz Criterion.
Variables (*but not their squares*) are defined so that the sample mean = 1.

Table 8.3 Cross-country equation 2: $\ln(I/Y)$

Variable	Model (1)		Model (2)	
	Coefficient	HCSE	Coefficient	HCSE
Constant	− 0.039	0.084	− 0.059	0.058
$\ln(X/Y)$	0.227	0.088	0.271	0.084[b]
$\ln(X/Y)^2$	0.193	0.087	0.214	0.124[a]
$\ln(D/Y)$	0.327	0.074	0.230	0.085[b]
$\ln(D/Y)^2$	0.116	0.055		
VAR	− 0.246	0.093	− 0.161	0.087[a]
VAR^2	− 0.217	0.193		
$\ln(M/A)$	0.067	0.239		
$\ln(M/A)^2$	− 0.039	0.085		
R^2		0.715		0.650
σ		0.205		0.207
$X^2(2)$ normality		1.54		1.23
SC		− 2.497		− 2.755

a Significant at 5%.
b Significant at 1%.

Table 8.4 Cross-country equation 3: IPC

Variable	Model (1)		Model (2)		Model (3)	
	Coeff.	*HCSE*	*Coeff.*	*HCSE*	*Coeff.*	*HCSE*
Constant	−0.138	0.415	−0.025	0.400	0.339	0.918
D/Y	0.441	0.286	0.422	0.292	0.216	0.058[a]
$(D/Y)^2$	−0.093	0.094	−0.074	0.093		
$\$GNPPC$	0.432	0.421	0.373	0.392		
$(\$GNPPC)^2$	0.201	0.148	0.229	0.138	0.357	0.023[a]
M/A	0.096	0.146	0.113	0.099	0.202	0.035[a]
M/A^2	0.018	0.021	0.014	0.020		
VAR	0.118	0.611	−0.081	0.522	−0.259	0.076[a]
VAR^2	−0.116	0.203	−0.061	0.203		
Nigerdum			0.708	0.073	0.743	0.074[a]
R^2	0.930		0.951		0.946	
σ	0.269		0.230		0.219	
$X^2(2)$ normality	4.16		3.20		2.14	
SC	−1.955		−2.200		−2.575	

a Significant at 1%.
Note: the error corresponding to the observation for Niger is an outlier, and if left untreated generates excess kurtosis in the error term in models 2–3 (the null of a normally distributed error term being rejected at 15% and 1% respectively), hence the inclusion of a dummy variable (Nigerdum) for this observation. Investment in Niger is inexplicably high.

Table 8.5 Cross-country equation 4: $\ln(IPC)$

Variable	Model (1)		Model (2)		Model (3)	
	Coeff.	*HCSE*	*Coeff.*	*HCSE*	*Coeff.*	*HCSE*
Constant	−0.103	0.178	−0.049	0.081	−0.009	0.076
$\ln(D/Y)$	0.315	0.128	0.418	0.073	0.461	0.079[b]
$\ln(D/Y)^2$	0.072	0.103	0.140	0.054	0.162	0.074[a]
$\ln(\$GNPPC)$	1.033	0.086	1.017	0.094	1.119	0.075[b]
$\ln(\$GPC)^2$	0.070	0.218	0.003	0.168		
$\ln(M/A)$	0.057	0.478	0.056	0.284		
$\ln(M/A)^2$	0.098	0.262	0.084	0.141		
VAR	−0.452	0.144	−0.621	0.086	−0.649	0.084[b]
VAR^2	−0.474	0.270	−0.695	0.181	−0.644	0.188[b]
Nigerdum			1.102	0.064	1.107	0.967
Sudandum			−0.710	0.083	−0.743	0.074[b]
R^2	0.877		0.964		0.955	
σ	0.328		0.187		0.197	
$X^2(2)$ normality	15.30[b]		0.79		0.26	
SC	−1.554		−2.552		−2.644	

a Significant at 5%.
b Significant at 1%.
Note: again, the observation for Niger produces an outlier; so too does the observation for Sudan, hence the inclusion of a dummy variable for that country (Sudandum). Investment in Sudan is inexplicably low.

Table 8.6 Summary statistics #1

Country	VAR	D/Y	PD/Y
Bénin[a]	0.235	1.364	0.476
Burkina Faso[a]	0.057	0.936	0.040
Cameroon[a]	0.069	0.607	0.109
Centrafrique[a]	0.108	0.818	0.054
Chad[a]	0.066	0.035	0.286
Congo Rep.[a]	0.041	2.698	1.718
Côte d'Ivoire[a]	0.072	1.283	0.647
Mali[a]	0.037	1.827	0.053
Niger[a]	0.197	0.862	0.150
Sénégal[a]	0.047	1.299	0.161
Togo[a]	0.069	1.479	0.144
Botswana	0.056	1.186	0.086
Burundi	0.209	1.137	0.046
Congo D.R.	0.192	0.822	0.119
Ghana	0.238	0.365	0.045
Guinea-Bissau	0.225	2.806	0.651
Kenya	0.042	0.953	0.139
Liberia	0.119	1.325	0.212
Madagascar	0.074	1.353	0.176
Malawi	0.056	1.396	0.120
Mauritius	0.101	0.668	0.118
Mauritania	0.208	3.802	0.276
Nigeria	0.083	0.305	0.230
Sierra Leone	0.176	0.688	0.123
Somalia	0.180	3.348	0.260
Sudan	0.103	1.261	0.187
Tanzania	0.112	0.929	0.161
Zambia	0.083	1.487	0.269
Zimbabwe	0.096	0.570	0.267

a Indicates membership of the CFA during the sample period.

sample period been 10 per cent higher. However, the model does indicate some of the factors that are important in explaining why investment is different in different countries.

Tables 8.6 and 8.7 show the values of explanatory variables used in the estimation of *I/Y* and *IPC*: *X/Y*, *GNPPC*, *D/Y* and *VAR*. Also included is *PD/Y*, measuring that part of *D/Y* which comes from private creditors (i.e. loans other than those from multilateral aid agencies and individual governments). They show that neither *per capita* income nor the ratio of primary commodity exports to GDP in the CFA is significantly different from the average for the rest of Sub-Saharan Africa. Given the wide disparity in natural resources in both groups of country, this is not surprising. Nor is the average value of the residual

Table 8.7 Summary statistics #2

Country	X/Y	$YPC
Bénin[a]	0.246	224
Burkina Faso[a]	0.147	139
Cameroon[a]	0.283	565
Centrafrique[a]	0.258	233
Chad[a]	0.186	138
Congo Rep.[a]	0.487	721
Côte d'Ivoire[a]	0.440	657
Mali[a]	0.158	155
Niger[a]	0.191	264
Sénégal[a]	0.351	361
Togo[a]	0.396	265
Botswana	0.898	608
Burundi	0.116	166
Congo D.R.	0.239	272
Ghana	0.223	331
Guinea-Bissau	0.080	176
Kenya	0.291	284
Liberia	0.532	458
Madagascar	0.183	237
Malawi	0.276	139
Mauritius	0.516	908
Mauritania	0.469	348
Nigeria	0.200	647
Sierra Leone	0.219	261
Somalia	0.196	141
Sudan	0.120	324
Tanzania	0.161	209
Zambia	0.420	484
Zimbabwe	0.286	586

a Indicates membership of the CFA during the sample period.

for CFA members in each estimated equation significantly different from zero (the mean is less than 0.2 times the standard deviation), so there is no evidence for a hidden 'X' factor favourable to CFA members. There must then be another explanation for the higher investment in the CFA.

The tables show that privately financed credit (as a fraction of GNP) is higher on average in the CFA than in the rest of Africa.[5] However, this difference depends on a very high ratio in just three countries: Bénin, Congo Republic and Côte d'Ivoire. Elsewhere in the CFA, the ratios are not significantly different from the average for the rest of Africa. Moreover, there is no significant difference between the ratios of total debt to GNP in the two groups: in fact, the ratio for the rest of

Africa is very slightly higher. Total credit is dominated by credit from public sources, and these sources do not favour the CFA.

The one variable for which a difference does appear is *VAR*, as Table 8.6 shows. The average value of *VAR* for the CFA is 0.091; for the rest of Africa it is 0.131.[6] The only CFA countries with a value of *VAR* higher than the average for the rest of Africa are Bénin and Niger. The others enjoy returns to investment which are markedly more stable than is typical for Africa, even in the economies of the Sahel, where investment is very low because of the scarcity of natural resources (which shows up in the regressions as low *X/Y* and low *GNPPC*): Burkina Faso, Mali, Sénégal and Chad. Here there is a definite benefit from CFA membership. An explanation for the higher rates of investment in the CFA must include an account of what it is that generates this stability.

8.2. The determinants of *VAR*

As a first step in investigating the relationship between CFA membership and the variability of returns to investment relative to the returns to investment in the West, it is useful to look at the components of the measure of variability. In particular, it is important to elaborate the role of the nominal exchange rate, *e*. Table 8.8 shows the value of three

Table 8.8 Exchange rate statistics (1970–87)

Country	$\mu[\,|\Delta e\,|\,]$	$Corr[e, P_I/P_I^*]$	$Corr[|\Delta e|, e - P_I/P_I^*|]$
Botswana	0.021	0.729	0.139
Burundi	0.082	0.253	0.458
Congo D.R.	2.032	0.983	0.975
Ghana	2.740	0.987	0.922
Guinea-B.	0.457	0.872	0.887
Kenya	0.080	0.966	0.448
Madagascar	0.172	0.835	0.930
Mauritius	0.040	0.773	−0.285
Mauritania	0.066	0.019	−0.344
Nigeria	0.365	0.960	0.992
Sierra Leone	1.519	0.991	0.997
Somalia	0.266	0.996	0.167
Sudan	0.296	0.996	0.447
Tanzania	0.416	0.974	0.937
Zambia	0.367	0.962	0.988
Zimbabwe	0.056	0.852	−0.042

variables for the non-CFA countries included in the model above: a measure of the variability of the nominal exchange rate – the mean of the absolute value of the first difference of e, $\mu_{|\Delta e|}$, the coefficient of correlation for e and P_I/P_I^*, and the correlation coefficient for $|\Delta e|$ and $|e - P_I/P_I^*|$.[7]

The correlation coefficient for e and P_I/P_I^* is between 0.85 and 1.00 for most of the countries in the table. This is because the money supply is expanding very rapidly in most countries, so there is high domestic inflation, including inflation of P_I, and upward pressure on e, to which e responds, at least to an order of magnitude. There are two exceptions, countries with no significant correlation between e and P_I/P_I^*: Burundi and Mauritania. Note that these are two of the countries with a value of *VAR* greater than 0.2: in these countries, neither the nominal exchange rate nor P_I respond to a rise in P_I^*, so P_I/eP_I^* can stray a long way from parity. In the case of e, this is to be expected, because the nominal exchange rate is being driven by other relative prices (e.g., of consumer goods), and is subject to government intervention. In the case of P_I, it may be the result of some imperfection in the capital goods market. The possible nature of such imperfections will be discussed below.

$|e - P_I/P_I^*|$ is included in order to discriminate between the other countries. It is a measure of exchange rate misalignment, assuming that there is no misalignment in 1980.[8] One hypothesis is that misalignment will be greater when e and P_I/P_I^* are moving more quickly, i.e. when $|\Delta e|$ is higher.[9] P_I may always adjust so that it is approximately equal to eP_I^*, but when both are moving rapidly, e.g., when P_I^* jumps in response to an oil price shock to world markets, or when e jumps in response to an external trade shock, P_I may exhibit some inertia, having difficulty 'catching up': so the magnitude of price changes is correlated with the degree of exchange rate misalignment. This hypothesis is confirmed for a number of countries: Ghana, Guinea-Bissau, Madagascar, Nigeria, Sierra Leone, Tanzania, Congo Democratic Republic and Zambia. Not surprisingly, it is these same countries which exhibit the highest $|\Delta e|$: in other countries, where movements in e and P_I/P_I^* are generally small, the relative inertia effect is not significant and so there is no significant correlation between the present speed of price changes and exchange rate misalignment.

Note that the very high correlation coefficients for $|\Delta e|$ and $|e - P_I/P_I^*|$ in Table 8.8 are partially due to the large rises in e

174   *CFA membership and price stability*

Table 8.9 Exchange rate statistics (1970–86)

Country	$\mu[\,|\Delta e\,|\,]$	$Corr[|\Delta e|, |e - P_I/P_I^*|]$
Botswana	0.045	0.387
Burundi	0.162	0.155
Congo D.R.	0.984	0.892
Ghana	3.426	0.945
Guinea-B.	0.471	0.822
Kenya	0.069	0.109
Madagascar	0.075	0.128
Malawi	0.038	0.652
Mauritius	0.039	− 0.339
Mauritania	0.060	− 0.345
Nigeria	0.135	0.946
Sierra Leone	0.219	0.504
Somalia	0.197	0.172
Sudan	0.183	0.179
Tanzania	0.183	0.562
Zambia	0.282	0.991
Zimbabwe	0.051	0.006

Liberia's exchange rate is pegged against the US$.

(and in exchange rate misalignment) experienced in 1987. However, similar results are obtained using 1970–86 as the sample period, as Table 8.9 illustrates.

So, one or two countries (Burundi, Mauritania) have a high *VAR* because the law of one price has completely broken down, at least where capital goods prices are concerned. Of the other countries with high *VAR* (i.e. greater than 0.15: Ghana, Guinea-Bissau, Somalia, Sierra Leone and Congo Democratic Republic), all but Somalia seem to suffer misalignment because prices and exchange rates are moving very rapidly: in periods of rapid adjustment, e diverges from P_I/P_I^*. Nominal exchange rate variability seems to be linked to relative price variability. One explanation for this is that when e is subject to a large shock, inertia in P_I prevents immediate adjustment of P_I/eP_I^* to unity. It is important to note also that countries in which Δe is high are also ones in which the rate of domestic consumer price inflation is high. In countries where the general rate of price increase is high, there tends also to be a greater degree of relative price misalignment, as some prices exhibit more inertia than others. However, inertia is not the whole story: some countries have a high correlation between $|\Delta e|$ and $|e - P_I/P_I^*|$ but, for Africa outside the CFA, low *VAR* (Madagascar, Nigeria, Tanzania, Zambia), while one

(Somalia) has a low correlation coefficient but high *VAR*. We need to find some other explanation for high variability of P_I/eP_I^*.

One point which we have neglected so far is that the law of one price does not necessarily entail that $P_I = eP_I^*$. If there are import tariffs or quotas, then P_I and eP_I^* will diverge, and it will be the case that $P_I = (1 + \tau)eP_I^*$, where τ is the tariff on imported capital goods or the implicit tariff equivalent of a quota. It may be that the lower variability of P_I/P_I^* in the CFA is as much to do with lower barriers to trade as with lower nominal exchange rate variability. High tariff levels are likely to be associated with high tariff variability, especially when the tariff is one implicit in an import quota: for a given quota, any fluctuation in supply or demand for the commodity will alter the tariff rate to which the quota is equivalent. In general, a more restrictive quota – one with a higher tariff equivalent – will produce more absolute tariff-equivalent variability for a given variance in supply and demand.[10]

No work has been done specifically on the openness of capital goods markets in the CFA. However, Geourjon (1988) presents a study of the magnitude of overall protection in Sub-Saharan Africa, using as indicators of this magnitude the following variables:

(i) Total customs receipts (*TCR*) as a fraction of total government receipts (*TRG*);
(ii) *TCR* plus fiscal receipts on imports (*FRI*) as a fraction of *TRG*;
(iii) *TCR* as a fraction of the total value of imports (*TVI*);
(iv) *TCR* plus *FRI* as a fraction of *TVI*.

There is no significant difference between the CFA and the rest of Sub-Saharan Africa with respect to these four measures over the period 1979–81. However, it is still possible that overall CFA trade restrictions are less Draconian than anglophone African restrictions, because most anglophone African governments use quotas rather than tariffs (Bevan et al., 1990a). Implicit rents on quotas are not included in any of Geourjon's four measures, but are probably much larger than tariff revenues. Moreover, the CFA does exhibit a significantly higher degree of import penetration (as measured by the ratio of non-fuel imports to total domestic supply) than the rest of Africa. Since most imports are industrial products, we should expect a smaller wedge between p and ep^* in the CFA, where p is the domestic price of industrial output and p^* its international price.

Table 8.10 Import taxes on intermediate and capital goods

Franc Zone		Others in Africa	
Burkina Faso	5% + fiscal taxes	Botswana	0–25%
Centrafrique	2.5–20%	Burundi	15–25%
Congo Rep.	2.5–20%	Congo D.R.	0–50%
Côte d'Ivoire	7–10%	Eq. Guinea[a]	9–48%
Gabon	2.5–20%	Ethiopia	0–60%
Mali[a]	5% + fiscal taxes	Gambia	0–30%
Niger	5% + fiscal taxes	Ghana	35%
Sénégal	40%	Guinea	3%
Chad	3.5–11%	Guinea-Bissau	0–25%
Togo	5–10%	Lesotho	0–25%
		Kenya	0–50%
		Liberia	0–45%
		Madagascar	0–15%
		Malawi	0–35%
		Mauritania	5–87%
		Mauritius	0–50%
		Mocambique	0–32%
		Nigeria	5–75%
		Rwanda	0–15%
		Seychelles	10–30%
		Sierra Leone	0–45%
		Somalia	0–10%
		Sudan	10–80%
		Swaziland	0–25%
		Tanzania	0–55%
		Uganda	0–30%
		Zambia	0–30%
		Zimbabwe	0–22.5%

a   Denotes membership of the CFA for part of the sample period.

No results are quoted for imports specifically of capital goods. However, UNCTAD data on tax bands for capital goods imports suggest a lower degree of protection, at least by means of tariffs, in the CFA. Table 8.10 lists the recorded tax bands as of 1987: single figure percentage tariffs are typical of CFA members. The only exception is Sénégal, with a rate of around 40 per cent for most capital goods. Outside the CFA, rates are more variable, and can rise beyond 75 per cent.

A second possibility is that high variability of P_I/eP_I^* is due to movements in the prices of non-traded capital goods (e.g., prices in the construction industry). There is no reason why the law of one price should apply to these goods, and the aggregate domestic price of non-traded capital goods (and therefore the cost of investing in the domestic economy) could be very different from that in other countries. One hypothesis is that non-traded capital goods prices are more variable outside the CFA than inside.

Why might this be the case? One explanation is that CFA members have better access to international financial markets, so that net domestic saving and borrowing in response to temporary rises and falls in domestic income is relatively easy. In response to a positive income shock, domestic residents increase their holdings of net foreign assets in aggregate; in response to a negative shock, they reduce their foreign asset holdings. Outside the CFA, with only limited access to international financial markets, changes in the ratio of consumption to income in response to a temporary shock can be accomplished only by changes in the investment ratio. For example, domestic investment will rise and fall in response to a positive income shock, and to the extent to which the investment is in non-traded capital, the price of non-traded capital goods will rise and fall. Capital goods price variability is a sign of limited access to international financial markets. Moreover, it will over the long run in itself reduce investment, since the returns to investment are more uncertain.[11]

We have seen in previous chapters that the distinction between CFA members and others in Africa with respect to financial market integration is not at all clear-cut. However, one might argue that even with an equal degree of integration, a non-CFA economy is likely to experience more variable investment and capital goods prices than a CFA economy. In the former, booms may be accompanied by expectations of exchange rate appreciation (or, more realistically, expectations of less future devaluation), and slumps by expectations of depreciation/devaluation. To the extent that capital markets are integrated, a higher (lower) future expected Δe will mean a lower (higher) domestic interest rate, via covered interest parity, and so more (less) investment, and higher (lower) non-traded capital goods prices.

Data on non-traded capital goods prices in Africa are limited. However, one comparison that it is possible to make is between the responses of Nigeria and Cameroon to their respective positive oil shocks. Figures 8.1 and 8.2 show capital goods price series for the two countries. The prices of traded and non-traded capital goods in Cameroon are taken from Devarajan (1991) – the major component of the non-traded capital is construction, and the major component of traded capital is equipment. The prices for Nigeria are taken from the

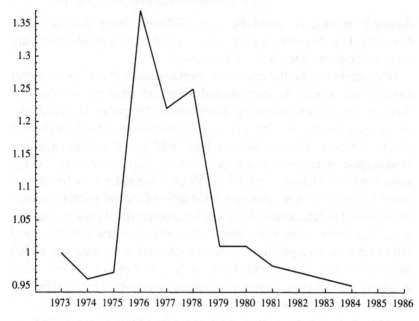

Figure 8.1 Nontradable–tradable capital goods price ratio for Nigeria, 1973 – 1.

Figure 8.2 Nontradable–tradable capital goods price ratio for Cameroon, 1978 – 1.

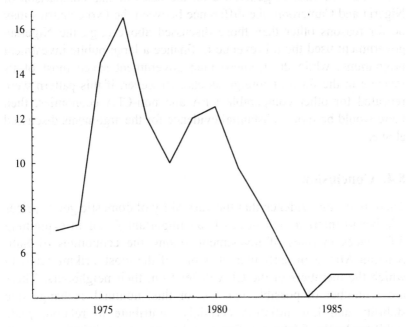

Figure 8.3 Gross national investment in Nigeria in billions of 1980 Naira.

Nigerian Digest of Statistics (various editions), which gives current and constant price investment series that are disaggregated into equipment and construction.

The Nigerian oil shock began in 1973–4. The figure shows a subsequent sharp rise in the price of non-traded capital relative to traded capital, and a sharp rise in P_I relative to eP_I^*, with the peak of both series in 1976. After 1978, both series are relatively stable. This is consistent with an investment boom following the first oil price shock (see Figure 8.3). The absence of a second peak after the second oil price shock reflects the fact that the increase in investment the second time round was much smaller.

In Cameroon, the oil price shock began with the oil discovery in the late 1970s, and the start of oil exports in 1978. Figure 8.2 shows that this boom did not have a noticeable determinate effect on relative capital goods prices. In fact, from 1978 to 1983, there is a spurious negative correlation between P_N/P_T and P_I/eP_I^*, since ΔP_N and ΔeP_I^* are relatively stable, while ΔP_T (and therefore ΔP_I) is more variable. The oil price shock here seems not to have generated the price instability it did in Nigeria.

It would be rash to generalise on the basis of this comparison of Nigeria and Cameroon: the difference between the two countries may be for reasons other than those discussed above (e.g., the Nigerian government used the oil revenue to finance a large public investment programme, while the Cameroonian government saved most of its revenue in the form of foreign assets). However, if this pattern were repeated for other comparable CFA and non-CFA economies, then there would be more substantial evidence for the arguments discussed above.

8.4. Conclusion

There is strong evidence that the variability of domestic goods prices relative to international prices is an important factor in explaining differences in rates of investment among the economies of Sub-Saharan Africa. In particular, it is one of the most striking ways in which the members of the CFA differ from their neighbours. There are a number of possible reasons for this: nominal exchange rate stability and low inflation certainly contribute to relative price stability. In the CFA, e is fixed, and there is low inflation, but P_I relative to other prices is flexible and, since CFA capital goods markets are relatively open, P_I adjusts so that P_I/eP_I^* is approximately unity. A flexible e would not improve on this mechanism, and might even make things worse by introducing another variable susceptible to short-run shocks.

Outside the CFA, capital goods markets are often insulated from the rest of the world by trade restrictions: P_I is determined by government fiscal policy and by conditions in the domestic market. A high proportion of non-traded capital goods in investment will amplify this effect. Insofar as these conditions are variable, there will be variability in P_I. So the continued equality of P_I and eP_I^* depends on compensating movements in e; but e is determined by other prices as well as P_I, and is subject to the influence of government intervention when the market exchange rate is seen as unacceptable. Moreover, with a flexible exchange rate, non-CFA governments are prone to rapid expansion of the money supply, which induces high inflation of all prices, and currency depreciation. So even if there is a degree of integration between domestic and international capital goods markets, and P_I tends to eP_I^* (or at least to a constant fraction of eP_I^*) then when all prices are changing rapidly, any difference between inertia in domestic prices and inertia in the exchange rate will lead to a gap between P_I and eP_I^* in the short run.

There is more work to be done in this area: it would be useful to quantify the impact of different variables – the nominal exchange rate, the rate of inflation, the magnitude of trade restrictions and the non-tradability of certain capital goods – on the variability of relative prices. However, this would require more data than is at present available on government trade policy and on disaggregated investment behaviour. Nevertheless, there is evidence that all these factors play a role.

Notes

1 That is, the price of foreign exchange in terms of the home currency. Outside the CFA, e is typically either floating, or subject to discretionary changes by the government.

2 All Sub-Saharan African countries for which data for the sample period exist are included in the model. These are, in the CFA: Bénin, Burkina Faso, Cameroon, Congo Republic, Centrafrique, Côte d'Ivoire, Mali, Niger, Sénégal, Chad and Togo; outside the CFA: Botswana, Burundi, Ghana, Kenya, Liberia, Madagascar, Malawi, Mauritania, Mauritius, Nigeria, Sierra Leone, Somalia, Sudan, Tanzania, Congo Democratic Republic, Zambia and Zimbabwe. Guinea-Bissau is also included; for the period covered by our data set, Guinea-Bissau was not part of the CFA.

3 See e.g. Guillaumont (1988).

4 The dollar value of a variable is taken to be its current domestic currency value converted at the official exchange rate. This will misrepresent the true value of the variable to the extent to which there is forex rationing. However, parallel exchange rates are not available in all countries in all years, so the official rate is used in all cases.

5 One possible explanation for this is that privately funded credit is influenced by VAR.

6 Both groups of countries have a standard deviation of $VAR = 0.065$, which yields a t ratio for a test of the significance of the difference between the two means of $t_{27} = 1.608$, which is significant at 15 per cent.

7 Both e and P_I/P_I^* are defined so that they are equal to unity in 1980.

8 $|e - P_I/P_I^*|$ measures exchange rate misalignment on the assumption that there was no misalignment in 1980. In fact, it matters little what base year between 1970 and 1980 is used: in all cases, $|e - P_I/P_I^*|$ turns out to be very small in the 1970s and much larger in the 1980s. The important assumption we are making is that there was negligible misalignment from 1970 to 1980, and increasing misalignment after that. The consensus of economic opinion is that this was the case – as demonstrated by the rapidly expanding gap between official and black market exchange rates for African countries in the last few years.

9 Since e and P_I/P_I^* are so highly correlated, using $|\Delta P_I/P_I^*|$ instead of $|\Delta e|$ in the correlation coefficient produces very similar results. Both indicate the speed with which prices are moving.

182   CFA membership and price stability

10 See Södersten and Reed (1994), pp 204ff.
11 See Bevan et al. (1990b) for a detailed account of the possible investment responses to a temporary trade shock.

References

Bevan, D., Collier, P. and Gunning, J. (1990a) *Controlled Open Economies*, Oxford: OUP.

Bevan, D., Collier, P. and Gunning, J. (1990b) 'The Macroeconomics of external shocks', in Balasubramanyan, V. and Lall, S. (eds), *Current Issues in Development Economics*, London: Macmillan.

Devarajan, S. (1991) 'Cameroon's oil boom of 1978–86', Seminar paper, Centre for the Study of African Economies.

Geourjon, A.-M. (1988) 'La protection commerciale', in Guillaumont, P. and Guillaumont, S. (eds), *Stratégies de Développement Conparées*, Paris: Economica.

Guillaumont, S. (1988) 'Taux d'investissement et productivité d'investissement', in Guillaumont, P. and Guillaumont, S. (eds), *Stratégies de Développement Conparées*, Paris: Economica.

9 Conclusion and suggestions for future policy

In Chapter 1 we considered three possible routes through which CFA membership might influence economic performance: (1) the impact of the fixed exchange rate on inflation; (2) the impact of the regulatory system on monetary policy and the monetary transmission mechanism; (3) the impact of currency convertibility, transferability and exchange harmonisation on investment and growth. We are now in a position to evaluate the strength of the arguments in favour of the importance of these routes.

9.1. The impact of the fixed exchange rate on inflation

We saw in Chapter 2 that across the developing world exchange rate pegs have been associated with lower average inflation, *ceteris paribus*. Countries that manage to adhere to a unilateral fixed peg can expect lower monetary growth delivering an average inflation rate over ten percentage points lower than under a crawling peg or float. A persuasive interpretation of this effect is that pegging the exchange rate solves (or partly solves) the monetary authorities' problem of how to commit credibly to low inflation, and to solve the time-inconsistency problem in monetary policy. However, membership of the CFA confers an extra advantage over and above that of a unilateral peg, with average monetary growth that is a further five percentage points lower. This difference corresponds to the unique degree of infrequency of devaluation of the CFA currencies: there has been only a single devaluation in the last fifty years.

There are two plausible reasons for this additional effect. First, it is much more difficult for CFA countries to re-peg their exchange rate – this requires the coordination of all the members of the monetary union – so both actual and anticipated re-peggings are much less frequent. Although speculation about forthcoming devaluation is not unknown in the CFA, it is very much less common than in most of the rest of the developing world. Secondly, a country that pegs unilaterally to the currency of an industrialised country will suffer when the industrialised country's business cycle diverges from that of the developing country. Political pressure on the peg will be particularly acute when the currency fails to depreciate when there is an adverse supply shock in the developing country, leading to persistent unemployment. This kind of pressure has been a feature of Latin American currency boards, for example (Fielding and Mizen, 2001). The fact that the CFA currencies have been pegged to the French Franc, and that they are now pegged to the Euro, does not entail such costs for CFA countries. The French Treasury guarantees the convertibility of the CFA Franc at a fixed rate, and provides overdraft facilities to the CFA central banks so that they have the ability to pursue a short-run stabilisation policy that diverges from that of France.

This is not to say that the stability of the CFA monetary system is never threatened: such instability was marked in the period leading up to the 1994 devaluation. But the strains on the system arise not from ties to the French economy, but from internal inconsistencies among the CFA members themselves that arise from failures in the regulatory system.

9.2. The impact of the regulatory system on monetary policy and the monetary transmission mechanism

The key mechanism by which the credibility of the CFA–French Franc peg is maintained is the Operations Account (described in Chapter 1). This account is in effect an overdraft facility for the Zone as a whole, allowing the two central banks of the continental African CFA the opportunity to pursue a short-run monetary policy that is independent of that of France. It also gives the central banks the ability to insulate monetary growth shocks to public debt. The ability to borrow from France in this way does not undermine the credibility of a low-inflation policy, since the implicit (if not explicit) rules of operation of the system prevent a build-up of debt over the medium term.

However, there are two main failings in the operation of this system. First (Chapter 3), central bank policy appears not to have fully insulated the money supply from shocks to public debt. This is true of, for example, borrowing by the Ivorian government from the BCEAO. The variability in the rate of growth of money appears to have been caused by inconsistencies between the average rate of growth of money and the average rate of growth of debt, which necessitate periodic accommodating shifts in the money base. These inconsistencies are not necessary: if the rate of growth of money could be maintained at the same rate as that of the growth of public debt, then the Operations Account facility could be used to insulate short-term shocks to debt. In fact, *some* anglophone central banks (for example, the Central Bank of Kenya) appear to have performed better in this regard, insulating the money supply from short-term borrowing shocks more efficiently than the BCEAO, and without recourse to a facility like the Operations Account. (The Kenyan central bank uses adjustments in its stock of foreign assets to accommodate most of the borrowing shocks.) Here, it seems to be the case that the monetary authorities of the CFA do not make optimal use of the institutional arrangements.

Second (Chapter 4), the fiscal and monetary prudence instilled by adherence to the CFA – which results in the low inflation recorded in Chapter 2 – applies only at the aggregate level: it is not true of each individual country. The regulations that are designed to constrain the borrowing of individual government from the central bank (in particular, the '20 per cent rule') are ineffective because they do not represent binding constraints. Governments can adhere to the regulations and still build up large quantities of debt. Chapter 4 examines how the absence of restraint at the national level coincides with the existence of a binding constraint at the aggregate level. Implicit in the *status quo* is an inequality between two groups of countries within the monetary union, some of which are running permanent deficits with respect to the central bank, and some of which are running surpluses. The first group consists mostly of the larger, more politically stable and more financially developed countries; the second consists of the poorest, least developed countries. This outcome is consistent with the Nash equilibrium of a game-theoretic model of monetary union in which the players are of different sizes. The inequalities arise not from political intrigue or corruption, but just from each government playing its Nash strategy when choosing – within the rules of the union – how much it would like to borrow.

These two failings entail economic costs that are potentially very large. The inequalities that have arisen between different CFA members have the potential to destabilise the monetary union. The inability of the central bank to insulate monetary growth from fiscal shocks has the potential to create financial instability that offsets the benefits of the low long-run inflation rate that the CFA undoubtedly delivers. Chapter 5, which examines the monetary transmission mechanism in one representative CFA country (Côte d'Ivoire), provides even more cause for worry, as the link between base money growth and the growth of wider monetary aggregates is far from stable. The impact of any money creation that arises from uninsulated increases in public debt will have monetary consequences that are difficult to predict with any precision.

9.3. The impact of currency convertibility, transferability and exchange harmonisation on investment and growth

9.3.1. Capital market integration and currency convertibility

It has been claimed that the CFA enjoys a greater degree of financial integration with the West than do other African economies. This may be partly because of better performance with respect to stability and convertibility, and partly because of the financial institutions of the CFA, for example, those accounts of the BEAC/BCEAO designed to facilitate private transactions between Africa and France.

However, these institutions do not operate perfectly, and the mechanics of transferring assets into and out of the CFA are sometimes quite complex. If, for example, a French company wishes to transfer a large sum of money to the bank account of an Ivorian company in Abidjan, the transaction has to be in the form of a 'transfer in treasury'. The sum is debited from the French agent's bank account and credited to the Banque de France in Paris. The same amount is then debited from the Banque de France and credited to the BCEAO in Dakar, from where it is transferred to the BCEAO regional office in Abidjan, and finally to the private bank account of the recipient. This process is sometimes subject to considerable delays. Delays also occur in movements of assets out of the CFA.[1]

The export of assets from the CFA is also subject to a number of taxes. There is a 0.25 per cent tax on short-run loan capital exiting the CFA (both regions). In addition, each country can impose a national surtax; the highest is that of Congo, 0.75 per cent. Even assets moving from one CFA member to another are subject to a 0.1 per cent tax. In the complex financial transactions of the sort described above, an asset can end up being taxed two or three times on its journey out of its country of origin.

In addition, governments impose a number of regulations on the asset holdings of private agents as well as of banks, which are not entirely in keeping with the principles of the Most CFA governments require that their exporters hold their export receipts in their own country. Private banks are 'encouraged' not to hold more money abroad than is necessary to meet their current requirements. Export receipts from Africans living abroad must be repatriated within a few weeks. Pressure is put on banks to hold all their assets in the national financial system, rather than in neighbouring CFA members. These regulations are designed to prevent Latin American style capital flight, but they also restrict the movement of capital within the CFA and between the CFA and France.

So it is not surprising that there is little econometric evidence of a greater degree of integration. Real interest rates in the CFA, as calculated using the Obstfeld model (Chapter 6) diverge just as much from French rates as do interest rates in other African countries, and a comparison of Kenya with Côte d'Ivoire (Chapter 7) shows that domestic investment in both is dependant on domestic saving, although the structure of the relationship differs between the two countries. The result that domestic savings still represent a constraint on investment and growth is particularly important in the light of existing research indicating that the CFA has not performed noticeably better than the rest of Africa in terms of gross domestic saving.[2]

However, the CFA does appear to make a difference to investment by ensuring currency convertibility. The investment model in Chapter 7 shows that even in an anglophone country such as Kenya, where the degree of foreign exchange rationing is relatively mild, the absence of currency convertibility and the shortage of foreign exchange have seriously damaged investment. In the CFA, whose members use a currency whose convertibility with the French Franc is guaranteed, there is no such obstacle to investment.

9.3.2. *Exchange rate stability and relative price stability*

The most striking results about the impact of CFA membership on investment performance are those concerning price stability. Time-series evidence in Chapter 7 indicates that the stability of domestic capital goods prices relative to foreign capital goods prices positively influences investment both inside and outside the CFA. The relative price series can be interpreted as a measure of the stability of the return to domestic investment relative to the return to foreign investment. Moreover, cross-country data suggest that high investment across Sub-Saharan Africa over the last twenty years is correlated with stable prices (Chapter 8).

Further, the indicators of stability used to explain differences in investment between countries and over time show a markedly higher degree of stability among CFA members, as compared with their neighbours. The reasons for this are not obvious. It is true that CFA members enjoy a fixed exchange rate between their currencies and the French Franc (and now the Euro) and, since France (the EU) is such an important trading partner, this leads to a more stable trade-weighted exchange rate. However, there is no a priori reason why this should lead to greater relative price stability, i.e. stability of P_I/eP_I^*.

Nevertheless, there does appear to be a link between on the one hand a low rate of exchange rate depreciation and low inflation rate, and on the other greater relative price stability. In some countries outside the CFA, expansion of the money supply and hyperinflation have been accommodated by exchange rate depreciation. Cross-country evidence indicates that in this case, where both P_I and e are moving much faster, P_I/eP_I^* is likely to be more variable. Small differences in the rates of growth of e and P_I, which will occur unless arbitrage in all relevant markets is perfect, will lead to large movements in P_I/eP_I^*.

However, this is not the whole story. Since P_I is only one of many prices in the economy, e adjustment will never guarantee absolute stability of P_I/eP_I^*: when the exchange rate is flexible, it is likely to be determined by many relative prices. Of course, exchange rate flexibility is the exception rather than the rule in Africa: most often, there is exchange rate pegging of some kind. Only with a flexible P_I in an open capital goods market will relative price variability be minimised. To the extent that the currency unions promote freer trade in goods – and the available data suggest that they do[3] – they will facilitate relative price stability.

9.4. Options for the future

On several occasions CFA ministers have 'reaffirmed their attachment to the monetary stability which the CFA has brought'.[4] Such attachment is well placed: there is strong evidence that this stability is a major factor in promoting long-term investment and growth. However, the institutions guaranteeing this stability are not perfect, as demonstrated particularly in Chapters 3 and 4. Evidence suggests that the CFA does not score particularly highly with respect to short-term adjustment and stabilisation. What improvements can be made?

The problems highlighted above in Section 9.2 are potentially soluble. In particular, more efficient stabilisation, and better insulation of the monetary system from shocks, would be promoted by a greater transparency in the process by which the different components of the central bank balance sheet are determined, at both the national and the union-wide level. The central bank could be set explicit instrument targets that are derived from a theory of optimal stabilisation, in order to improve the poor stabilisation performance illustrated in Chapter 3. However, such a theory does not yet exist. There is no parallel in the development economics literature to the stabilisation theory that has evolved in response to the problems of industrialised economies, and there is a great deal of scope for refining the benchmark model of optimal monetary policy discussed in Chapter 3.

In addition to greater transparency in the decision rules followed by the central banks, the banks could also be given greater power to restrict the borrowing of individual governments, in order to limit the fiscal inequalities highlighted in Chapter 4. It is possible to replace the 20 per cent rule with rules that do represent binding constraints. For example, there could be a rule that would put an upper bound on the stock of a government's debt in relation to its revenue or the country's GDP, instead of on the annual increase in this stock. Such a tightening of the rules would reduce both the need for monetary insulation by reducing the magnitude of shocks to public borrowing and the potentially damaging inequalities between countries that have built up in recent years.

However, such institutional modifications are unlikely to solve completely the problems that arise from the heterogeneity of the current members of the two CFA monetary unions. Indeed, member governments are becoming increasingly aware of the tensions that result from such diversity. In the words of one report, 'The CFA encompasses both countries amongst the least developed in the World and those termed "middle income". Ministers were anxious to see the situation of the latter taken into account'.[5]

The CFA already comprises two separate monetary unions, plus Comoros. These unions can instigate different monetary policies, including, if necessary, devaluation. The value of the Comorian Franc has been changed more often than that of the BEAC/BCEAO currency. This potential flexibility has not been exploited to the full, because both unions comprise a wide variety of economies. Regrouping the CFA countries along (1) economic lines – so all members are likely to be subject to the same external shocks[6] – or (2) the basis of size (which would prevent a large country hijacking the Operations Account) would introduce more flexibility into the system, allowing monetary policy which was appropriate for a particular type of economy. The historical accident that is the CFA has served many of its members well; but if the institution is to perform efficiently in the future, its institutions must be based not on its colonial inheritance but on the economic characteristics of its member states.

Notes

1 For example, in the mid-1980s ABECOR advised European exporters, 'Although Franc Zone membership has been conducive to smoother payments, the pressure on international liquidity brought about by sustained current account deficits has led to payments delays, and the situation should be kept under review.' (ABECOR report on the Sahel, 1986.)
2 See for example Boissonade and Guillaumont (1988).
3 See for example Guillaumont (1988).
4 See for example Secrétariat du Comité Monétaire de la Zone Franc (1989).
5 Secrétariat du Comité Monétaire de la Zone Franc (1989).
6 See for example Fielding and Shields (2001).

References

Boissonade, M. and Guillaumont, S. (1988) 'L'effort d'épargne', in Guillaumont, P. and Guillaumont, S. (eds) *Stratégies de Développement Comparées*, Economica: Paris.
Fielding, D. and Mizen, P. (2001) 'Seigniorage revenue and self-fulfilling currency crises', *Journal of Development Economics*, **65**: 81–93.
Fielding, D. and Shields, K. (2001) 'Modeling macroeconomic shocks in the CFA Franc Zone', *Journal of Development Economics* (forthcoming).
Guillaumont, P. (1988) 'L'ouverture commerciale sur l'extérieur mesurée á partir au taux d'exportation', in Guillaumont, P. and Guillaumont, S. (eds) *Stratégies de Développement Comparées*, Economica: Paris.
Secrétariat du Comité Monétaire de la Zone Franc (1989) *La Zone Franc Rapport*, Paris.

Index

For Product Safety Concerns and Information please contact our
EU representative GPSR@taylorandfrancis.com Taylor & Francis
Verlag GmbH, Kaufingerstraße 24, 80331 München, Germany